HOSTING *the* PRESENCE *Every Day*

DESTINY IMAGE BOOKS BY BILL JOHNSON

Hosting the Presence

A Life of Miracles

Dreaming with God

Release the Power of Jesus

Strengthen Yourself in the Lord

The Supernatural Power of a Transformed Mind

When Heaven Invades Earth

Bill Johnson

HOSTING *the* PRESENCE *Every Day*

365 Days to Unveiling Heaven's Agenda for Your Life

 Please note that Destiny Image's publishing style capitalizes certain pronouns in Scripture that refer to the Father, Son, and Holy Spirit, and may differ from some publishers' styles. Take note that the name satan and related names are not capitalized. We choose not to acknowledge him, even to the point of violating grammatical rules.

DESTINY IMAGE® PUBLISHERS, INC.
P.O. Box 310, Shippensburg, PA 17257-0310
"Promoting Inspired Lives."

This book and all other Destiny Image, Revival Press, MercyPlace, Fresh Bread, Destiny Image Fiction, and Treasure House books are available at Christian bookstores and distributors worldwide.

For a U.S. bookstore nearest you, call 1-800-722-6774.
For more information on foreign distributors, call 717-532-3040.
Reach us on the Internet: www.destinyimage.com.

ISBN 13 HC: 978-0-7684-0524-8
ISBN 13 TP: 978-0-7684-0754-9
ISBN 13 Ebook: 978-0-7684-0525-5

For Worldwide Distribution, Printed in the U.S.A.
2 3 4 5 6 7 8 / 18 17 16

HOW TO USE THIS DEVOTIONAL

THE QUEST TO host God's Presence does not begin with formulas or principles. It starts with an increasing awareness of *Who* lives within you.

When you were born again, you became the temple of the Holy Spirit (see 1 Cor. 6:19). Jesus' blood made it possible for God to come and take up residence in your heart in the Person of the Holy Spirit. Though this truth is absolutely stunning and, at the same time, confounding, it is nevertheless the reality for every single person who has said the ultimate "Yes" to Jesus.

It is the Cross that provided your entryway into the Kingdom. Now, it is time for us to learn how to host the Presence of the One Who shows us how to live out the resurrected life.

The Spirit who lives within you desires to also rest upon you. He lives within you for your sake. However, He rests upon you for the sake of others.

As you discover how to host His Presence every day, you will take one step after the next into practically living the Kingdom lifestyle. Remember, it is not simply a matter of implementing the right Kingdom principles to experience a desired result. This quest is about developing deeper intimacy with a Person. He is the prize. *He is the breakthrough.*

Daily Scripture Reading

These verses and passages of Scripture will reinforce the topic covered during a particular day. You may see some verses repeated. This is intentional. The key is not study or even memorization; it is meditation. The vision is internalizing and, ultimately, living out the biblical truth that you are feasting upon. Remember, His words are spirit and they are life! (See John 6:63.)

Prayer

These prayers are tools to help you give voice to what you discover each day. They are not comprehensive. Instead, they are launching pads designed to help you talk with the Holy Spirit about what you discovered about hosting His Presence.

JANUARY

Your Ultimate Assignment

January 1

There was something different about the atmosphere that surrounded the apostle Peter. His lifestyle changed quite dramatically after he was baptized in the Holy Spirit.

ONE MOMENT, PETER stood fearful, intimidated, and trembling before a servant girl, denying that he ever knew Jesus. It was only after he was transformed by the Presence that his true identity was awakened and he became the rock Jesus saw him as in Matthew 16.

When you are empowered by the Presence of God, Heaven awakens your true potential, positioning you to step out and be the person you were divinely designed to be. You are a completely new creation—a human being possessed by God. This truth alone should embolden you to step out, absolutely confident that the Greater One lives within you and that everything He has called you to be and everything His Word describes you as—*this is who you really are.* Remember, the One Who identifies you also inhabits you!

Daily Scripture Reading

MATTHEW 26:69-70 ▪ ACTS 5:15

Prayer

Holy Spirit, come....Show me the person Your empowering Presence has anointed me to be.

January 2

People not only were healed when he prayed for them, they just seemed to get well when they were near him.

PETER'S SHADOW RELEASED the Presence of the One Who overshadowed him. This apostle lived from a place where having the Spirit dwelling *within* him was glorious, yes, but not enough. He desired to walk in a dimension where this Presence Who indwelt him also rested *upon* him and changed the environment *around* him. This is why Peter's very shadow was charged with supernatural healing power. This same reality is available to you because you have access to the same Holy Spirit Peter had access to.

The challenge: Will you take the steps that Peter did to make this transition? All believers have the Holy Spirit living within them. He makes salvation possible and is the gift we receive *when* we are born again. However, there is a difference between living with the Spirit dwelling within us and walking with His empowering Presence resting upon us.

Daily Scripture Reading

Acts 5:15

Prayer

Holy Spirit, I cry out for more. I know You live inside of me. I ask, please show me what it looks like to live with Your Presence and power resting upon me.

January 3

The anointing is a Person.

THE PRESENCE OF God, or *the anointing,* is not an abstract concept; it is a living reality for every single believer. In order to walk in the power of God's Presence, you must first discover Who the Presence really is. The Presence is not another member of the Trinity. We are not discussing a force, a wind, or even some kind of physical manifestation. The Presence of God is the Person of the Holy Spirit.

In the Book of Acts where Peter's shadow carried and released supernatural healing power, the apostle was not merely walking under the influence of some kind of energy. He was inhabited by a Divine Person called *Holy Spirit*. This Person is as much God as both the Father and the Son. He is not an "it." The Holy Spirit is God Almighty fulfilling the promise He made in Ezekiel 36:27, "*I will put My Spirit within you.*"

DAILY SCRIPTURE READING

EZEKIEL 36:24-28

PRAYER

Father, increase my awareness of the One Who lives inside of me and empower me to represent Jesus well in the earth.

January 4

***For He dwells with you and will be in you* (John 14:17).**

As you come into a deeper understanding that God's anointing lives inside of you, you will begin to recognize more and more that the Presence is actually the Person of God, *the Holy Spirit*. When introducing us to the Holy Spirit's ministry, Jesus introduced Him as a "*He*" not an "it." *He* would dwell with us, live inside of us, and bring us into greater revelation of Who the Father is. *How*? Because the Person of the Holy Spirit is actually the Person of God, and God is the One Who is most qualified to reveal Himself!

The more you know God—study His attributes, encounter His nature, and review His characteristics—the more you receive deeper revelation of Who the One living inside you truly is. Remember, God the Father, God the Son, and God the Spirit are one. This is the mission of the Holy Spirit within you—*to represent Jesus accurately in both word and demonstration,* which brings great glory to your Father in Heaven.

Daily Scripture Reading

John 14:15-18

Prayer

Lord, open my eyes to the wondrous reality that You—the Maker of Heaven and earth—live inside of me through the Person and Presence of the Holy Spirit.

January 5

Jesus was known for healing people with and without prayer. There were times when it looked as though He was not involved at all in the miracle that happened through Him.

CONSIDER THE WOMAN with the nonstop blood flow in Mark 5. In approaching Jesus for healing, she was not trying to implement some type of miracle formula. Neither was she responding to some teaching she received on the "Five Keys to Get Your Healing."

She simply said to herself, "*If only I may touch His clothes, I shall be made well*" (Mark 5:28). The point of emphasis in this story is *not* Jesus' clothes; rather, it is what made His clothes the woman's point of contact. Her faith was not in the hem of a garment, but in the One whose very Presence caused the garment to be charged with healing power.

DAILY SCRIPTURE READING

MARK 5:25-34

PRAYER

Thank You, Holy Spirit, that Your Presence releases Your power. More than anything, I hunger for Your Presence, Your nearness, and Your closeness. May You and You alone be my life's great pursuit.

January 6

Extraordinary miracles operate at a higher level of mystery, anointing, and authority.

JOHN 14:12 EXTENDS an incredible invitation to all believers throughout all generations. Jesus tells us, "*Most assuredly, I say to you, he who believes in Me, the works that I do he will do also; and greater works than these he will do, because I go to My Father*" (NKJV).

While the Holy Spirit has been bringing the body of Christ into a place where the works of Jesus are becoming embraced and experienced again, there is also a call to operate in the greater works. Though our natural minds may have trouble processing these words, this does not make them any less relevant to our lives today. As a people filled with God, we have been empowered to do the same works as Jesus—and yes, even greater works—*because* the same Holy Spirit Who anointed Jesus with supernatural power has fallen upon us.

DAILY SCRIPTURE READING

JOHN 14:12

PRAYER

Holy Spirit, You have invited me to not only do the same works that Jesus did, but also to pursue and expect even greater works. Thank You for this amazing invitation.

There was a time in the apostle Paul's ministry when he graduated from miracles to extraordinary miracles.

"God was performing extraordinary miracles by the hands of Paul, so that handkerchiefs or aprons were even carried from his body to the sick, and the diseases left them and the evil spirits went out" (Acts 19:11-12 NASB).

IN THIS SCRIPTURE, we are given a preview of what the greater works actually look like! Luke, the author of the Book of Acts, classifies them as extraordinary miracles.

Why call these miracles *extraordinary*? Consider Jesus. The sick touched the hem of His garment and they were healed. Flip over to Acts 19. Now, people are actually taking the clothes and sweatbands off of Paul's body, placing them on the sick and tormented, and watching them experience wholeness. Again, it had nothing to do with Paul or Paul's clothing. There was nothing special about the cloths that were taken from Paul's body. He was simply a man completely saturated in the Presence of God. As a result, every area of his life was marked because of the anointing—including his physical body!

DAILY SCRIPTURE READING

ACTS 19:11-12

PRAYER

Holy Spirit, come and saturate every area of my life with Your Presence. Position me to walk in the extraordinary miracles that Your Word promises, not because of my performance, but because of Your anointing upon me.

January 8

It's amazing that the miracle realm can become so normal that Luke, under the inspiration of the Holy Spirit, had to create a separate category to describe the new miracles.

THE WORKS OF Jesus are becoming more and more normal for us. This absolutely makes sense. When we study the life and ministry of Jesus and recognize our commission to model what He did, we cannot escape the mandate to walk in the miraculous as normative—not the exception. We cannot live this supernatural lifestyle apart from the One Jesus called *the Advantage*—the Holy Spirit (see John 16:7).

As Jesus was explaining this *Advantage* to the disciples, I have to think they were in a state of shock and disbelief. After all, Jesus—God Incarnate—was telling them that it would be *better* for them if He was to go away and leave the scene. They simply could not process it, but Jesus knew that the key to the disciples following His example and, ultimately, stepping into those realms of extraordinary miracles had everything to do with the shift that would take place because of the Cross.

When Jesus calls us to do the same works that He did and *even greater*, the concept is inseparable from the reality of Him leaving the earth and going to the Father (see John 14:12). Jesus' departure only meant the coming of Another—*Heaven's Advantage*—the Presence and power of the Holy Spirit.

Daily Scripture Reading

John 16:5-7

Prayer

Father, thank You for sending the Holy Spirit. He is my Advantage and gives me the ability to do the works of Jesus. He is a glorious Person and your empowering Presence in my life.

January 9

We have yet to live in what has already been revealed.

JESUS GAVE US a model that was attainable for anyone cleansed of sin and filled with the Holy Spirit. This is exactly what the body of Christ is being called into. The example of the normal Christian life, as presented by Jesus Christ, is the inheritance of every believer.

All one needs to do is look at Jesus for any questions or confusion concerning the will of God to be immediately answered. While there are specifics that pertain to the more detailed nuances of your life, there is a clear blueprint that we have been given to follow no matter where we are or what we are doing. Businessperson? Pastor? Banker? Doctor? Lawyer? Artist? Here is God's revealed will for your life:

> *And as you go, preach, saying, "The kingdom of heaven is at hand." Heal the sick, cleanse the lepers, raise the dead, cast out demons. Freely you have received, freely give* (Matthew 10:7-8).

DAILY SCRIPTURE READING

MATTHEW 10:7-8

PRAYER

Thank You for the example of Jesus and the clarity He brings to Your will for my life. This is my inheritance as a believer. I know there are other details and specifics; I simply trust those to You as I step out and start following the model of Jesus in my life today.

January 10

Faith sees and responds to unseen realities.

WALKING BY FAITH and not by sight is the believer's lifestyle. Our vision needs to be tuned in to the unseen in order to appropriately respond to the seen. In other words, we need to learn how to watch the Holy Spirit and align ourselves with His movement.

Unusual methods used by the Holy Spirit give us glimpses of how He works and acts. In one instance, He may use the anointed clothing of Paul to set a demonized person free. On another occasion, He may direct you to lay hands on someone and pray for their healing. It might be that by simply sharing a word of knowledge, the condition or affliction is broken. The problem is that we have a bent toward developing systems and formulas around what we think produces results, when in fact the Holy Spirit is a relational Person Who simply wants to tune our spiritual ears in to His frequency.

Different methods are not intended to tie us to a particular way or strategy. Instead, they remind us of the need for moment by moment relationship with the Spirit of God. Remember, His movements will change—and at times may appear quite unusual—but His ways are always consistent.

Daily Scripture Reading

2 Corinthians 5:7

Prayer

Sharpen my eyes to see Your movements, Holy Spirit. Tune my ears to hear Your voice. And grant me grace to obey You, follow Your lead, and work with You to accomplish Your purposes.

January 11

Faith doesn't come from the mind; it comes from the heart. Yet a renewed mind enhances our faith through an understanding of the unseen.

FAITH IS BIRTHED in the heart by the Holy Spirit. Remember, it is a gift from God (see Eph. 2:8). However, when our minds are renewed and transformed by the Presence of God operating in us, we start to understand how the unseen realm operates. Faith actually has a transformative impact on our thinking if we allow it to. What God deposited into our hearts at salvation was never meant to simply remain there, but to change every area of our lives—particularly the way we think. When the faith that God deposited into my heart begins to shape my thought life, this is a sure sign that my mind is being renewed.

The renewed mind sees the impossible as logical. This is because we have decided to yield our minds to the influence of the One dwelling inside of us. When we remove the natural constraints from our thinking and actually embrace the thought life of God, realities that used to drive us to fear, unbelief, and anxiety become opportunities for the miraculous invasions of God.

Daily Scripture Reading

Romans 12:1-2

Prayer

Holy Spirit, renew my mind. Change the way I think so that the impossible becomes logical and the circumstances that used to drive me to fear, worry, or anxiety would actually draw me closer to Your empowering Presence.

January 12

It's time for these exceptional stories to no longer be the exception. It's time for them to become the rule—THE NEW NORM.

IN THE CONTEXT of the Gospels and the Book of Acts, miracles were normal. A blueprint was established for what the Christian life was supposed to look and operate like. As the Holy Spirit continues to move in great power through believers today, people often look at His supernatural work and brand it as something new.

It is only new in the sense that it has been so long since signs, wonders, and miracles have defined the expression of the normal Christian life. The Holy Spirit has never stopped moving and flowing through the church since the Day of Pentecost. His power has always been available. The question is, who will return to the blueprint and actually believe that what Scripture revealed in the life of Jesus and in the Book of Acts is available to us today?

Jesus has sent you in the same way that He was sent by the Father! This invites us to return to His life and ministry and ask, *How was Jesus sent*? This gives us the most accurate blueprint of what our lives should look like today.

Daily Scripture Reading

John 20:21-22

Prayer

As You sent Jesus, so You are sending me! Give me a clear vision of what Jesus' life and ministry looked like so that, through the power of the Holy Spirit, I can walk out the supernatural lifestyle that He made available to me.

January 13

The apostles learned from Jesus' example that the greatest treasure was the Presence of the Holy Spirit resting upon Him.

THE PRESENCE OF the Holy Spirit that rested upon the Son of God was guarded as the most precious treasure. Jesus knew that His words and actions, demonstrated through the enabling of the Spirit, were constantly creating a template that was meant to be followed from generation to generation. While the redemptive work of Calvary is eternally exclusive to Jesus with Him being the only worthy Lamb, we must pay careful attention to the model He was building during His life and public ministry. This model was *not* meant to be exclusive to just Him, but designed to be followed by all who would believe in Him.

While Jesus was journeying toward the Cross, He was also giving humankind a glimpse of the life that would become possible *after* the Cross. Jesus was the only Man in history—up to this point—perfectly compatible to be filled with the Holy Spirit's Presence because He was without sin. Because of His redemptive work, Jesus made it possible for everyone who received His gift of salvation to be forgiven of sin and, ultimately, be filled with the same Spirit He was filled with.

Daily Scripture Reading

John 1:32-34

Prayer

Thank You for the Cross, Father. Thank You for making it possible for me to be cleansed of sin and become fit to be indwelt by the precious Spirit of God.

January 14

Jesus' ultimate priority in life was doing the Father's business.

FROM A YOUNG age, Jesus was faithful to fulfill His commission to do the works of the Father. He had eyes fixed on another world, where He saw the Father's works and heard the Father's voice. Time after time, Jesus revealed the ultimate priority of every believer: To be one who sees and hears from Heaven. While doing the Father's business, Jesus was faithfully representing the heart, nature, and will of God to an onlooking world. He is rightly named *the Faithful and True Witness* (see Rev. 3:14), meaning that Jesus has the final, ultimate say on Who the Father is. While walking the earth, Jesus was on a mission to show the world Who God truly was. This same world is looking at you, desperate to catch a glimpse of the Father.

Because of the Presence dwelling in you, the Father's business is also your business. When, under the influence of the Holy Spirit, you do the works of Jesus, those works faithfully reveal the Father to the world.

Daily Scripture Reading

John 5:19

Prayer

Father, give me eyes to see what You are doing. Thank You for the empowering of the Holy Spirit to follow the model of Jesus and, in doing so, to show the world Who you are and what You are like.

January 15

There is no greater privilege than being a host to God Himself. Neither is there a greater responsibility.

IT IS ONE thing to host friends or family in your home; it is something of an entirely different level to consider the reality of hosting God in the *home* that is your physical frame. This is one of those scriptural truths that we often quote, cite, and discuss, but I am not sure if we allow the full weight of it to resonate in our hearts.

Your body is a tabernacle—a temple for God on the earth (see 1 Cor. 6:19). With His precious blood, Jesus paid an exceedingly high price so that you could be completely forgiven of sin *and* become a fit dwelling place for God's Presence. With so high a privilege comes an equally great responsibility. Consider this. When we host guests in our homes, we have certain responsibilities—namely, to create an inviting, welcoming atmosphere for them to feel comfortable. Likewise, we have this same responsibility with the Holy Spirit, as He is the ultimate guest. He has not only come to visit; He has come to abide with us forever (see John 14:16).

Daily Scripture Reading

1 Corinthians 6:19

Prayer

Increase my awareness of what it means to host Your Presence with my life. Thank You, Holy Spirit, for making my body Your dwelling place. Show me how to accommodate You in every way, making every step with Your Presence in mind.

January 16

Few are aware of the assignment to host Him. Fewer yet have said "Yes."

HOSTING GOD IS not a decision to be taken lightly. In fact, it is all-consuming and completely demanding. And yet, whatever we give up in exchange for experiencing a constant awareness of the Spirit's abiding Presence makes any sacrifice more than worth it. The prize gained is a man or woman completely possessed by God where the Holy Spirit impacts and shapes every area of life. Nothing is off limits. Our thoughts, our words, our emotions, our motives, and yes, even our physical bodies exude His Presence. This is truly what happens when a people experience the Spirit's Presence resting *upon* them.

This is what Simon the Sorcerer saw resting upon the apostles and foolishly tried to offer money for—the abiding Presence and power of the Holy Spirit (see Acts 8:18-19). No natural currency could be exchanged to obtain so glorious a gift. And to think, this gift is not exclusive to certain select Christians whom God singles out. This great invitation has been extended to all. The question is posed: *Who will respond to the invitation by saying "yes"?*

Scripture Reading

Acts 8:18-19

Prayer

Holy Spirit, I ask You to rest upon me. Just as You were upon Jesus, and just as Your Presence was so powerfully upon the disciples, show me how to walk in this same expression of power.

January 17

He planted us here with a purpose. Yet it's a purpose we can't accomplish without Him.

WE HAVE BEEN placed on earth for a divine purpose. In fact, you were specifically planted in this moment, this generation, and this season to fulfill a unique calling. What God designed you to release to the world has been strategically ordained for this moment in history.

So, what is the key to stepping into your purpose, living in constant response to God's indwelling Presence? His Presence is the key to you fulfilling your purpose. You were knit together by a supernatural God. He formed you to be inhabited by Himself. This means that whatever you were designed to accomplish and release to this world is linked to your identity as one filled with God, for it is His Presence that empowers you to fulfill divine destiny.

Daily Scripture Reading

Acts 17:24-28

Prayer

Thank You for appointing me to live in this time in history and in this place. In You I live and move and have my being. Fully fill me with Your Presence and enable me to fulfill my purpose on this planet.

January 18

Our true nature and personality will never come to fullness apart from His manifest Presence.

BECAUSE WE WERE created by God and for God, who we really are will not find ultimate expression until we live as men and women who consciously host His Presence. It was, after all, His Presence that made you fully alive to begin with. The Holy Spirit is the One Who made salvation possible for you. He opened our eyes and ears to the glories of the Gospel. The Spirit quickened our dead hearts to say "Yes" to Jesus' call to follow after Him.

Could it be there are many believers, sleepwalking through the motions of life, who are not enjoying the *fully alive* reality that they were born again into? Sooner or later, we need to fully believe in what took place when we got saved. Our sins were forgiven so that we could be indwelt and inhabited by the Presence of the Holy God. It is in Him that we live, move, and have our being, and it is through His Presence that we walk this earth as men and women *fully alive* in Christ. The key is maintaining *awareness* of His Presence.

Daily Scripture Reading

Psalm 16

Prayer

God, it is in You that I find fullness of joy and become the best version of who You've created me to be. I know You are always with me, but please help me to become more aware of Your tangible Presence.

January 19

Learning to host Him is at the center of our assignment.

WHEN IT COMES to considering our assignment, we are quick to want to *do* something. However, before we *do* anything, we must place our great emphasis on the God we host, even more than the works we set out to accomplish in His Name.

This is a vital switch because there are so many believers out in the world who are trying to work very hard *for* God. They believe that the more they do, the greater effectiveness their "doing" will bring to their lives. The center of our assignment is not in *what* we accomplish for God, but Whom we live mindful of. It is all too possible for us to fall into a cycle of working in our own strength and not drawing from the Presence of the One we host with our lives. This is why it is so vital to make hosting God's Presence the center of our assignment. When our awareness is *first* directed toward the Holy Spirit rather than external acts of spiritual service, what we do externally will have far greater impact than it did previously. We have made hosting God our primary pursuit and have learned to draw limitless supernatural resources from His transforming Presence.

Daily Scripture Reading

Luke 10:38-42

Prayer

Holy Spirit, thank You for loving me for who I am and not for what I do for You. I want to host You well by spending time with You and letting You love me. Help me to be like Mary and sit at Your feet instead of like Martha compulsively doing things for You that You never asked me to do. Give me a greater revelation of Your love for me as a son/daughter.

January 20

In one moment we find ourselves rejoicing in the dance, arms raised with heads lifted high. In the next we are bowed low, not because someone suggested it would be an appropriate response, but because the fear of God has filled the room.

WHEN HIS PRESENCE comes, everything changes. We know that God is already with us. The Holy Spirit lives inside of us because of Christ's work on the Cross. This is a given for all believers. But as we have been discovering more and more, the One Who lives within His people also moves among them.

Remember, the Presence is not a force or a thing—the anointing is a Person. The Holy Spirit is a Person with feeling, emotions, and yes, an agenda. He is not static and His ways are not stagnant. He may move one way *one day*, but then move differently the next. The key word is *differently*, not contrarily. This does not mean God is ever-changing; it simply means that this glorious God Whose character and nature is boundless in every way has decided to let you and I in on how He is feeling and what He is doing—*in this moment of time.*

There are times during a gathering where everything appears to be going in one direction, but then *He comes*. Even though He was already there because God is omnipresent, He draws close to the point where the atmosphere noticeably changes. Something obvious takes place in that unique space. This same shift can take place wherever you are, from being in a church gathering to talking with friends at a restaurant. Everything appears to go one way, and then *He shows up*. His movements are different and His methods can vary, but in the end the same Glorious One has given us the awesome privilege to respond to His movement in that moment. May our hearts always be postured to receive and welcome how He is moving.

Daily Scripture Reading

Revelation 1:9-18 ▪ Revelation 4

Prayer

Holy Spirit, help me to be attuned to how You are showing up, so I can follow Your lead.

January 21

God is a Person, not a machine. He longs for fellowship.

If you are a believer, fellowship with God is your inheritance. Because the Presence of God lives within you, it is your decision whether or not to enjoy this wonderful intimacy that He has made available to you through the Holy Spirit.

We live beneath this measure of glory when we reduce Christianity to principle-based formulas. While there are time-tested scriptural principles that we are responsible to both teach and observe, Jesus did not purchase us to simply follow protocol; His blood ushered us into the very Presence of God and, yes, made provision for the Presence of God to take up residence within us.

In fact, it is the one who recognizes this priceless indwelling that lives according to the principles. Except now, principles are not laws that cause us to *try* and earn God's good graces. No. His good grace is what brought us into intimate fellowship with Himself. Everything we do, we do *from love*. We don't work for God's love or acceptance, as we already have this. Truly, one of the great evidences of God's acceptance for us is the seal of the Spirit. Consider this. God's Presence living within you is proof that you are forgiven, loved, and accepted by the Father!

Daily Scripture Reading

Ephesians 1:13-14 ▪ 2 Corinthians 13:14

Prayer

Thank You for the seal of the Holy Spirit that enables me to have fellowship with You, God. Thank You that You aren't far away and that I don't have to do x, y, and z to appease You or convince You not to punish me. It is amazing to think about how much You love me and want a relationship with me. Help me to have a greater grasp of the depth of Your love.

January 22

Hosting God is filled with honor and pleasure, cost and mystery. He is subtle, and even sometimes silent. He can also be extremely obvious, aggressive, and overtly purposeful.

SOONER OR LATER, it is bound to register that God actually does live inside of His people. While some of the logistics are far beyond our natural comprehension—how God can live in Heaven, yet also on earth in us—we have been invited to embrace this adventure by faith, not by sight or natural human logic.

Adventure is never reasonable. It is not reasonable to scale Mount Everest or journey into outer space or dive into the ocean's depths. There is risk involved. Such activities are *not* normal and thus invite participants to embrace a new dimension of "reason." God is likewise inviting His people to embrace the adventure of hosting His Presence; however, walking out this Presence-indwelt life should make every earthly thrill and rush seem like an utter bore. Hosting God's Presence is an incomparable adventure, as nothing on earth can even measure beside it. There is no accurate scale of comparison! It would be like taking the experience of climbing Mount Everest, putting it inside of your body, and living with that every moment of your life. And yet, such an abstract method of comparison still falls tremendously short, because the One Who dwells within you actually formed and fashioned the highest mountain peaks.

This is your inheritance. *This* is your adventure! Let's never reduce what is available to us to the level of our current experience. Just because you are not presently experiencing every blessing of this incomparable adventure does *not* mean it is unavailable to you. It becomes increasingly available to us as we are willing to increasingly embrace the adventure.

Daily Scripture Reading

Philippians 3:10-14

Prayer

Holy Spirit, help me to become increasingly aware of who You are inside of me, so that I can tap into everything that You've given to me as an inheritance.

He is a guest with an agenda—Father to Son. Heaven to earth.

HOSTING GOD IS an incomparable adventure for many reasons. For one, the assignment we have been given is absolutely stunning. *On earth as it is in Heaven*. This assignment is *your* assignment, and *your* assignment is ultimately backed by Heaven's agenda.

What does God want? *His world to transform this one*. God's heart has been a planet that is filled with His glory (see Num. 14:21). His agenda is your assignment. What greater meaning could we have in life than to participate with God and bring His agenda to pass? Many people—Christians included—are searching for their purpose in life, when in fact we often neglect the assignment that has been given to each one of us. Yes, there are specifics. There are places to go, people to meet, and tasks to perform. At the center of it all, though, there is a motivating desire for the Maker of Heaven and earth to use *you* as an ambassador to re-create the climate of Heaven on earth.

Holy Spirit is truly a guest with an agenda, because He is the One Who gives you power to be a witness of God's ways and God's world in your world (see Acts 1:8).

DAILY SCRIPTURE READING

MATTHEW 6:9-13

PRAYER

Father, thank You for the privilege of being Your ambassador on earth and for empowering me with the Holy Spirit. Let Your will be done on earth as it is in Heaven, and use me to accomplish this in whatever way I can. Show me specific ways that I can bring Heaven to earth every day... starting today.

January 24

What generation will host Him until the kingdom of this world becomes the Kingdom of our Lord and Christ?

THERE IS A day when Jesus Christ will visibly and physically return to planet earth. There is a longing within each of us for this *ultimate* and *final* merger of two worlds, Heaven and earth, when it will be said that all of the kingdoms of this world are under the influence of Christ. However, this last day represents the *conclusion*, not the unfolding process.

Right now, we are all living in the process and have an essential role to play in preparing for the conclusive last day. In the meantime, we are living in a season recognized as the *last days* (see Acts 2:17). Notice that these days are not singular, they are plural. The last days represent a season, while the last day is a definitive moment of conclusion. Heaven is our destination, but the earth—this unique moment that we have been born into—is our assignment. We trust the logistics of the "last day" conclusion to God, but we must steward the commission we have been given.

DAILY SCRIPTURE READING

REVELATION 11:15-19 ▪ ACTS 2:16-21

PRAYER

I want to live a life that will give You the glory You deserve. I want to give my all to You for the rest of my days on earth. I can't wait to see You face to face in Heaven and for Your Kingdom to fully come. In the meantime, help me to steward the short time I have on earth well, for Your Name's sake.

January 25

He longs for fellowship. He loves to love.

GOD LIVING INSIDE of you demonstrates His longing for intimate fellowship *with* you. There is no closer He could come to you. In the Old Testament, people experienced seasonal anointings by the Spirit or were graced with divine empowerment for a specific task. Yet, even during these temporary graces, there is little language of fellowship or intimacy. Under the Old Covenant, people were practically anointed. God had a task for them to fulfill, and apart from the supernatural empowerment of His Presence they were unable to complete their specific assignment. Now, everything has changed.

Jesus clearly described the Holy Spirit as One Who would be both with us and in us. At the time, the disciples may not have been able to wrap their minds around the massive implication—*God in us*—but this was the plan. While it is easy for us to get caught up in the wonderful demonstrations of power that the Spirit's Presence brings, we must never lose sight of the deep intimacy that God has now made available to us. The One Who, for so long, could only dwell *with* His people now lives *within* us. I pray we would receive a fresh revelation of the wonderful fellowship the Holy Spirit has brought us into.

DAILY SCRIPTURE READING

JUDGES 14:6,19 ▪ 1 JOHN 2:27

PRAYER

Jesus, thank You for making a way for me to have permanent fellowship and anointing through the Holy Spirit. Help me to get a greater revelation of the intimacy You made available.

January 26

The invasion of God into impossible situations comes through a people who have received power from on high and have learned to release it into the circumstances of life.

We have received the Spirit's Presence to experience and release His power to the world around us. Power is given to us for a purpose. In fact, those who tend to walk in greater demonstrations of Kingdom power are those who steward the Presence they have already received.

Many are crying out for *more* when we neglect to steward what we have already received. This begs the question, *why do we receive to begin with*? Yes, because the Giver loves us, but also so the Gift could benefit those around us. Is there any greater gift we could receive than that of God Himself? Yet, this is exactly Who we have received by receiving the Presence of the Holy Spirit in our lives. Such a priceless gift demands an equally serious stewardship.

Daily Scripture Reading

Luke 11:9-13

Prayer

Holy Spirit, I welcome You to show up in power in my life. I welcome You to be in me and upon me...both when I'm by myself and when I am with people. I don't want to keep You all to myself. I want to give You away as best I can. Show me how to do that moment by moment.

January 27

If I have a power encounter with God, which we are required to pursue, then I am equipped to give it away to others.

POWER ENCOUNTERS IN God's Presence are multi-purposed. What we experience becomes what we offer. If we encounter God for ourselves, then we offer the world an encounter with God. We cannot give away what we have not first received. When we do receive, it is absolutely necessary for us to give it away. While we all enjoy riding the waves of encounter in God's Presence, such waves are powerful reminders of what we carry on the inside of us.

The Christian life is not just about riding those refreshing sovereign waves of God's Presence, but also learning how to *start* waves. Even though such a concept leaves the realm of comfortable analogy, it is the Kingdom privilege that every Spirit-filled believer gets to enjoy. We experience waves of His Presence as a reminder of His love for us and also His love for others. After all, what we experience during a power encounter is a glimpse of what we carry inside of us as those privileged to host the Holy Spirit.

DAILY SCRIPTURE READING

ROMANS 15:17-19

PRAYER

God, wash over me with waves of Your Presence. Give me a fresh touch from Heaven. Thank You for the manifestation of what I carry inside of me. Show me when it is appropriate to ride the waves of Your Presence and when it is appropriate to start waves.

January 28

We were designed to rule like God rules—in generosity and kindness, not self-serving, but always for the higher good of others.

WHAT IS OUR task as ambassadors of Jesus? *Reconciliation.* We are servants of reconciliation, empowered by the Holy Spirit to bring the people, systems, and kingdoms of this world into a transformative encounter with King Jesus. This does not happen through overthrow or takeover—it is released through servanthood.

Even though the first disciples were looking for military victory, Jesus had to clearly define the expression of their commission. Through love and service, a different form of conquest would be taking place. Darkness would be driven out of cities. Disease would be healed. Torment would be relieved. Families would be restored. This is how the kingdoms of this world will become the kingdoms of the Lord Jesus Christ. Until the last day comes, this is God's mission for us—to overthrow darkness through loving people, serving our cities, and carrying the Presence of the Holy Spirit. The Spirit empowers us to serve, as our Savior was the ultimate servant.

Daily Scripture Reading

2 Corinthians 5:17-21 ▪ John 13:1-17

Prayer

Jesus, You are the ultimate example of a servant leader. As I go out with power to reconcile Your lost sons and daughters to You, give me an attitude of a humble servant. Help me to love and serve selflessly like You showed us when You washed Your disciples' feet.

January 29

The heart of God is for partnership with His created likeness. He's the ultimate King who loves to empower.

GOD INHABITS US so that we can effectively collaborate together. Serving in the Kingdom is not all about working *for God*. Although we never graduate beyond being servants, at the same time Jesus brought us into divine friendship. This does not cancel out our servanthood. Instead, our service is fueled by intimacy. We are not working *for* love, but working *from* love. We do not serve God to become His friends; we serve Him because we are His friends. Also, we do not serve as *just* servants any longer. Mere servants do not know what the Master is doing. And yet, Jesus brought us into this unique expression of service where, as friends of God, we become intimately aware of what the Master is doing.

We partner with God to accomplish His purposes on the earth. While the King is sovereign, He has nevertheless established a system where His purposes would be accomplished in the earth through a unique partnership birthed out of intimacy and friendship. As intimates, we catch a glimpse of what the Master is doing. As servants, we joyfully participate with Him in bringing His Kingdom work to pass. It is the Holy Spirit Who uniquely empowers God's friends to accomplish His work. Beyond empowerment, the Presence is not just God enabling us to do something—it is Him working with us, His current pulsing through our hands, our feet, and our lips. He empowers, yes, but He also works *through* us. I cannot think of a more intimate partnership than what we experience with the Holy Spirit.

DAILY SCRIPTURE READING

JOHN 15:12-17

PRAYER

God, thank You for choosing me first and allowing me to be Your friend. Thank You for empowering me to bring Your Kingdom to earth. It is my joy to partner with You!

January 30

It's important that we all find the "one thing" that can become the reference point for the rest of the issues of life. And that one thing is the Presence of the Almighty God, resting upon us.

LIVING MINDFUL OF the reality of God within you and God upon you constantly reorients your life. *God within* is a truth that we have certainly embraced in theology and doctrine, but *God upon* is another dimension we have yet to experience in full measure. The Holy Spirit wants to touch and transform every area of your life, conforming it into the likeness of Jesus Christ. Many of us recognize this, in theory, but when it comes to identifying what this actually looks like in a measurable, practical way, we tend to be without clear vision.

Even though we become a Presence-indwelt people at the moment of salvation, it is over the course of a lifetime that we continue to taste of what it means to be Presence-empowered. This is the process where the gift we received at the new birth begins to produce a series of "new births" in our lives. No, this is not saying that we need to get saved over and over again. Simply put, God wants to birth His nature, character, and power in your life as you surrender each area of your life over to the Spirit's loving control. God wants to birth new thought patterns and attitudes. He wants to birth new perspectives on impossibility and courage. This is what it means to live out the resurrected life. As we discover what it means to host God's Presence with our lives and let the Spirit Who lives inside of us rest *upon* us, it will become difficult to ever "change the subject." The *one thing* that drives us will be a desire to see the glorious Holy Spirit of God transform every area of our lives to look, sound, act, and operate more like Jesus. After all, *this* is what a Presence-indwelt life has made available to you.

Daily Scripture Reading

Romans 8:28-29 ▪ Galatians 5:22-25

Prayer

Lord, I surrender myself to You once again. Conform me to be more like Jesus. I am teachable. I submit to You any area of my life that is not what it should be and ask You to change me supernaturally.

January 31

***The more people carry God's Presence into all the earth as joyful servants of the Most High, the more we will be positioned to see one of Heaven's major mile markers*—THE EARTH COVERED WITH THE GLORY OF THE LORD.**

IMAGINE THIS—AN ENTIRE planet filled with people who host and carry God's Presence. Because it is Heaven's desire that none should perish and that *all* might be adopted into God's family, this is the reality we are called to press into. This must be the vision of God, because He Himself said that "*truly, as I live, all the earth shall be filled with the glory of the Lord*" (Num. 14:21).

He desires that none would be lost, but that all would experience eternal life. Receiving this life through the redemptive work of Christ is the key to seeing His glory transform a people and cover the planet. By bending our knee before the Cross, saying the ultimate "Yes" to the atoning work of Christ, and yielding our lives to follow Him, we position ourselves to be those fit to cover the earth with His glory. The key is stewarding this position. We are saved completely and utterly by grace. Even on our "best day," we can never earn our way to becoming worthy enough to be filled with God's Presence. Only the work of God can qualify someone to be filled with God. This is exactly what has created a company of people who are forgiven of sin, filled with the Holy Spirit, and qualified to carry God's Presence throughout the nations, *covering* the earth with His glory.

DAILY SCRIPTURE READING

HABAKKUK 2:14 ▪ PSALM 2:8

PRAYER

I say "Yes" to Your glory covering the whole earth. I want to be part of fulfilling Your vision by bringing people into Your Kingdom family. Please show me practical strategies of how I can do this in my city as well as in other nations, for Your glory.

FEBRUARY

Restored by the Presence to Represent the Father

February 1

The ones made in God's image would rule over the earth and represent Him in personality and function.

IN THE BEGINNING, humankind was created in the image and likeness of God. Sin caused us to fall short of living in this measure of glory. This is one of the reasons Jesus came to the earth. He was on a mission to "seek and save" that which was lost. Yes, people were lost, but there was also a position that was lost because of the transaction that took place in the Garden. Humankind gave the keys of earthly authority over to the devil when Adam and Eve rebelled. When Jesus was tempted by the devil for forty days, one of the temptations involved the enemy offering Jesus the kingdoms of the world. Jesus did not refute the devil's invitation, because authority over these earthly kingdoms was exchanged in Eden. According to Paul, the devil was the "god of this age" (see 2 Cor. 4:4).

Yet, Jesus was on a mission to restore you to your originally created position. You were made in God's image to represent His likeness and, yes, His rule over the earth. In fact, in representing God's unique expression of authority, redeemed humanity is giving expression to the uniqueness of God's nature. Remember, He rules in love and justice. He is completely good, entirely trustworthy, and eternally unchanging. The Sovereign King is also the Servant of All. As redemption has purchased us out of darkness and brought us back into a place of authority, it is necessary for us to model the example of the Redeemer. He was the only Man in history ever qualified to strip the devil of his tyranny over the nations. In turn, Jesus reclaimed the keys of authority from the enemy and has given them to you and to me.

Daily Scripture Reading

Matthew 16:19

Prayer

Jesus, thank You for giving me the keys of authority. I want to represent You well on the earth as I wield the authority You have given me to make disciples of all nations. Help me to understand both my position of authority and how to use it well.

February 2

Adam and Eve and all their descendants were to represent God on earth to the rest of creation.

WHAT DOES IT look like to walk in authority? If Eden exemplifies the exchange that took place between fallen man and the evil one, then the Cross signifies the exchange between Christ and redeemed humanity. In Eden, man handed the keys of authority over to the devil through sin. At the Cross, Christ reclaimed those lost keys so He could give them *back* to man. Until redemption, man was not qualified to be given a commission of authority as delivered by Christ in Matthew 28. This is because humankind was not able to accurately represent God until God dwelt inside of them. That was the Father's great plan. Jesus endured the Cross for the *joy* that was set before Him—a new reality that His sacrifice would usher people into. His joy was in obeying the Father, but also, His joy was in the vision of a community of people filled with the same Spirit that lived within Him. The pain of Calvary made necessary provision for the glory of Pentecost.

To represent God on the earth, humankind needed more than a seasonal or task-specific empowerment. This worked under the Old Covenant, but mainly to accomplish particular tasks. The work of Christ made it possible for humankind to actually be indwelt and possessed by God. Sin always stood as an ominous barrier that prevented deep intimacy between Heaven and earth, God and man. Jesus destroyed this barrier, making it possible for you to be filled with His Spirit. The veil in the temple was torn down the middle, revealing that the Presence that was kept behind that curtain for so long had now been unleashed. A work was accomplished that made it possible for the Presence to be released out of the old system and take up residence in a completely *new* temple. A new house: Redeemed men and women throughout the ages.

Daily Scripture Reading

Hebrews 12:1-2 ▪ Luke 19:10

Prayer

Jesus, thank You for dying on the Cross so that I could have a relationship with God and also house the Holy Spirit.

February 3

We can only release the benefit of God's rule flowing through us to the degree that His rule is over us.

GOD DOES NOT entrust His authority to rebels. We cannot rule well if we cannot first be ruled well. This is not a call to mindlessly submit ourselves to controlling or harmful authority; rather, it is first and foremost a necessary reminder that the One we call Savior is also our Lord. He is our ruler. Yes, we are His friends. However, friendship does not cancel out the function of servanthood; it only enhances it. It leaves us without excuse, actually. We serve God, not just because He tells us to do something, but because He reveals His heart to us. How can we not obey the One we profess to love above all others?

Those who submit to the rule of God *over* them actually qualify themselves to experience the rule of God *through* them. Too many are trying to walk in authority when they do not even understand how authority works. We submit to God's rule because we honor Him supremely, but we should also understand that in the process of submitting to God's authority we are discovering how divine rule operates through our lives. One of the great examples of this is seen in the Gospel of Matthew where the Roman centurion asks Jesus to heal his servant. Because the centurion understood authority, he was able to tap in to a dimension of faith that, up until that point, Jesus had not even experienced—not even in *all of Israel* (see Matt. 8:10). The centurion understood how authority operated and in turn was able to access a breakthrough for his servant as Jesus simply spoke the word and the man was healed (see Matt. 8:13).

Daily Scripture Reading

Matthew 8:5-13

Prayer

God, I know that there are different facets to our relationship including friendship and servanthood. As I grow in authority and demonstrate Your power on earth, help me to remain completely dependent on You. I never want to be haughty or selfish. I acknowledge that You are my Lord and Master.

February 4

Adam was brought into the creation picture as a co-laborer. He was actually given the responsibility to help define the nature of the world he was going to live in.

IN GENESIS 2:19, we are introduced to an incredible vision of God's collaborative partnership with man. God brings the animals to Adam to *see what he would call them*. Whatever name Adam gave the animal ended up defining the unique expression of its nature. It seems as though the Creator was actually inviting the creation into the process as a co-creator with Him. Was Adam fit to occupy such a role? Scripture tells us that man was created in the image and likeness of the Creator, so the potential to create was written into Adam's very DNA. This same potential is likewise etched into the essence of our true humanity.

Redeemed or not, people are still creating. Art. The written word. Film. Architecture. This creative ability has not been revoked. However, as those filled with the Presence of God, we have an unparalleled opportunity to create *with* God instead of creating apart from His influence and inspiration. This is a key area that we have been designed to rule in—the realm of creative arts. The rule is not expressed by overthrowing what we consider to be "dark" or "unredeemed" art. Rather, we represent the rule of God through creativity as we dream with Him, invent in His Presence, and collaborate with Him to produce works of art that can only be described as those birthed in another world.

Daily Scripture Reading

Genesis 2:19-20

Prayer

Father, I want to rule with You through expressing creativity. Remind me of the ways I love to create. I am open to new ideas as well. As You release Your creative inspiration, I won't be scared to step out and try to do whatever You show me.

February 5

God did not create us to be robots. We were made in His image as co-laborers, working with Him to demonstrate His goodness over all that He made.

EVEN THOUGH GOD could have created humankind to be robotic in nature, void of any type of free will, He took the risk and made free agents. It is incredible to consider that God risked everything to have that one treasure—those who would worship Him, not as robots, not merely out of command, but out of relationship.

The reason that Jesus does not show up in bodily form during our church services and manifest His full glory is that such an act would make worship involuntary. There is something fragrant about worship that is offered up through choice, by free decision. Such worship can only exist in the context of an intimate relationship between man and God.

Daily Scripture Reading

Genesis 2:15-17

Prayer

Thank You, God, for creating me with a free will. I use my will and choose to serve and love You because You are so good! Help me to make good decisions and co-labor with You to show people how good You really are.

February 6

The Garden itself demonstrated Heaven on earth.

Everything in the Garden of Eden was considered "good" by the Creator Himself. This represented God's template for the whole of created order. Remember, all that God created was perfect in every way. His creation was good because it carried the very essence of the Creator. Not even God could improve its design, function, or purpose, because all of it came out of Him. Eden was a picture of *on earth as it is in Heaven.*

And the reason for the placement of such an extraordinary place of peace and divine order was extreme—the rebellion of satan brought a scar into what was otherwise a perfect creation. And now peace, the substance of Heaven's atmosphere, was to take on a military function. Disorder had tarnished God's creation. It was now light against darkness, order versus chaos, and glory against that which is inferior, lacking, and hollow. This explains why Adam was given the unique commission that he was charged with. Likewise, the environment of Eden is a prophetic picture for why you and I have been given a commission to disciple nations. *Expansion.* God desired Eden to define the entire landscape of planet earth, particularly the areas that were in disorder because of darkness. In the same way, God desires His ambassadors to define *this world* by the culture of *His world.* Peace. Wholeness. Healing. Joy. Fullness. Freedom. Purpose.

Daily Scripture Reading

Genesis 1 ▪ Romans 14:17

Prayer

Thank You that I get to be Your ambassador who brings righteousness, peace, and joy in the Holy Spirit every place that I go. Fill me up so I can overflow with all of Your goodness and dispel darkness around me with light.

February 7

Adam's immediate responsibility was to tend the Garden. His ultimate responsibility was to bring the same order to the rest of the planet.

Adam's commission was to ensure that the culture and climate that defined Eden was spread throughout the rest of the planet. This is why God instructed him to "subdue" the earth, as there were elements that would need to be brought into subjection to the divine order that the Creator had originally established. The implication was that outside of the Garden there was not the same order that existed on the inside. This makes a lot of sense when we remember that the serpent came into the Garden to tempt Adam and Eve. He was already on the planet.

The world outside of the Garden was not perfect; it suffered under the influence of the rebellious one, satan, and his agenda to destroy, tarnish, and maim all that was beautiful and good. Humankind was not only instructed to steward Eden; they were called to advance and enforce Eden's culture throughout the whole of creation. This is the essence of *on earth as it is in Heaven.*

Daily Scripture Reading

Genesis 1:26-31

Prayer

I may not be able to influence the entire planet, but I know I can influence the people in my day-to-day world. Father, give me creative ways even now on how I can use the platform You have given me to bring the Kingdom of Heaven to earth.

God created order in the midst of disorder so that those made in His image might represent Him well by extending the borders of the Garden until the whole planet would be covered by God's rule through His delegated ones.

EDEN WAS WHERE humankind was planted—this was their territory. This would strongly suggest that the Garden of Eden was man's normal. Everything outside of this Garden revealed a world in opposition to the structure that God sovereignly set up which defined Eden. Anything beyond the borders of perfection needed to be transformed. Paradise was normal, not abnormal. Perfection was the standard, not the exception.

This is why God gave specific instructions to the man and woman *to "fill the earth and subdue it"* (Gen. 1:28). The very use of the "subdue" language reminds us that there was an enemy that needed to be defeated. There was darkness present that was alien to a planet fashioned for perfection. Even though there were opposing forces present on the earth beyond the confines of the Garden, God had equipped His appointed ones to successfully rule in His Name. Humanity was designed to *rule* over the earth—not just in the midst of perfection, but imperfection and resistance. Divine authority empowers humanity to enforce victory over darkness.

Daily Scripture Reading

1 John 5:1-5 ▪ Revelation 12:10-11

Prayer

Thank You for granting me victory over the enemy through Jesus Christ. I claim my full inheritance as a son/daughter of God and declare that I am an overcomer by the blood of the Lamb. Thank You for Your divine protection and the authority You've given to me.

February 9

Never at any time has satan been a threat to God. God is ultimate in power and might, beauty and glory. He is eternal with unlimited measures of all that is good. He is uncreated—has always existed. Satan is limited in every way.

THE DEVIL IS a created being that you have authority over. Satan has never been a threat to God. Heaven is not intimidated by the works of darkness. If God is not threatened by the enemy, you should not be either. In and of yourself, you may be no match against the powers of darkness. On the other hand, you are not waging warfare from a posture of human being to spiritual being. Of course the spiritual being will always triumph. The truth is, in Christ you are a new creation! The Victorious One actually lives within you and this means that "*greater is He who is in you than he who is in the world*" (1 John 4:4).

God is quite literally without equal. He is uncreated—has always existed. Your enemy, satan, is limited in every way. He is ever at the disadvantage. God gave him his gifts and abilities at his own creation. There has never been a battle between God and satan. The entire realm of darkness could be forever wiped out with a word. But God chose to defeat him through those made in His own likeness—those who would worship God by choice.

DAILY SCRIPTURE READING

1 JOHN 4:1-4 ▪ DEUTERONOMY 33:26-27

PRAYER

God, it is amazing to me that You would choose to include me in the battle against the enemy here on earth. Thank You for equipping me with Holy Spirit power and with angelic help and protection so I don't need to be afraid. I'll gladly stand against the enemy with Your Word and the power of Your Presence. You are the Victorious One and You live inside of me.

February 10

God didn't give Adam and Eve any instructions on spiritual warfare. There is no known teaching on the power of the name Jesus, no instruction on the power of their praise, nor is there any known emphasis on the power of His Word. These tools would be a great benefit later in the story. But right now their entire life was focused on maintaining divine order through relationship with God and spreading it through representing Him well.

ADAM AND EVE were to live responsibly and be productive, have children who would have children who would have children etc., and expand the borders of the Garden until the planet was covered by their rule. All of this flowed from their fellowship with God, *walking with Him in the cool of the evening.* This was their culture—their *normal.* We have much to glean in this picture of how to re-approach spiritual warfare in the day in which we live.

I understand that since sin entered the equation the devil did, in fact, become a point of focus. But the Garden is worth reexamining, as Jesus made provision to bring us back into relationship with the Creator. Between Eden and the Cross, relationship was severed, and thus the Garden would not prove an accurate template for what was accessible to the people under this era. Things have since changed. In fact, the author of Hebrews reminds us time after time that the New Covenant in Christ's blood has brought us into *better* and *greater.*

Daily Scripture Reading

Hebrews 8

Prayer

Thank You, God, for the New Covenant that has made a way for me to be in relationship with You like Adam and Eve were before the fall. I want to be aware of Your nearness and talk to You all throughout the day. Would You remind me just how close You are throughout the day?

February 11

We must be mindful of the enemy's tools. But even so, my strength is putting on the full armor of Christ. Christ is my armor!

I **BECOME CONCERNED BY** an *over*emphasis by some on the subject of spiritual warfare. Spiritual conflict is a reality that is not to be ignored. Paul admonishes us to not be unaware of the enemy's devices (see 2 Cor. 2:11).

If we have inherited a Covenant defined by better promises and a life of access to divine Presence, it goes without saying that the overemphasis we place on a defeated devil is a sign that we are walking below this new level of living. Jesus brought us into relationship with the Father. In Eden, everything was defined by relationship. Satan was never the focus for Adam and Eve. He didn't need to be, as he had no authority. In the same manner, he should not be a main focus for us either—*Christ must be!*

Daily Scripture Reading

2 Corinthians 2:11,14-15 ▪ 2 Corinthians 10:3-5

Prayer

Lord, help me to never be more impressed with the devil than I am with You because the devil has already been defeated. You are the risen King who reigns now and forever! As I focus my attention on You, Your Presence will permeate the atmosphere around me and dispel the darkness.

February 12

Adam and Eve, the ones who saw God the clearest, had no instructions on warfare, as their dominion repulsed the enemy in the same way that light drives away darkness without a fight.

SATAN COULDN'T COME into the Garden of Eden and violently take possession of Adam and Eve. That would have been a laughable impossibility. He had no authority or dominion where he had no agreement, either in the Garden or in Adam and Eve. Dominion is power. And because humanity was given the keys of dominion over the planet, the devil would have to get authority from humans. We see this transaction played out in Genesis 3, where man hands over the keys of authority to the serpent.

Fast forward to Jesus' resurrection and ascension into Heaven. The Great Commission involved Jesus making the bold announcement that *all* authority belonged to Him. *This* is the same authority that He commissioned us to disciple nations in. Jesus reversed the exchange that took place in the Garden by securing the keys of authority from the evil one and giving them back to those who were designed to represent God on earth. That original agenda had never been revoked. Sin, however, made its execution impossible for those under the tyranny of sin. That is, until Jesus gave us the keys!

DAILY SCRIPTURE READING

MATTHEW 28:18-20

PRAYER

Thank You, God, for making what was impossible possible through the sacrifice of Jesus. Without Jesus we would all be disempowered and under satan's rule. But instead You made a way for us to have relationship with You and dominion over the earth again. Thank You for making it easy to exercise dominion over the sphere of influence You've given me.

February 13

I can't afford to live in reaction to darkness. If I do, darkness has had a role in setting the agenda for my life.

IN THE ORIGINAL purpose of God, humankind was to rule over creation. But then sin entered our domain. Because of sin, creation has been infected by darkness—disease, sickness, afflicting spirits, poverty, natural disasters, demonic influence, etc. While our rule is still over creation, it has become focused on exposing and undoing the works of the devil. That is the ministry of Jesus that we inherited in His commission.

The key to undoing the works of the enemy is remaining focused on the blueprint of Heaven. This is not simply a matter of adhering to principles, but living in response to Presence. In the Lord's Prayer, *deliver us from the evil one* is listed after *Our Father in Heaven*—the very statement that begins the prayer. We are the greatest threat to the works of darkness when our gaze is continually fixed upon our Father in Heaven. This is the model that Jesus gave us, as He was One whose eyes and ears were consistently in tune with the Father. To constantly live in response to darkness, we are elevating the very thing we wish to resist or destroy. Darkness should not be a governing force in our lives; it was not for Jesus. He destroyed the works of the devil, not by being consumed with the task to dismantle demonic powers, but rather by constantly looking at the Father and seeing what He was doing. When we live in response to the Father, following the model of Jesus, by default we will destroy the works of darkness.

Daily Scripture Reading

John 5:16-23

Prayer

Father, help me keep my eyes fixed on You and not the enemy or the circumstances around me. I want to see from Your perspective. Take me higher in my thinking so I can be on the same page as You and bring Your heavenly strategies to earth.

February 14

All our actions come from one of two basic emotions—fear or love. Jesus did everything from love.

JESUS DID EVERYTHING from love. So much of what is called warfare comes out of fear. I've done it more than I care to admit. We would never worship or give honor to the devil. But remember, like the child needing attention in the classroom, if the enemy can't get it for something good, then at least he'll get it for something bad. He wants to become our object of focus and point of emphasis. Perhaps one of the greatest and yet most underused spiritual warfare strategies is to keep our eyes fixed on the Father's love. This is not a call to ignore conflict. Instead, it is a summons to see darkness from the right perspective.

The problem is, too much of what we call spiritual conflict involves an unfortunate shift of perspective. We fall into fear when we move away from love. Scripture tells us that perfect love casts out fear (see 1 John 4:18). I am convinced that we will become less fearful of darkness and more of a threat to it when we start experiencing greater measures of the Father's love. The One Who loves also protects. He walks with us. He never leaves us or forsakes us. In fact, the One Who loves us also dwells *within* us. Out of love, He has ensured that we are well-equipped for victory in every arena of life. The conflict must never distract us from the Father's love. When it does, we step into fear and fear distorts our perception. Fear is what magnifies darkness beyond its realistic position. In truth, darkness has been disarmed and you are filled with the Presence of its Conqueror!

Daily Scripture Reading

1 John 4:7-19

Prayer

Father, I choose to step toward Your loving embrace and away from fear. I choose to rest my head on Your chest and receive Your love. In Your Presence all fear disappears. What do you want to say to me today about the fear that has been nagging at me?

February 15

Jesus lived in response to the Father. I must learn to do the same. That is the only example worth following.

JESUS DID WHAT He saw the Father doing. He spoke what He first heard the Father saying. The Son of God never lived in reaction to darkness—He always operated in response to the Father. To walk in victory, we must follow this model. It is worth noting that this model is not entirely principle-based or formula-driven. The model that Jesus gives us of His response to the Father is a blueprint, yes, but it is completely motivated by intimacy. Jesus did not simply spend time with the Father to get the latest revelation, strategy, or formula for success in life.

Yes, Jesus personified a lifestyle of victory. He did not do this by following some seven-step process, though. A lifestyle of breakthrough is the organic byproduct of the lifestyle of intimacy with the Father. Jesus was able to see what the Father was doing because He walked closely with the Father. Jesus heard the sounds of Heaven because He was more at home in that world than He was in this world—although He never became "too heavenly minded to be of earthly good." It was Jesus' intimate connection with the Father in Heaven that positioned Him to bring that world to this one. In the same way, we can live in response to the Father in Heaven as we enjoy intimate fellowship and friendship with Him, just as Jesus did. Remember, Jesus is both our Savior and our example. God became a man, so that God could show man how to relate back to God. This is what we see in Jesus' relationship with the Father. Though He was and is eternally God, He also lived as a man in right relationship with God, giving believers throughout the ages a clear example of what the connection between man and God should look like.

Daily Scripture Reading

Luke 5:12-16 ▪ Matthew 14:22-33

Prayer

God, I don't want to be too busy to come away and spend time with You. Help me set boundaries in my life to protect my private time with You, just like Jesus did. In Your Presence is where I find life. You're my best friend and I want to spend time with You.

February 16

The devil doesn't mind negative attention. He'll let us chase him all day long in the name of "warfare." But it's a place of weakness. God calls us into a place of strength—rediscovering our place in the Garden.

SPIRITUAL WARFARE MUST always begin from a position of victory. We do not fight for victory, but rather we fight *from* victory. The difference is significant. When we are trying to fight for victory, we place a heavy demand on ourselves. If our prayers, confessions, declarations, and various spiritual warfare strategies do not overcome darkness, we call it defeat. The problem is that when we become overly focused on our efforts, we bypass the only effort that is of any substantial value—Christ's effort. He already won the victory.

When spiritual warfare is all about trying to secure victory, then we will always be fighting a losing battle. We do not have the power to prevail against darkness. This is one of the reasons that God sent Jesus to the earth in our place. Jesus was and is the only Man qualified to secure victory against the devil. Instead of us trying to fight for something that is impossible for us to obtain, let us start standing in the place of victory that was already paid for, in full, by Jesus. This perspective changes everything when we approach the necessary reality of spiritual warfare.

Daily Scripture Reading

Romans 8:31-39 ▪ Matthew 11:25-30

Prayer

Jesus, I choose to rest in the price You already paid at the Cross to secure victory against the devil. There is nothing else I need to do besides believe and do what You show me to do from that place. Thank You for not placing a heavy burden on my shoulders, but instead You give me supernatural rest and Your easy and light yoke. Thank You for freedom in Your Presence.

February 17

It is from the place of intimacy that true warfare is experienced.

THE DEEPER THE intimacy we enjoy with God, the more clearly we understand that the victory has already been purchased—and that the Victor actually indwells us. The place of intimacy reminds us of how close the victory truly is because the One who *is* victorious dwells within us. Think about it. Jesus Christ, the Champion of Heaven, lives inside of every believer through the power of the Holy Spirit. His victory is our victory; His resurrection is our resurrection!

When we exchange fighting for intimacy and start enjoying our relationship with God, we step into a new dimension of warfare. This is not license to ignore the reality of spiritual conflict. Make no mistake, we are in a battle. Paul reminds us not to be ignorant of the devil's devices. At the same time, Paul does not call us to become overly consumed with the enemy's schemes and strategies either. Warfare from intimacy is always victorious because we have decided to rest in the fact that the Greater One within us is already victorious. This suggests that our first directive in warfare is to change our agreement. We need to cease agreeing with the enemy, who tells us that we need to fight for our victory, and instead agree with the One who definitively stated, "It is finished."

Daily Scripture Reading

John 19:28-30 ▪ Romans 8:9-11

Prayer

Thank You, Jesus, for securing the final victory on the Cross. Thank You, Holy Spirit, for living inside of me. Give me a greater revelation of who You are in me so I can release You to the world around me.

February 18

At the table of fellowship, our relationship with God deepens and overflows into a life of victory in conflict with the powers of darkness.

GOD CALLS US into a place of strength—rediscovering our place in the Garden, walking with Him *in the cool of the evening.* This would suggest that true warfare is experienced in a place of intimate fellowship. Perhaps it was for that reason that David, Israel's great warrior and king, wrote, *"You prepare a table before me in the presence of my enemies"* (Ps. 23:5). The place of fellowship and intimacy with God is seen as the table of the Lord—yet it is placed in front of his enemies.

This is a strange picture indeed. But until we understand this concept, we will unintentionally elevate the devil's place much higher than it should be. This kind of romance strikes terror in the heart of the devil and his hosts. The enemy cannot stomach watching people enjoy deep intimacy with the Father. In the Garden, Adam and Eve ruled from this place of closeness. They saw what God was like in the place of intimacy and mirrored His character by following His instructions to have dominion over created order. Surely this aggravated the serpent beyond belief, as he was expelled from heaven because of his lust for a position of authority. He was banished to the earth, now a "creeping thing" that was placed under the dominion of man and woman—those created in God's image. The devil naively assumed that the fall would change everything. He attempted to disrupt God's design for man to rule in His image and likeness. To his utter disappointment, the Man, Christ Jesus, won back the keys of authority and dominion. He gave them to you and me so that we would assume our rightful place as those who *subdue* every expression of darkness in the planet.

Daily Scripture Reading

Psalm 23

Prayer

Thank You, Lord, for putting the devil under my feet by giving me authority over him in Jesus' Name. No matter what tough circumstances are in front of me, I know You are going to work them out for good, because of Your great love for me. I declare that the enemy is defeated in Jesus' Name.

February 19

We were created in God's image, for intimacy, that our dominion over the earth might be expressed through loving relationship with Him.

THE CREATION OF humankind was in a sense the beginning of a romance. We were created in God's image, *for intimacy*, that our dominion over the earth might be expressed through loving relationship with God. It is from this revelation of dominion through love that we are to learn to walk as His ambassadors, thus defeating the "prince of this world." The stage was set for all of the powers of darkness to fall as Adam and Eve exercised their godly influence over creation. But instead, *they* fell.

Jesus became a Man so that He could legally enter the human race and break the contaminating power of sin that kept us from enjoying the place of intimacy with the Father. He removed this impurity, making us fit to be inhabited by His holy Presence. Our commission as those indwelt by the Presence is to advance the rule of His Kingdom throughout the earth. This happens very uniquely. Just as the disciples were confused about how the Kingdom would be expressed, so many believers today have conflicting views about what an *advancing Kingdom* should look like. We express our authority in Christ by loving and serving those created in His image. This love can take on a number of different demonstrations. We meet practical needs, such as feeding the hungry, providing shelter for the homeless, and caring for orphans. These are beautiful expressions of the Kingdom—but there is more. We also carry the love of this Kingdom by seeing disease healed, torment lifted, bondage broken, and the captives set free. Authority and power have been restored to us for a glorious purpose—to show the world how good and loving the Father *truly* is.

DAILY SCRIPTURE READING

MARK 16:14-20

PRAYER

Thank You for empowering me to advance Your Kingdom by carrying Your Presence!

February 20

The enemy has no authority or dominion where he has no agreement.

IT'S IMPORTANT TO realize that even today satan is still empowered through our agreement. He cannot just overthrow your life at a moment's whim. Such is a flawed view of the adversary, giving him power that he does not possess.

Because the devil had no authority over Adam and Eve, all he could do was talk. This is often what he will do until he can secure our agreement. In Eden, he suggested that they eat the forbidden fruit, as it would make them like God. And they listened. Adam and Eve tried to become like God, but they did so through disobedience. And that disobedience cost them what they already had by design—Godlikeness. When we try to get through our efforts what we already have by grace, we voluntarily put ourselves under the power of law. This was the devil's attempt to get Adam and Eve to agree with him in opposition to God, thus empowering the devil himself. Through agreement, he is enabled to *kill, steal, and destroy* (see John 10:10). The great weapon against the devil's lies is God's truth. During his forty-day temptation, Jesus silenced the enemy every single time, wielding the sword of the Spirit—the Word of God. This same power is not only in your possession; it is upon your lips. It is in your mind. It is in you and it is near you. The same power that Jesus used to break every offer of demonic agreement is available to you today!

Daily Scripture Reading

Luke 4:1-13

Prayer

Jesus, help me to recognize the plots of the enemy to steal, kill, and destroy, and help me to use the Word of God like You did to overcome his lies. Holy Spirit, bring to mind Scripture verses that I have studied and heard so that I can align myself with the truth. Thank You for giving me such a powerful weapon!

February 21

God had given the entire Promised Land to the children of Israel. It all belonged to them all at once. It was their inheritance by promise. But they possessed only what they had the ability to manage.

THE EXPRESSION OF God's dominion flowed through the children of Israel according to their ability to rule well. They ruled well according to how well they were ruled. God told them why He wouldn't give them the fullness of the land all at once. If He did, the beasts would become too numerous for them and they would be defeated (see Exod. 23:29; Deut. 7:22). Instead, they were to grow into possessing the fullness of their inheritance. God advances His people in accordance with their ability to steward what they are stepping into. There are times when God promotes us beyond our ability, because He knows what it is inside of us. He recognizes that the potential within us is strong enough to accommodate the promotion that He is bringing us into. By and large, He promotes based on how we steward what is already in our possession.

The same principle applies to us today. From the Garden of Eden to Israel and the Promised Land to the believers of this hour, it's all ours. But what we possess now is according to our capacity to steward in the way that He would.

Daily Scripture Reading

Exodus 23:20-31 ▪ Deuteronomy 7:17-24

Prayer

God, thank You that You won't give me more than I can handle at a given moment. Thank You for Your grace that sets me up to succeed and not to fail. You know where I'm going and what the best plan is for me. I trust You and thank You in advance for Your good plans for my life. Help me to be a good steward of all the things in my possession.

February 22

There is no contest in a battle between God and satan. The devil is nothing compared with the Almighty One.

THE BATTLE HAS never been between God and the devil—there is no legitimate battle in that context. Such would be an unfair fight to the enemy, as God has the eternal advantage of power and victory over him. Rather, the conflict is between the devil and man, the ones made in God's image.

When sin entered the human condition, it became necessary for God's Son to become a Man to fight on our behalf. It was an unusual fight. First, He displayed absolute authority over the powers of darkness by healing and delivering every person who came to Him. Second, He lived victoriously and purely. There was nothing of sin that was enticing to Jesus because there was nothing in Jesus that valued sin. Third, He used His authority only for serving others. He did not use His power for Himself. And finally, He did the unthinkable: He gave Himself up to die in our place. That sounds like a strange way to win a war, but it was key. In doing so, He gave Himself entirely to bring salvation to all humanity.

Daily Scripture Reading

Colossians 2:11-15

Prayer

Jesus, thank You for fighting and winning the war against hell on my behalf. You are the ultimate victor. I am so thankful for my position in You as a victorious son/daughter who can partner with You to see You get Your full reward.

February 23

God's people are to manifest the beauty of His rule to a world in unbelief.

EVERYTHING GOD CREATED was made for His pleasure. He is a God of extravagant joy. He enjoys everything He made. Humanity has a unique place in His creation, though, in that we are the only part of His creation actually made like God. Likeness was made for the purpose of fellowship—intimate communion. Through relationship with God, the finite ones would be grafted into His eternal perfect past and obtain through promise an eternal perfect future. Even the realm of impossibilities could be breached by those created to be like Him. *"All things are possible to him who believes"* (Mark 9:23). No other part of creation has been given access to that realm. We have been invited in a "place" known only by God.

The heart of God must be celebrated at this point: He longs for partnership. He risked everything to have that one treasure—those who would worship Him, not as robots, not merely out of command, but out of relationship. This is how we manifest the beauty of His Kingdom throughout the earth. By choice, we worship. Not because we are forced to, but because everything about Him awakens everything within us. We have been chosen for this very purpose. Not because we're better, but because we're the ones who signed up for the ultimate quest—hosting His Presence. He enlists everyone who is *available* to learn to carry His Presence until all is changed.

Daily Scripture Reading

Mark 9:17-27

Prayer

Father, You risked it all to be in relationship with me. It is my great delight to honor, worship, and love You. I will do anything for You. I believe You can do anything, and that I can do the impossible because of the Holy Spirit Who lives inside of me.

February 24

There is always a difference between what's in our account and what's in our possession.

NOW IN THE same way God had given Adam and Eve the entire planet to rule over, they only had possession of the Garden of Eden.

The rest would be brought under their charge as they multiplied and increased their ability to represent God well. This would be seen in manifesting dominion over the entire planet. They, too, were to grow into their inheritance. They owned it all by promise. But their control was equal to their maturity. They possessed only what they could steward well.

DAILY SCRIPTURE READING

EPHESIANS 1

PRAYER

I praise You, Father, for the great inheritance that is already in my account because of Jesus. I want to more fully possess and utilize what is in my account. Thank You for the things I have already seen You do through me. Please continue to use me as a conduit to bring Heaven to earth in an increasing measure.

People were lost because of sin—so was their place of rule over God's creation. Jesus came to recapture both.

JESUS CAME TO seek and save that which was lost. This includes both humankind and what humankind delivered over to the enemy in Eden—*keys of authority.* Examine Jesus' conversation with satan during His 40-day temptation. At one point, the devil offers Jesus the kingdoms of the earth in exchange for worship. He explains, *"All this authority I will give You, and their glory; for this has been delivered to me, and I give it to whomever I wish. Therefore, if You will worship before me, all will be Yours"* (Luke 4:6-7). Notice the phrase *"for this has been delivered to me."* Satan could not steal it. It was forfeited over to the enemy when Adam left God's dominion for the sentence of death. This happened in much the same way as when Esau gave away his inheritance (long term) for the gratification of a meal (immediate) (see Gen. 25:29-34). It was an abandonment of a call, purpose, and inheritance.

The dialogue between Jesus and satan was fascinating. It was as though the devil was saying to Jesus, "I know what *You* came for. You know what *I* want. Worship me, and I'll give back the keys of authority that You came for." The devil blinked, so to speak. In this moment, he acknowledged that he knew what Jesus came for. Keys! Jesus held His course, rejecting the opportunity for any kind of shortcut to victory. He had come to die, and in doing so He would reclaim the keys of authority that God gave to Adam in the Garden.

DAILY SCRIPTURE READING

ACTS 2:22-36 ▪ EPHESIANS 1:20-23 ▪ REVELATION 1:18

PRAYER

Jesus, You are seated far above every principality, and You have all the authority. It is amazing to me that You have granted me the authority to use Your Name to drive out the enemy and see impossible situations submit to You. How would You like me to use the authority You've given me today?

February 26

The invasion of God into impossible situations comes through a people who have received power from on high and have learned to release it into the circumstances of life.

THE HEART OF God is for partnership with His created likeness. He's the ultimate King who loves to empower. His heart from day one was to have a people who lived like Him, loved like Him, created and ruled like Him. From day one, God's desire has been to be with His creation as the invited Landlord to look over their increased capacity to rule, making this world like His. In His world, His glory is the center.

The more people carry His Presence into all the earth as joyful servants of the Most High, the more we will be positioned to see one of Heaven's major mile markers—the earth covered with the glory of the Lord.

Daily Scripture Reading

Psalm 46-47

Prayer

God, You rule over the nations and You are highly exalted. You could have chosen to rule over us without a relationship with us or without including us in Your plans. Thank You for Your heart and strategy to empower me to rule with You. As I get to be part of seeing Heaven invade earth, I pray that every impossible situation would bow before You and give You the glory!

Jesus defeated the devil with His sinless life, defeated him in His death by paying for our sins with His blood, and again, in the resurrection, by rising triumphant with the keys of authority over death and hell, as well as everything else that God originally intended for man that will be revealed in the ages to come.

JESUS, THE VICTORIOUS One, declared, *"All authority has been given to Me in heaven and on earth. Go therefore..."* (Matt. 28:18-19). In other words: I got the keys back! Now go use them and reclaim humankind.

It is in this moment that Jesus fulfills the promise He gave to His disciples when He said, *"I will give you the keys of the kingdom of heaven"* (Matt. 16:19). God never cancelled the original plan. It could only be fully realized once and for all after the resurrection and ascension of Jesus. Another thing to take note of: If Jesus has all authority, then the devil has none! We have then been completely restored to the original assignment of ruling as a people made in God's image, people who would learn how to enforce the victory obtained at Calvary: *"The God of peace will soon crush Satan under your feet"* (Rom. 16:20 NIV).

DAILY SCRIPTURE READING

LUKE 19:1-10 ▪ ROMANS 16:17-20

PRAYER

Thank You, Jesus, for coming to seek and save me. You reign victorious and have given me victory over the plans of the enemy. I speak to the situations in my life that need a supernatural touch from God and say, "Submit to the Name of Jesus and come into alignment with Heaven's plan!"

February 28

Had the devil known that killing Jesus the Christ (the Anointed One) would make it possible for millions of "anointed ones" to fill the earth as the fruit of Jesus' death, he never would have crucified Him.

ONE OF THE beautiful truths so often overlooked is that on his best day the devil can only play into God's hand. Knowing the devil's hatred for humanity and knowing his hatred for the Son of God, it was easy to set the devil up to crucify Jesus. Incredibly, by trying to destroy the Son of God the devil was actually setting up his own demise. Even so, every strategy of the enemy in setting up Jesus' death was anticipated and divinely manipulated.

It's important to note that the devil didn't take Jesus' life. This would reinforce the deception that the devil has more power than he actually possesses. Jesus willingly laid down His own life (see 1 John 3:16). On numerous occasions the religious leaders planned to kill Jesus. But He had the habit of disappearing while they were pursuing Him. It wasn't the right time for Him to die. However, when the time was right, He gave Himself as a sheep to be slaughtered. Surely, the devil thought that he had secured a victory by eliminating the Anointed One. To his utter disappointment, the Prince of Glory was not the only one to rise up out of the grave. Because of the divine plan of God, you and I get to partake in His resurrection. His victory is our victory. As we receive the work of Christ on the Cross for salvation by faith, we become grafted into Jesus' personal victory over sin, the devil, death, and the grave.

Daily Scripture Reading

1 Corinthians 2:6-8 ▪ 1 John 3:16

Prayer

God, you are wisdom and brilliance personified! Would You impart to me some brilliant strategies for the people, possessions, and situations that I'm in charge of today? I am open for divine ideas. Help me to be brilliant and humble simultaneously, just like Christ.

If Jesus did His great miracles as God, I'm still impressed. But I'm impressed as an observer. When I discover that He did them as Man, then suddenly I am completely unsatisfied with life as I've known it. I am now compelled to follow this Jesus until the same things start happening in my life.

JESUS IS THE eternal Son of God. He is not a created being who somehow ascended to divinity, as some cults claim. He is entirely God, entirely Man. But both His life and death were lived as Man. What that means is that He set aside His divine privileges to live as a human being. He was without sin and was completely dependent on the Holy Spirit. In doing this, He became a model that we could follow.

The supernatural works of Jesus are not off-limits to you and me. If He performed miracles out of His divinity, then the possibility of you and I doing the *same works* that He did would be outlandish. "*Only God can do that*" would be our rote response to what we see Jesus doing in the Scriptures. Such would be a reasonable response if it were not for what took place at Jesus' water baptism. This event is one of the most significant examples for believers throughout history. Jesus did not *need* to be baptized, as He was without sin. Rather, He was baptized in both water and with the Holy Spirit for *our benefit and example.* This is what commenced His earthly ministry which was followed by signs, wonders, and miracles. Though He remained (and remains) God, He walked in the miraculous because of the Spirit. The Holy Spirit Who rested and remained upon Jesus is the same Presence Who took up residence within us the day we gave our wholehearted "Yes" to God. You automatically became qualified to do the same works as Jesus because you received the same Holy Spirit that He did!

DAILY SCRIPTURE READING

PHILIPPIANS 2:5-11

PRAYER

Thank You, Father, for the revelation that I can do the same works that Jesus did— empowered by the same Holy Spirit! Let nothing hold me back from attempting to do the same things Jesus did.

MARCH

Your Significance in God's Presence

March 1

Any time we look to ourselves, we will buy into the lie of insignificance.

AFTER GOD GAVE Moses a most impossible assignment, Moses asked God the question, *"Who am I?"* (Exod. 3:11). The same question has been asked countless times since. God comes to you with an impossible assignment and you view the assignment in light of your natural abilities or your perception of significance. Introspection, if unchecked, can lead us down a dangerous path. God calls us to do the impossible. Rather than instantly obeying, trusting that His calling assures empowerment, we become like Moses, looking to ourselves and asking the question, "Who am I?"

Moses knew he lacked all the necessary qualifications that one should have to be used by God for something so significant as leading God's own people out of slavery into freedom. When God chooses any of us for something like this, the same question should come to mind. It will if we see the call of God correctly. But God, knowing Moses intimately, was neither troubled nor impressed with who Moses was or wasn't. It was a non-essential. *"Certainly I will be with you"* was God's reply to Moses (Exod. 3:12 NASB). The same is true for you today. The same Presence that accompanied Moses lives inside of you! *Who are you?* You are one whom God walks with and lives inside! This truth should strengthen you for the assignment at hand.

Daily Scripture Reading

Exodus 3:1-14 ▪ Hebrews 12:1-3

Prayer

Thank You, Lord, for the testimonies in the Word of God that give me grace to step into breakthrough. Give me impossible dreams to be part of fulfilling on earth. Help me not to be fearful of seemingly impossible assignments, but help me to keep my eyes on You, Jesus, the Author and Finisher of faith.

March 2

Moses may not have known who he was. But God knew whose he was.

INITIALLY IT LOOKS like God ignored Moses' "Who am I?" question. But perhaps He didn't. It seems that he was letting Moses know that his whole identity was not to be in his skills, training, or popularity. It wasn't his gifts or even his anointing. It boiled down to one thing: "You're the one I want to be with." Who was Moses? The guy God liked to hang around.

Scripture shows us that Moses was a friend of God, one whom God spoke with *face to face*. After Abraham, Moses was the only one identified as God's friend until the New Testament. Because of Jesus, we have all been brought into friendship with God. The same Presence Moses enjoyed communion with and that empowered Moses to accomplish the impossible is the Presence Who lives inside of you. God knows you, not by what you consider to be your faults, hang-ups, and struggles, but by the significance He has assigned to your life. Just remember, like Moses you are one who God likes to hang around. This was demonstrated when God sent His very Spirit to take up residence within you. Never question your significance. As a believer, you need look no further than the Presence of the One dwelling within you for encouragement!

DAILY SCRIPTURE READING

DEUTERONOMY 34

PRAYER

God, thank You for the privilege of being able to speak to You face to face. Give me a clear vision of how much You like to be with me as my friend. Help my identity to be grounded in who I am to You, not what I can do for You.

March 3

When you're willing to do what you're unqualified to do, that's what qualifies you.

Both qualifications and significance appear different here on earth than they do from Heaven's perspective. Just as humility welcomes exaltation, so weakness qualifies us for strength. Weakness places you in a posture to receive supernatural strength. When we depend on our personal strength, there is only so far that natural currency can take us. As human beings, there are certain things that our natural abilities can accomplish, and then there are certain things that are well beyond the potential of our abilities. God is summoning His people to live beyond their ability, for only then can we tap in to His ability. What qualifies us to experience God's ability? Willingness to do what we are naturally unable to do. God is looking for a people who say "Yes" to Him, even when their minds cannot safely wrap around what He is calling them to do. This demonstrates trust, which is key to faith.

To walk in God's ability, we must be confident in the significance that He has assigned to us. Focusing on our own significance will always leave us discouraged, for if our significance is measured by our ability it has clear limitations. But God has assigned significance to your life, not because of what you can do, but because of Who has been deposited within you—the limitless Holy Spirit.

Daily Scripture Reading

Colossians 1:9-14

Prayer

Thank You, God, for qualifying me to share in the inheritance of the saints and do the same works that Jesus did. I say "Yes" to the plans and purposes You have for me. Give me Your heavenly perspective of the limitless potential and power available through the Holy Spirit.

March 4

God often answers the prayers of His people by raising up a person He favors.

MANY IF NOT most Jews hold Moses in the highest place of respect as compared with any other individual in their history. And for good reason. He brought the Law to them (the Word from God), he led them through the wilderness to their inheritance, and equal in importance from my perspective, he modeled a yielded life. His encounters with God remain a high-water mark. This man, Moses, was actually God's answer to Israel's cry for deliverance.

Scripture tells us that creation is groaning, desperate for the sons and daughters of God to be revealed. Though Moses enjoyed a special measure of God's favor, being uniquely chosen to deliver Israel, you and I have access to the same Spirit of God. In fact, that very Spirit that raised Jesus Christ from the dead lives within us. This tells me that we are more than qualified to take our place and answer the cries of enslaved humanity. This is represented through sickness, torment, hopelessness, fear, anxiety, discord, and a host of other ills that have plagued the human condition because of sin. The Holy Spirit Who anointed Jesus to bring deliverance, freedom, healing, and liberation is the very Spirit Who has empowered you and me to fulfill this same mission. God continues to answers prayers today using His people. Let's keep our lives postured to be used in this most wonderful way!

DAILY SCRIPTURE READING

LUKE 4:16-21

PRAYER

Holy Spirit, I want to be part of Your answer to people's prayers. Use me to bring good news to the poor, freedom to the oppressed, restoration and healing to the hurting, and miracles to the sick in Jesus' mighty Name. Thank You in advance for setting me up for divine appointments that will change people's lives for the better.

March 5

God often chooses people knowing that they are the key to touching other people's lives.

GOD IS SOVEREIGN. He can do whatever He wants and move however He likes. And yet, the Sovereign One has established a structure where His Presence and power flow through anointed people. His standard mode of operation seems to be using people to touch the lives of other people. Such was the case with David, king of Israel. The Scripture tells us that God exalted David *for the sake of His people Israel.* This is a prime example of how God uses people—in this case, King David—as conduits to release His blessing. This produces a divine "trickle-down effect" where everyone in Israel was blessed because of David.

Everyone reading these words was chosen first because of God's love for you. But make no mistake. You are uniquely positioned in this world because of the cry of other people. His favor is upon you so you can be a part of His plan of distributing that same favor to others.

Daily Scripture Reading

2 Samuel 5:6-12

Prayer

God, thank You for the favor that is on my life. Show me how I can use the influence that You've given me to be a blessing to other people. Thank You for using people to speak and pour into my life. Help me to do the same for others.

March 6

All meaningful relationships require such vulnerability.

MOSES LIVED FOR 120 years—40 years in Pharaoh's house raised as a son, 40 years in the wilderness leading sheep, and 40 years leading Israel to the Promised Land. If the first 80 years weren't extreme enough, from the palace to the wilderness, the last 40 years were even more so—success and failure, visitations and encounters with God followed by horrible run-ins with the demonic realm, the worship of false gods, and the corresponding devilish activity.

His conversation with Pharaoh alone is enough on which to write a book. God actually told Moses, *"I make you as God to Pharaoh"* (Exod. 7:1 NASB). That's quite a statement for God to say to someone. Unlike anyone previous, God positioned Himself to do as Moses acted and/or declared. It's a rare thing to find God so willing to make Himself vulnerable to a man. But it is His heart to have that kind of relationship with man—with *you*! God trusts you because He trusts Himself. Moses gives us a picture of the interaction we can enjoy with God today. God trusts those He has given Himself to. God has given you His very Presence, the Holy Spirit. This required incredible vulnerability on His end. Such demonstrates the Father's extravagant love which is utterly beyond the realm of comprehension.

DAILY SCRIPTURE READING

EXODUS 7:1-5 ▪ LUKE 10:1-20

PRAYER

Father, thank You for trusting me. Thank You for the gift of the Holy Spirit in me, the mind of Christ, and for the ability to hear You speak. As I obey, You empower me to make good decisions. I want to do a good job of stewarding the trust You've given to me. Continue to teach me to recognize Your voice and know when You're leading me a certain way and when You're leaving the decision up to me.

March 7

God draws us into our destinies by revealing Himself to us.

WHEN GOD REVEALS Himself to us, this stirs up our hunger—hunger that can only be satisfied by Him. Revelation comes piece by piece, layer upon layer, to generation after generation. Moses stepped into a dimension of God that was new to humankind. *"God spoke further to Moses and said to him, 'I am the Lord; and I appeared to Abraham, Isaac, and Jacob, as God Almighty, but by My name, Lord, I did not make Myself known to them'"* (Exod. 6:2-3 NASB).

God revealed Himself to Moses in a way that not even Abraham, the father of faith, had received. And God was letting Moses know the place of favor he had entered into. Each bit of increased understanding is both an invitation for relationship and a new high-water mark to be sustained by the following generation.

Daily Scripture Reading

Exodus 6:2-3 ▪ Exodus 33:7-23

Prayer

God, thank You for the realms of glory and understanding that I can step into because of other saints who have gone before me. Bring me into the high places of encounter and intimacy with You so I can give it away to the next generation—who will go even higher.

March 8

Revelation is initially for relationship and ultimately for the transformation of our lives.

WE ARE TRANSFORMED through a renewed mind (see Rom. 12:2). And transformed people transform cities.

God is not that interested in our increased understanding of theological concepts if there's no relationship increasing with it. When God gives us revelation, He is inviting us to a new place of experience—knowing Him in a deeper, more intimate way. *"To know the love of Christ which passes knowledge; that you may be filled with all the fullness of God"* (Eph. 3:19). This verse states that we can know by *experience* what surpasses knowledge or, more specifically, *comprehension*.

Daily Scripture Reading

Ephesians 3:14-21

Prayer

Lord, help me to experience the great love of Christ and be filled with the fullness of Your Presence! Overwhelm me with Your infinite goodness. I am so grateful that You can do above and beyond all that I could ever ask or think.

March 9

Moses' response to God moved Him out of the "what's possible" position to a highly favored position.

Moses' role was a frightening one for sure. But he was unique—unique in the sense that he responded to God as few have in history. My football coach would have described him as one who gave 110 percent—more than what is seemingly possible. The verse *"many are called, but few are chosen"* (Matt. 22:14) comes to mind in this context.

So much of the increased favor we get from God is really according to what we've done with the favor we already have. Moses had been called, but now he was chosen. He was one who took what God offered and ran with it with what some might consider *reckless abandon.*

How are you using the favor that God has already given you? This is often a strong indicator of the level of favor that He will usher you into.

Daily Scripture Reading

Matthew 25:14-30

Prayer

Lord, thank You for the favor and influence You have entrusted to me—like the parable of the talents. I believe that You are for me, not a harsh master waiting for me to mess up so You can punish me. I choose to step into and use the favor that You have entrusted to me, just like Moses did.

March 10

Each generation has access to more than the previous.

King David would later discover some things about God's response to worship that were unknown in Moses' time. This reveals how each generation has access to more than the previous generation did. It is God's law of compound interest. Specifically, David recognized how God responds to the praises of His people. God responds with His Presence—He comes. This call of God upon the nation of Israel was to leave Egypt in order to worship. They were becoming a people who would be known by the Presence of God. He would become the distinguishing factor.

God's heart was for His entire nation of Israel to become priests. In fact, He commanded Moses to tell Israel of His desire. *"And you shall be to Me a kingdom of priests and a holy nation"* (Exod. 19:6). Priests minister to God. The plan of God having a people of His Presence was well underway. In fact, this plan has been fulfilled through the work of Jesus. According to the New Testament, you and I are a kingdom of priests. We look back to Israel to receive a prophetic blueprint of the fullness we are now able to walk in.

Daily Scripture Reading

Exodus 19:3-6 ▪ Revelation 1:4-6 ▪ Revelation 5:8-10

Prayer

What an honor it is to be called Your priest. Thank You for the privilege of being able to minister to You and to other people. Keep me holy, pure, and blameless through the blood of Jesus. Show me what it looks like to minister to You on a day-to-day, moment-by-moment basis.

March 11

The devil is very afraid of a worshiping people.

WORSHIP IS POWERFUL for many reasons. One of the most important is that we always become like the One we worship. This by itself would take Israel to new levels. But this call of God upon the nation of God would not go unnoticed. The enemy is fearful of worshipers because of what worship summons them into—becoming increasingly transformed into God's likeness by experiencing His glory.

The enemy actually doesn't mind complacent worship, as it seems to work opposite to the real thing—it deadens our sensitivities to the Holy Spirit of God. It works completely opposite to the effects of sold out, passionate worship. Complacent worship is an oxymoron. Satan's strategy against God's people and their call as God's intimates has never been clearer than when he revealed his hand through Pharaoh's words: "*Go, sacrifice to your God in the land*" (Exod. 8:25). Moses was trying to bring Israel *out* of the land of Egypt, while Pharaoh was proposing a costless compromise: *Just stay here and worship.*

Convenience and sacrifice cannot coexist. The *going* is a sacrifice, and a non-sacrificial people are of no consequence to the devil. The enemy knows there's power in the offering and will do whatever he can to distract us from giving it.

Daily Scripture Reading

Exodus 8:25-28 ▪ 2 Samuel 24:18-25

Prayer

God, I am not afraid to sacrifice something if it means I get more of You in return. Show me what it means to offer up the sacrifice of praise and be an extravagant worshiper before You.

March 12

Sometimes we fail to reach our destiny because we insist on it happening where we are—within reason, with little effort involved on our end.

WE OFTEN CANNOT get to a new place in worship until we get to a new place in God. I've heard so many people say through the years, "If it is God's will to move powerfully in my life (or church) He knows we're hungry, and He knows where we are." Foolishness! He's not a cosmic bellhop, bouncing around the universe to fulfill our every wish. He has a plan. And we must move into His plan. Wise men still travel, both in the natural and figuratively speaking.

So many mistakenly think that if God is moving somewhere, there is really no purpose in visiting that place. After all, the God Who moves in one geography is more than capable of moving in a different geography. Here is the problem with such a perspective—it is void of hunger. When we are hungry for God's Presence, we will move where He is moving. This is not always a summons to leave everything and relocate to a new church or state or place in the world. Sometimes it might be. Most of the time, it is God's divine summons. Our response to the summons of outpouring reveals what's in our hearts. If we write it out before Him, claiming that *if God wants to move, He knows where to find us*, the first and most necessary "new place" has not been reached. If we want to walk in new places in God's Presence and experience fresh expressions of His power, our hearts first need to go to a new place in God—a place of humility and hunger.

Jesus describes this place in the Sermon on the Mount as He says, "*Blessed are those who hunger and thirst*" (Matt. 5:6).

Daily Scripture Reading

Matthew 5:1-10

Prayer

God, call me out of my comfort zone to go to new places where I can learn and experience You in new ways...even if it costs me something.

March 13

The only way to follow the One who died on the Cross in our place is to mirror His devotion!

THE FEAR OF fanaticism has kept many believers from stepping into their destiny. The Extreme One is calling out to extreme ones to come and follow Him. It is with that group He will change the world.

Deep still calls to deep—the deep of God is still looking for people who have a similar depth in their hearts to respond equally to Him (see Ps. 42:7). Wasn't it the one with no depth in himself that Jesus warned us of in the parable of the seed and the sower? *"Yet he has no firm root in himself, but is only temporary, and when affliction or persecution arises because of the word, immediately he falls away"* (Matt. 13:21 NASB).

God's invitation has been extended. Will you step into your identity as one of His *extreme ones* and respond to His *extreme call*? This is the only way we will ever experience the normal reality of His world transforming this one. Remember, what is extreme for us is quite normal to God. We call extreme what He labels as "reasonable." As we respond to God's invitation into the reasonable, we will likewise step into His version of normal.

DAILY SCRIPTURE READING

PSALM 42

PRAYER

God, I will follow You no matter what. I'm not afraid to be called extravagant and wasteful in my worship for Jesus. Introduce me to other burning ones who are following after You at any cost so we can encourage and partner with each other to see Your Kingdom come.

March 14

Nothing is as fierce an opponent to the powers of darkness as the unified offering to God from multiple generations.

THIS IS ONE of the places where we see the mystery of compound interest in effect in the things of the Spirit. The fact that the devil puts so much effort into dividing the family unit and splintering the generations should testify to us of its importance.

It has become all too common for one member of the family to stand out as the spiritual one, while the rest of the family is known for complacency. Tragically, the spiritual one often gets exalted in pride, which brings division, or they lower the standard of their passion to fit the lowest common denominator in the family. Neither route is effective.

The purpose of Heaven is connectedness among generations. This is the vehicle through which revival will be sustained—continuing on from one generation to the next. What one generation receives as a revelation, the next will step into as a reality.

DAILY SCRIPTURE READING

PSALM 145

PRAYER

Lord, I don't want there to be division in my family, in my church, or in the larger body of Christ. I pray for a spirit of unity and humility to permeate all of us, so that the stronger ones can pull the weaker ones up. I want to receive from the generation that went before me so I don't have to start from scratch. Help guide me to people and resources from people who have gone before me who can impart revelation to me.

March 15

When we add the supernatural power of the resurrected Christ to a people unified to His purpose and one another, nothing they purpose to do will be impossible for them.

BURN WITH PASSION no matter what, but maintain humility, being the servant of all. The momentum gained through the generations working together creates a spiritual wealth that truly makes nothing impossible for those who believe. Even the unity *outside* of Christ is powerful. Consider the Tower of Babel. We see that the people said:

> *"Come, let us build for ourselves a city, and a tower whose top will reach into heaven...." The Lord said, "Behold, they are one people...and now nothing which they purpose to do will be impossible for them"* (Genesis 11:4,6 NASB).

Just consider the power of unity *in* Christ. It was unity that positioned one hundred and twenty people in the upper room to change the landscape of the known world. Surely there were disagreements among them. I cannot imagine that in the context of one hundred and twenty people, everyone was on the exact same page all of the time about everything. But something positioned their hearts to be so knit together that it became possible for them to maintain the humility necessary to sustain hunger to receive what Jesus prophesied would come.

These people were waiting with hunger and expectancy for the Promise of the Father that Jesus told them about. Undoubtedly, there were fears, doubts, concerns, and questions also assaulting their minds. But in that place of unity, there was encouragement. There was edification. There was a mutual strengthening. There was iron sharpening iron. Unity preserved this company of people, and unity prepared them to receive power for the supernatural task that was ahead.

DAILY SCRIPTURE READING

ACTS 1-2

PRAYER

God, I ask for a supernatural unity to take place among my family, church, and ministry team members.

March 16

True worship involves my whole being. It is physical, emotional, spiritual, intellectual, and financial.

THE OFFERING GIVEN from convenience protects form, ritual, and image. None of these things threaten the devil. He'll even attend the meetings where such priorities exist. And strangely, he'll go unnoticed. True worship is all-encompassing. It involves my relationships and my family, and it has a major impact on the boundaries I've set for how I want to live.

Worship has a complete focus—God and His worth. It really is all about Him. It's about Presence. Israel, a generation of slaves up until their deliverance from Egypt, was called to greatness. And their first step into such greatness was to worship Him extravagantly! They could not cater to Pharaoh's shallow invitation to costless worship. It was impossible, for the One calling Israel out of bondage was the One worthy of it all. Moses recognized this. He was not willing to compromise with Pharaoh, for the worship God was calling Moses and the people of Israel to demanded everything. He was calling them out of Egypt in every way. Physically. Spiritually. Emotionally. Mentally. Israel's culture and society would change dramatically because of the Exodus. While this is undeniably a story of deliverance and freedom, it is just as much an expression of sacrificial worship. Remember, Israel was not just being called to the Promised Land. First, they were being brought to the Mountain of God to worship.

DAILY SCRIPTURE READING

JOHN 4:21-24 ▪ ROMANS 12:1

PRAYER

Lord, I surrender all to You. You're the One whom it all came from, so I lay it back down at Your feet. I don't want to just worship You on Sunday morning. I want to worship you 24/7. Give me creative ideas on how I can worship You extravagantly every day of my life.

March 17

Moses was a prototype in that he modeled a lifestyle that was above the Law.

MOSES WAS NOT *above the Law* in the sense that the Law didn't apply to him. But he was above the Law in the sense that he had access to the Presence of God in a way that was forbidden by the Law, even for the tribe of priests, the Levites. As such there's a part of Moses' lifestyle that gives you and I a prophetic picture of what would become possible under the New Covenant that was yet to come.

As I look at Israel's journey and the experiences with God from the many leaders in the Old Testament, Exodus 33 is the Bible's standout chapter in my perspective. Moses had several face-to-face encounters with God. But only one time that he came down from his meeting with God on the mountain did his face shine with the Presence of God. He literally radiated God's Presence (see Exod. 34:30). Not until Jesus, on the Mount of Transfiguration, would we see that phenomenon again (see Matt. 17:2).

This man with whom God spoke face to face gives expression to what Paul told the Corinthians, "*But we all, with unveiled face, beholding as in a mirror the glory of the Lord, are being transformed into the same image from glory to glory, just as by the Spirit of the Lord*" (2 Cor. 3:18). Until Jesus, the Law had kept the people of God from entering into His Presence and living as a company of priests. Moses was a glimpse of what would become available because of the Cross. Redeemed men and women, indwelt by God, were given all-access to the transforming, shining Presence of the Lord. Amazing how God invited Moses "above the Law" to give us a glimpse of what life would look like.

DAILY SCRIPTURE READING

EXODUS 34:29-35 ▪ 2 CORINTHIANS 3:7-18

PRAYER

Thank You, God, for the opportunity to have access to Your Presence like Moses did. Fill me up during my time with You. I want to experience You in the fullness of Your glory and release Your glory to those You long to encounter.

March 18

A revelation of God's goodness will change our countenance.

THERE WAS ONE significant difference in the outcome of Moses' encounter with God in Exodus 33. This is the time he asked to see the glory of God, and God let all His goodness pass before his eyes (see Exod. 33:19). The outcome was that Moses' face shone because of seeing God's goodness. God wants to change the face of His Church once again through a revelation of His goodness.

Even today, beholding God's goodness changes everything about us. If we approach life from a perspective that God is angry, upset, and ever ready to unleash judgment, our countenance will actually reflect our revelation of God's nature. Our words will communicate this. Our thoughts will be influenced by this framework. On the other hand, if we start modeling the God Who is good, everything about us will shine His nature to those we are constantly interacting with. He must be seen as the Good Father He truly is.

DAILY SCRIPTURE READING

ROMANS 8:15-16 ▪ MATTHEW 7:7-11 ▪ 1 JOHN 3:1

PRAYER

God, thank You for being a better Father than any parent in the whole world. You are more kind, generous, and loving than any human being. Please give me a greater revelation of just how good You are.

March 19

God longs to raise up a people who will not just carry good news in the form of words. He longs to raise up a people who carry the good news in power, which is a Person.

THE GOSPEL IS undeniably a message communicated through words, but it is also a demonstration of power. Paul the apostle knew this. He could not disconnect his preaching from the demonstration of power. He told the Corinthians that even his proclamation of the Gospel *message* came about not through natural eloquence or superior communication skills. It was the demonstration of supernatural power that validated that Paul's message was of another world and another Kingdom (see 1 Cor. 2:1-5).

Paul was not just another philosopher or poet coming through town, as the Corinthians had been well used to. He was not coming in the prose of rhetoric, but in supernatural demonstration of power that only came through the Holy Spirit's Presence. This made the Gospel far more than spoken words of good news. The good news was announced through words and then demonstrated through power. Gospel words became Gospel realities before their very eyes.

DAILY SCRIPTURE READING

1 CORINTHIANS 2:1-5

PRAYER

God, I want to be a messenger who brings the good news of the Gospel, but I don't want to have intellectual discussions only. I want there to be demonstrations of Your power and love accompanying the good news, so that people actually see how amazing and real You are. I give You permission at any time to flow through me to unleash the reality of Your Kigngdom.

We must expect superior things from a superior covenant.

MANY NEW COVENANT believers reminisce about Old Covenant realities that they have never experienced. They assume that what was experienced in a *former day* cannot be surpassed—or even attained—in our day. As a result of believing this, we have come to expect less from everything God made available to us in the New Covenant.

We will always expect less from our New Covenant inheritance as long as we continue to view them as nice words on a page. Nice words might inspire us for a moment or even a season, but they will always fail to bring us into a superior reality. God's Word is full of power; the lack is never on His end, but rather on the end of humankind's perspective of and approach to the glorious New Covenant promises.

I am sure Paul was doing everything he possibly could to communicate to believers, both in Corinth and those who would be reading for generations to come, the unfathomable glory that we have all been brought into because of Jesus:

> *But if the ministry of death, in letters engraved on stones, came with glory, so that the sons of Israel could not look intently at the face of Moses because of the glory of his face, fading as it was, how will the ministry of the Spirit fail to be even more with glory?* (2 Corinthians 3:7-8 NASB)

We must expect and press in for more!

DAILY SCRIPTURE READING

LUKE 22:14-20 ▪ HEBREWS 12:18-24 ▪ 2 PETER 1:1-4

PRAYER

God, thank You for all of the precious promises available to me through the blood of Jesus in the New Covenant. Help me to understand exactly what is available to me in this superior New Covenant reality. I ask for more of You!

March 21

If you could chose one thing to be known for, one thing that would distinguish you from everyone else, what would it be?

HOW DO YOU want people to remember you? People work so hard to create an image and form a reputation for themselves. For some it's their beauty or their skills. For others it's their significance or their place in society. And still others work hard to create an image from the spiritual gifts they operate in. The Bible even teaches us the value of a good name (see Prov. 22:1). It is obviously important if it's done correctly.

God chose Israel's reputation for them. At least He chose what He wanted it to be. They were the least of all, the most insignificant of all, the weakest of all nations. There was nothing about their natural qualities that made them stand out from any other people group. But there was this one thing that was to set them apart. *"And He said, 'My presence will go with you, and I will give you rest'"* (Exod. 33:14). It would actually be the glory of God—His manifested Presence—that would be their distinguishing mark. In the same manner that God's Presence gave Israel significance, He has also distinguished you using the same glory. Remember, the Presence that *went with* Israel lives *within* you. This is the glory of your New Covenant inheritance!

Daily Scripture Reading

Exodus 33:12-17

Prayer

God, thank You for the gift of Your Presence that lives within me and goes with me wherever I go. Let Your Presence be the distinguishing mark on my life that will transform atmospheres and people around me.

March 22

CHURCH HISTORY IS filled with people who obtained favor from the Lord in unusual ways. Most of us have favorites—those we have admired for various reasons, many according to our own history and background. These heroes of the faith reached places in God that we long for. Their place of great breakthrough is always to become the new norm as their example welcomes us to pursue Him in the same fashion. He still welcomes all.

Daily Scripture Reading

Hebrews 11–12:1

Prayer

Lord, thank You for the amazing legacies that heroes of the faith have given the body of Christ to step into. Help me to see their victories not as impossibly high ceilings, but as easily attainable floors that I get to build upon. Give me the grace to glean from these saints' victories so I can carry on the momentum they started. What an incredible spiritual heritage You have brought me into!

March 23

ONE OF THESE heroes I admire most is Kathryn Kuhlman. I actually had the privilege to see her on several occasions as a young man. I respect her so much, for so many reasons. The miracles that came forth in her meetings are certainly one of reasons. But let's lay that aside for a moment.

Without being disrespectful, I'd like to tell you what Kathryn wasn't. She wasn't known as a great Bible teacher or a great preacher, although she could do both. She didn't have natural beauty that seems to exalt others to a place of favor with man ahead of their appointed time. She wasn't a great singer, moving crowds with an amazing voice. And the list goes on.

What could she do? She just seemed to be the person God liked to be with. She is known for the Presence. The miracles came from that one thing. The mass conversions came from that one thing. The high places of worship that were experienced in her meetings came from that one thing.

She was a Presence woman.

Daily Scripture Reading

PHILIPPIANS 3:1-11

Prayer

Jesus, it is so encouraging to know that I don't have to be extraordinary at many things. I can just be extraordinary at hosting You so You can show up and do what You do best. Help me be someone who values Your Presence above any other earthly quality or certification, because when I do this, massive things will happen because Your Holy Spirit is given His rightful place in my life.

March 24

To be all we can be requires that we are more dependent on God.

I STILL GET TEARY-EYED when I watch the video where Kathryn Kuhlman talks about her point of absolute surrender to the Holy Spirit. It is a sobering moment indeed. She testifies of the precise moment, the precise location where she said the ultimate "Yes" to God. Those moments don't reveal our strength. They actually reveal our weaknesses. They demonstrate our utter need for God's Presence.

The incredible collision takes place when we recognize complete dependency on God's Presence and respond to this state of dependency with hunger. Some try to suppress dependency because it does reveal weakness. We must celebrate this rather than be ashamed of it. Weakness qualifies us to yield to His Presence. We are all weak. The question is, how are we going to respond to our weak condition? Will we attempt to continue in our own strength and effort, desperate to shield the world from what we assume to be a major shortcoming? Or will a confrontation with our weakness drive us into the secret place where we cry out for His power to be made perfect in our weakness?

We cannot cover up our shortcomings, the greatest of which is our inability to do anything significant apart from His anointing. This does not mean we are worthless people. I, for one, am amazed that God considered us worthy of His very Spirit. The Holy One tore open the heavens on the Day of Pentecost and released His Presence into a new temple—flawed people of flesh and blood. The question: Will we depend on His Presence working through us, or will we continue to try and pull our own weight?

Daily Scripture Reading

2 Corinthians 12:1-10 ▪ Jeremiah 9:23-24

Prayer

Holy Spirit, I never want to boast about my own ability or take pride in what I can do apart from You. I absolutely need You now and will always need You.

March 25

So many try to wear Saul's armor in an attempt to operate in someone else's gift.

KNOW WHO YOU are *not*. This is a powerful key to operating in the anointing because God created you to be uniquely *you*. The longer we try to be someone else, the longer we are avoiding placing our complete reliance upon the empowering Presence of God within us. We can either depend on God or depend on our own strength to try and become something we are not. This is a counterfeit response to weakness.

Could it be that your point of greatest weakness might be the area through which God releases the greatest breakthrough? So many respond to weakness incorrectly. We sense there are areas unique to us that God wants to work through. At the same time, we confront the fact that we are weak in these areas. We are inefficient. We are unskilled. We are unlearned. We have not arrived. We are unqualified. Because of this, we look at other people, watching them flourish in their giftings. We see them being used by God and desire to be used in the same way. The desire to be used by God is healthy; the assumption that the way to be used by God is to try and mimic someone else's gifting is dangerous. This is us trying to "put on Saul's armor." When David was getting ready to face Goliath, they tried to suit him up with Saul's battle gear. It did not fit. God was not going to manifest Himself through David as He would have through Saul; this was going to be a unique demonstration of His power through a shepherd boy with a slingshot and a few smooth stones.

Often, we see a person we admire and often jealously try to become them or surpass them. *Anyone who knows who God made them to be will never try to be someone else.*

DAILY SCRIPTURE READING

1 SAMUEL 17:31-54

PRAYER

Thank You, God, for the way that You uniquely made me.

March 26

It is improper to expect superior blessings from an inferior covenant

Moses' life stands today as an invitation for all to enter a deeper place with God. The amazing part is that all that Moses experienced happened under an inferior covenant. Jesus inaugurated a new and better covenant (see Heb. 8:6). It is vital for us to understand how the New and the Old interact. For one, the New does not abolish the Old. Jesus did not come to do away with the Law and the Prophets; He came to *fulfill* them (see Matt. 5:17). What Moses experienced in shadow, we have been given license to pursue in substance. The Old Covenant should not be seen as the high-water mark of Christian experience, but rather a significant starting place.

Consider Moses again. His accomplishments and experiences should be held in high esteem by the Church. It would be foolish for us to do otherwise. But it would be equally foolish to ignore that fact that the high-water mark of the Old Testament was not to remain the high-water mark for the New. This is what it means to expect superior blessing from an inferior covenant. It is easy for us to distance ourselves from what *they*, the key figures of the Old Covenant, experienced in God. This distance is the result of not recognizing the glorious superiority of the Covenant we have been brought into through Jesus' blood.

Our New Testament heroes of the faith understood this. This is what gave them permission to press in for more.

Daily Scripture Reading

Matthew 5:14-20 ▪ Psalm 78

Prayer

God, You did truly amazing things with the children of Israel, but I am so glad I am living in the New Covenant instead of the Old. Thank You that You don't see me as righteous because I obey You, but You see me as righteous because of the blood of Jesus. Thank You that You aren't angry with me and You will never be angry at me. Your love never fails me.

March 27

The death of Christ satisfied the requirements of the Old Covenant while igniting the fires of the New.

"THIS CUP IS *the new covenant in My blood. This do, as often as you drink it, in remembrance of Me"* (1 Cor. 11:25). When Jesus died, He paved the way for people to come directly into the Presence of God daily. This was unheard of in Moses' day. Only the high priest could do that, and it happened only one day a year—the Day of Atonement.

It is without question that the New Covenant in Jesus' blood has ushered us into superior blessings. Perhaps the greatest grace of this new reality is our unrestricted access to God's Presence. The Presence that demanded strict adherence to protocol is now accessible to all who receive the redemptive work of Christ. Under the Old Covenant, when sinful people entered the Presence unworthily, this meant death. Because of Jesus, this same Presence touches unworthy sinners and transforms them into the righteousness of God in Christ Jesus (see 2 Cor. 5:21).

Daily Scripture Reading

Hebrews 9–10:25

Prayer

Thank You, Jesus, for being the perfect sacrifice Who made atonement for my sin. Thank You that I don't have to offer sacrifices for my sin any longer. However, I do offer my whole self—body, soul, and spirit, to You as an offering. I want to honor You with everything I do, say, and think.

March 28

The blood of Jesus made it possible to be a people of His Presence.

THE BLOOD OF Jesus brought us into the very Presence of God and, likewise, brought the very Presence of God *into* us. We live out the resurrected life through the empowerment of God's indwelling Presence. It is absolutely vital if we are to live the Christian life. The Cross is our entryway *into* the Christian life, which is exemplified by the resurrection. While it is absolutely impossible to even start the Christian life without the Cross, it is equally impossible to *live* the Christian life without understanding the resurrection.

Pentecost is what makes the resurrection of Jesus Christ a lifestyle that each of us can experience rather than just commemorate as a holiday. The Spirit that raised Jesus from the dead also raised you from the dead (see Rom. 8:11). This means that the same Presence of God that was responsible for the resurrection of Jesus lives inside of you, enabling you to live a resurrected life following the Savior's model. You have been raised *with* Christ, according to Colossians 3:1. As a result, we must truly start thinking and living as a resurrected people.

Daily Scripture Reading

Colossians 3:1-17

Prayer

Holy Spirit, without You empowering me there would be no way I could ever life a life that resembles Jesus. Apart from Your Presence, I could not love well, forgive, or live a pure life. It's all because of You. Thank You, Holy Spirit, for dwelling inside of me.

March 29

Understanding God's nature sets the parameters for our faith.

"THE FOOL HAS *said in his heart, 'There is no God'"* (Ps. 14:1). Even so, *many* question God's existence, and His nature is questioned by *most* of the rest. One can believe that God exists but, at the same time, not know *Who* this God really is. Knowing the nature of faith and the tension in this dilemma, the writer of Hebrews said, *"He who comes to God must believe that He is, and that He is a rewarder of those who diligently seek Him"* (Heb. 11:6).

Confidence in His existence *and His nature* are the essentials to active faith. Faith thrives when we get those two issues settled. And it's not just a knowing He exists, somewhere out there. It's a knowing He is present, here and now. This kind of knowing is revealed by our response—*diligently seeking Him*. This is what sets the parameters for our faith. Our faith will go only as far as our revelation of God's nature.

Daily Scripture Reading

Acts 17:27 ▪ Ephesians 1:15-21 ▪ Ephesians 3:14-19

Prayer

God, You know where my faith is at and what needs to happen for me to go to the next level. Show Yourself to me so I can understand Your nature and love in even a greater measure.

March 30

It's not a rumor; God really is good, always good. And discovering His goodness gives me the grace to serve Him with reckless abandon.

MOSES HAD A series of life-altering encounters with God. The most notable was when he saw the fullness of God's *goodness*. There is no greater vacuum in the hearts and minds of humankind than understanding God's nature, especially as it pertains to the goodness of God. It seems that you can't even talk about the extreme kindness of God without someone voicing concern for "sloppy agape" as they used to say, or an "anything goes" kind of Christianity. Unfortunately, the fear of exaggerating His goodness has kept many a heart from the liberty that He purchased on their behalf. It is extreme. His goodness cannot be exaggerated. Such truth is not an invitation into a lifestyle of reckless disobedience and sin at the expense of God's goodness. To even consider such a response is to fundamentally misunderstand this life-altering revelation.

When we discover God's goodness, we cannot help but give Him complete control. Our desire is to imitate Him, for we have gazed into the eyes of pure and undefiled goodness. We serve Him wholeheartedly because we have absolute confidence in the nature of the One we have given our lives over to.

Daily Scripture Reading

Psalm 34

Prayer

You are such a good God! I have tasted and seen how good You have been to me and I say thank You. You continue to outdo Yourself the more I boast in You and thank You. There is no end to Your goodness. I know that I can always trust You and am confident that You have good plans for me.

March 31

Everyone wants a king like Jesus.

JESUS IS REFERRED to as *"the Desire of All Nations"* (Hag. 2:7). That tells me that everyone wants a king like Jesus—ultimately. Humankind was actually designed for rulership, both to rule and *be ruled.* Even though sin entered the equation, enslaving humankind to a heart of rebellion, the desire to be ruled by absolute goodness continued to exist in the deepest places of our being. Only God Himself can fill this void. It is in the experience of being born again that the blinded eyes of humanity finally behold the One worthy to rule every area of life.

Jesus is what everyone longs for, yet has come to doubt even exists. The Church represents Jesus, which basically means to re-present Him. This is our glorious responsibility as carriers of His Presence. If we can host Him and in the process become like Him, then perhaps the world will actually experience "it's My kindness that leads you to repentance" (see Rom. 2:4). Oh, that by seeing His image made manifest through our lives they would be able to exclaim, "I've tasted and seen that the Lord is good!" (See Psalm 34:8.)

Daily Scripture Reading

Haggai 2:1-9

Prayer

Lord, I want everyone to come to know You and experience Your wonderful goodness! It is my privilege to show and tell people about who You really are. Demonstrate Your love through my life in ways that You know will touch people deeply and show them the reality of Your deep love for them.

APRIL

Experience God's Empowering Presence

April 1

The most feared and respected people in the Old Testament were the prophets.

IN ORDER TO get an accurate view of the measure of empowerment we have received in the Holy Spirit, it is necessary to go back. Reflect on the Old Testament prophets for a moment.

When they spoke, things happened. Their interactions with God produced a very healthy fear of God that often had a great impact on how people thought and lived. There was one thing that separated them from the rest of the crowd. It was that *the Spirit of the Lord came upon them*. Everything changed in that moment. They went from a respected citizen of a city to a feared citizen of Heaven. There's no doubt they had a *gift* from God that was unusual. They could *see*. Yet it was *the Spirit of God upon them* that had the most overwhelming influence. God spoke through them, backing His word with signs and wonders. These unusual people brought about some of history's most bizarre moments. And we are richer because of them.

Daily Scripture Reading

1 Kings 18 ▪ Amos 1:1-2

Prayer

God, Your raw power was displayed through ordinary people who became extraordinary prophets in the Old Testament. It is amazing that the same power that came upon them to do signs and wonders and prophesy is upon me because of Jesus.

April 2

The prophets were the most feared because the Spirit of the Lord came upon them.

EVEN IN THE context of the Old Testament, this reality is absolutely stunning. The Spirit of God, One who, Himself, saturates Heaven with His Presence, rests upon people. And when He does, things happen.

The Old Testament prophets carried the Presence of God in a way that was rare, especially for their day. Their role is still often misunderstood in ours. They played a vital role in the increasing revelation of the interaction of God's abiding Presence and the purpose of man on earth. If we can see their history clearly and recognize the momentum created by these great men and women of God, we will be positioned to more readily embrace the assignment for our day.

Ours is to be a greater day just as God has promised: *"The latter glory of this house will be greater than the former"* (Hag. 2:9 NASB). Plus, we are to have the benefit of greater clarity of heart and mind through advances that previous generations have obtained for us.

Daily Scripture Reading

Jonah 3 ▪ Zechariah 1:1-6 ▪ 1 Peter 1:20-21

Prayer

Lord, grant me a greater understanding of what it means to have Your Presence resting upon me, like You did on the Old Testament prophets. Show me the difference between how You manifested Yourself and Your words in them and how You wish to manifest Yourself in and through me.

April 3

There is an obvious progression in the revelation of God for His people and an increase in His manifest Presence and glory.

GOD MEANT IT when He said, *"Of the increase of His government and of peace there will be no end"* (Isa. 9:7). There has only been increase since those words were spoken. More and more, *on earth as it is in Heaven* is becoming a reality in our midst. We have to adjust how we think and see to not only realize it but cooperate with what God is doing. His Kingdom is one of increase and expansion. This work will continue until Numbers 14:21 comes to pass: *"all the earth shall be filled with the glory of the Lord."*

Again Scripture says of us, *"But the path of the righteous is like the light of dawn, that shines brighter and brighter until the full day"* (Prov. 4:18 NASB). We should and must expect progress. After all, we are citizens of an unshakeable Kingdom that has no end. Our very purpose in life is intertwined with the in-breaking of God's Kingdom and the unveiling of God's glory. Wherever you are, whatever you are doing, *you* have a vital role in being one who participates in the increase of *His* government.

Daily Scripture Reading

Isaiah 9:1-7

Prayer

Father, thank You for the commission to be part of increasing Your Kingdom on the earth. Show me what this looks like in my life today and how I can spread Your goodness, love, joy, peace, healing, and justice in my sphere of influence.

April 4

Too many things get swept under the carpet called the Sovereignty of God.

IN A FALSE understanding of sovereignty, God gets blamed for whatever happens in life. People often assume everything that happens must be His will because He is God. This perspective does not consider the exchange that took place in Eden, nor does it bring to mind Jesus' own words to the devil during His temptation. There is an enemy with an agenda of his own. He is not all-powerful, but he is certainly cunning. He is ever looking for an inroad of agreement. He talks and talks until we actually buy in to his deception. Much of what we mistakenly brand as the *sovereignty* of God is actually the world operating under demonic influence. From disease to disaster, we must reconsider how we approach everything that steals, kills, and destroys.

The problem is when we identify these things as *God's sovereign will*. That simply isn't true. God is *"not willing that any should perish but that all should come to repentance"* (2 Peter 3:9). Is anyone perishing? Yes. Is it God's will? No. Because of that, I tend to emphasize the role that we play in the outcome of things. From the outset, God formed man to collaborate with. This tells me that we play a vital role in the unfolding of Heaven's agenda on earth. God is not powerless, waiting for man to dictate His next move. This is the other side of imbalance. By sovereign decision, God Almighty has set up a system where man, indwelt by His Presence, has been restored to a position of authority on the earth. It is time for us to step into this identity even more to bring about God's restorative solutions into a world marred by the consequences of sin.

DAILY SCRIPTURE READING

2 PETER 3:8-9

PRAYER

Lord, teach me what things I can actually change for the better by praying or declaring or by taking action. As I step out to play a part in bringing Heaven to earth, thank You for encouraging me through testimonies and answered prayers. These continue to strengthen my faith and cause me to keep taking risks.

I've learned God will not violate His Word. But He doesn't seem to mind violating our understanding of His Word.

WE CANNOT ASSUME that our natural minds have wrapped around the fullness of God's Word. Such is arrogance that positions us to live void of humility and true spiritual hunger. No, God will not operate contrarily to His Word, which ultimately unveils His nature. However, He is renowned for confronting our *understanding* of His Word. Perhaps we thought we were 100 percent sure of how God operated in a certain way—until He moved *differently*. His character remained the same, but how He did something was completely beyond our familiarity and understanding.

I once went to speak at a YWAM base in Colorado. Kris Vallotton, a businessman at the time, came with me to help. (He is now a very seasoned prophet on an international level who works on our staff at Bethel.) We watched the Spirit of God come upon many people in very wonderful ways. But He rested uniquely and powerfully upon a young lady who had no background in spiritual gifts, especially the prophetic. In fact, she didn't even believe they existed. God came upon her in ways that startled everyone. He wanted to speak through her. To be honest, I can't even say she was willing. She had no clue what was happening to and through her until it was over. It was so glorious, yet so sobering. The word of the Lord through her was powerful and pure. Her extremely conservative background had kept her pure from many of the things that contaminate that generation. We walked her around the room to pray for people (the anointing for this was obviously on her, not us). Each person we took her to was powerfully touched by the Lord through her words. Was it wonderful? Yes. Glorious? Yes, even beyond words.

Daily Scripture Reading

Isaiah 55:8-11

Prayer

God, give me eyes to see Your movement even when it doesn't make sense to me.

April 6

So many people have no one to go to when God touches them in an unusual way.

THE COMMON RESPONSE with many in the Church is to try to stay average, so our experience in God gets dumbed down to the lowest common denominator. People often unknowingly turn away from the anointing in their life to preserve their sense of control. The other extreme is they sometimes think they're going crazy because their experience seems so different from everyone else's. The enemy works to isolate us, and that's one of his tricks. We then end up sabotaging what God is actually doing. People in this position need help to process and learn of the gift that is in them.

We must create a culture that has an understanding of how the Spirit of God moves. Likewise, we must also remain a teachable people (teachable, above all, by the Holy Spirit). One prerequisite to being teachable is hunger. When we remain hungry for God, we are more likely to shield ourselves from spiritual arrogance. The key mix is hunger and humility. Humility recognizes that God is God and that there are vast expanses of knowledge and revelation about Him that have yet to be experienced. Hunger is what sets our hearts on a journey to know this God as much as possible, even at the expense of God personally confronting our theologies. We will create safe places for people to come when God touches them as we live in humility and hunger.

Daily Scripture Reading

Psalm 86:1-13

Prayer

Holy Spirit, as You do things that are off the grid in me, through me, and around me, teach me what it is You are saying and doing. Send people across my path who have more wisdom and experience than me regarding things of the Spirit, who can also teach me. I desire to stay humble and hungry before you.

April 7

Read your Bible. God does what He pleases. He is God and will not fit into our boxes.

I KNOW THERE ARE many who think that certain kinds of encounters couldn't be God. After all, the Holy Spirit is a gentleman. At least that's what I was told throughout the wonderful years of the Charismatic Renewal of the '60s, '70s, and early '80s. A gentleman? My response is perhaps, but by His own definition of the word *gentleman*. Remember, this *Gentleman* knocked Saul of Tarsus off his donkey (see Acts 9).

There are many who are very much afraid that God would do such a thing to them and as a result, they would fail to enter a place of total surrender. And then there's a whole other crowd that thinks if God would touch them that way, it would fix everything. God knows us inside out. He knows our greatest need and our greatest desire. As a perfect Father He longs to provide the very thing that is needed to take us to the next level. But He also knows what would detract us from our purpose and development. We must trust Him to arrange that part of our lives, while making sure that we hunger for and pursue all He makes available to us.

Daily Scripture Reading

Psalm 115

Prayer

God, I don't need some physical manifestation to believe You are real and doing something in my life. I trust You to take me to the next level spiritually, and I freshly surrender myself to You. I give You permission to touch me however, whenever and wherever. Do what You will in and through me.

April 8

I wish so much that we would learn to recognize when the Spirit of God is actually moving on someone else.

OVER THE NEXT few days, we are going to look at some examples in the life of King Saul. Saul started as a good king. He had zeal for the Lord and rose up with righteous indignation when the enemies of Israel threatened the safety of His people. But he isn't remembered for that. He's remembered for his failures, as he eventually became a wicked king. A very wicked king. Even though God knew what was in Saul's heart from the beginning, He gave him every opportunity to do well. At the start, Samuel the prophet told him about an encounter he would have that would change everything.

> *Afterward you will come to the hill of God where the Philistine garrison is; and it shall be as soon as you have come there to the city, that you will meet a group of prophets coming down from the high place with harp, tambourine, flute, and a lyre before them, and they will be prophesying. Then the Spirit of the Lord will come upon you mightily, and you shall prophesy with them and be changed into another man* (1 Samuel 10:5-6 NASB).

The Spirit of the Lord was already on the prophets. When Saul came into their atmosphere, what was on them got on him. In the same way, many are powerfully touched by the Presence of God today. Unfortunately, their experience is not sustained. This is not because of God's unwillingness or because the encounter was defective. The defect tends to be in the discipleship. To bring effective discipleship, we must learn to recognize the Spirit of God moving in the lives of others and help them steward His activity in their lives. Perhaps with honor we could learn how to avail ourselves to what He is doing in and through them so that we, too, would be impacted more intentionally by His Presence.

Daily Scripture Reading

1 Samuel 10:1-16

Prayer

Holy Spirit, Help me to also celebrate and glean from other people's breakthroughs.

April 9

Two are better than one, if united.
Two are less than one if divided.

THE SPIRIT OF God upon a person creates a heavenly atmosphere here and now. In the case of King Saul, it was a group of prophets, so we have the exponential increase of Presence and power that can only come through unity. Two are better than one, if united. Two are less than one if divided. Learning to recognize this is essential for us to go where He has planned. It is called a *corporate anointing.*

Unity creates an infrastructure for an increased demonstration of Presence. This is the message of Psalm 133, where the anointing is likened to the "*precious oil upon the head, running down...the beard of Aaron*" (Ps. 133:2). Scripture celebrates the corporate agreement of believers, with the psalmist expressing, "*Behold, how good and how pleasant it is for brethren to dwell together in unity!*" (Ps. 133:1). Two or more living in the place of agreement sets the stage for this compound release of anointing, while two or more in the place of division is worse than just one.

Daily Scripture Reading

Psalm 133

Prayer

Lord, I ask for You to increase the unity among the people in my family, ministry, and church. I know the enemy wants to get a foothold by creating division. I pray that our spiritual eyes would be opened to see any divisive schemes so we don't fall prey to them. When we are feeling angry, offended, hurt, or annoyed, help us not to partner with those feelings but to tell the enemy he has no place and declare the opposite spirit. Create an environment of love and honesty instead of bitterness and gossip. When there are times I need to communicate how I've been hurt to someone, help me to say it in love and be brave in my communication.

April 10

Gifts are free; maturity is expensive.

KING SAUL'S ENCOUNTER with the prophets was to set him up to be the kind of king Israel needed. When the Spirit of God came upon him, he was changed into another man. This encounter truly changed everything about him. God initiated; now it was time for Saul to respond. It was up to him to "tend the new garden" that God had planted in his heart. We always have a role in our development.

"And let it be, when these signs come to you, that you do as the occasion demands; for God is with you" (1 Sam. 10:7). This Holy Spirit realm would be necessary for Saul to accomplish what God intended as he led Israel to both safety and peace. Through these means, he would have access to the realms in God to *do what the occasion required*. This is a call for us to be good stewards of the divine *occasions* that God brings us into. He always takes the first step. He even comes with grace and strength, enabling us to live out what these divine occasions bring us into. When all is said and done, whether or not we go forward and actually increase in empowering grace, divine favor, and momentum is our responsibility.

Daily Scripture Reading

1 Corinthians 4:1-2 ▪ 1 Corinthians 14:1-20

Prayer

God, thank You for entrusting me with Your mysteries. Bring to mind even now some mysteries I learned about in the past that You want me to do something with starting today.

April 11

All of Heaven has been assigned to make sure we have everything we need to reach our God-designed destinies. God is not responsible for our potential.

SAUL'S ENCOUNTER HAPPENED just as the prophet Samuel said it would. And it enabled Saul to start well. He had a much-needed sense of humility as well as a significant zeal for the Name of the Lord. This encounter with the prophets no doubt changed him into the man that God needed in that position. Without a doubt, Saul had an incredible assignment; but he was responsible for fulfilling his potential.

The word of the Lord has been spoken. And we must act. We must steward what we have been given. Saul is not merely an example of poor stewardship. The result of his disastrous choices positioned him to become the untrustworthy king of Israel. This caused God to seek out another one—the one after His heart. What we need to reach our God-designed destiny is a supreme value for His Presence. It is God Himself who grants us the supernatural ability to fulfill divine potential. To release it, we must receive it. To step into our destiny, we must draw from the limitless reservoir of His indwelling Presence. This starts by simply valuing the gift of His Presence.

One of the most frightening statements one could possibly hear is, *"But the Spirit of the Lord departed from Saul"* (1 Sam. 16:14). The great gift and the great responsibility has everything to do with His Presence. Saul did not value the Presence and as a result did not fulfill his potential. Could it be that this is one of the reasons why, later in David's own life, we hear him cry out, *"Do not take Your Holy Spirit from me"* (Ps. 51:11)? The Presence of God must be our prize!

Daily Scripture Reading

Psalm 84

Prayer

Holy Spirit, I want to reach the fullness of my potential, but I am fully dependant on Your empowerment. I am so thankful for Your endless wisdom, inspiration, grace, peace, and love. Without You, I will just be going through the motions.

April 12

When the Spirit of God comes upon people, they do extraordinary things in His Name. The Spirit of God coming upon a group of people automatically charges the atmosphere.

IT IS YEARS later and Saul is now a very wicked king. He hates the anointing and especially hates the anointed one—David. It became obvious to him that God had chosen another man to serve as king because Saul had abused his position. Saul was jealous of David and tried to kill him. So he sent servants to capture David so he could get rid of the one who reminded him of what he had lost.

Yet, we catch a glimpse of something very unusual in First Samuel 19:20-24. In Saul's attempts to seize David, he sends messengers over to where the prophets were prophesying. In that environment, charged by the Spirit of God, the men sent to capture David were themselves captured. They were overwhelmed by the anointing and began to prophesy, just as the company of prophets were. When God moves upon a person, we must expect the extraordinary to take place. After all, as the Holy One comes down in *any* measure of glory and collides with humanity of flesh and blood, *something* supernatural is bound to take place.

Daily Scripture Reading

1 Samuel 19:15-24

Prayer

Lord, You are so amazing. I love seeing You show up in power. I invite You to move miraculously in my life and take me to places where You're showing up in supernatural ways. I long to partner with the Holy Spirit in fulfilling Your purposes on the Earth!

April 13

There are many instances in the Old Testament that are actually pictures of New Testament realities.

SAUL'S PROPHETIC ENCOUNTER in First Samuel 19:23-24 is an amazing picture of grace. Grace is most often defined as *unmerited favor.* And that's the perfect place to start in defining this significant word. But a more complete definition is, it's the *unmerited favor that brings God's enabling Presence.* In the case with Saul and his servants, the enabling Presence of God was giving people a chance to taste of life in its fullness. Certainly this gave Saul's servants a chance to rethink how they wanted to live their lives. They'd tasted of life in the Spirit. Hopefully they were now ruined for anything else. This is a prophetic glimpse of grace.

Saul finally decides to go himself. And even though he is in such a horrible condition, with a heart filled with wickedness, he comes into the atmosphere of the manifest Presence of God upon the prophets and *prophesies continually.* Unfortunately, it didn't stick. You can have a perfectly planted garden. But without continual maintenance, the garden will become a garden of weeds in no time at all.

Daily Scripture Reading

Acts 4:31-33 ▪ 2 Corinthians 3:17-18

Prayer

God, I have experienced Your empowering grace on my life at various times and I am hungry for more. I want to live a life empowered by Your Spirit. I don't want to live for mountaintop experiences every so often with You. I want to go from glory to glory by hosting Your Presence and continuing to practice the things You've shown me and let me experience.

April 14

We must steward the life that God gives us.

"FROM EVERYONE WHO *has been given much, much will be required*" (Luke 12:48 NASB). King Solomon experienced disaster in his own life because he failed at this one thing. God gave him more than anyone to ever live. The one verse about him that pierces my heart more than any other is, *"So the Lord became angry with Solomon, because his heart had turned from the Lord God of Israel, who had appeared to him twice"* (1 Kings 11:9).

God gave Solomon the most unusual encounters with Him, twice, but their effect didn't last. It is important for us to remember that we are accountable for what we've been given. This is the essence of Kingdom stewardship.

DAILY SCRIPTURE READING

1 KINGS 11:1-13 ▪ LUKE 12:35-48

PRAYER

God, I never want to treat what You say to me and show me flippantly. Help me to recognize Your voice and listen well when You speak to me. I don't want to miss what You are saying, and I especially don't want to forget what You have said. Give me practical strategies for stewarding what You show me and help me to freely give as I have freely received.

April 15

It is up to us to keep the impact of an old experience current.

I'VE SEEN PEOPLE receive a dramatic touch from the Lord. And when they don't steward that touch, things go sour in their lives. Critics of revival tend to want to discount the touch of God and say, "See, I told you, that wasn't really God's touch on his life in the first place."

Should God be questioned because of man's poor response? Jesus talked about healing ten lepers. Only one returned to give thanks (see Luke 17:15-18). Does that mean that the other nine didn't really receive a touch from God? Of course not. Every touch of God contains seeds of transformation. God touches; man decides whether or not he wants a *touch* or a *transformation*.

Daily Scripture Reading

Luke 17:11-19

Prayer

God, help me to not judge You as less than faithful because of someone's poor stewardship. I don't want just a touch; I want to be transformed by Your touch. I long to see Your Presence reorient how I live.

April 16

The validity of God's work is never determined by man's response, good or bad.

GOD'S WORK IS measured by this: They had leprosy, and now they don't. Or, *"Though I was blind, now I see"* (John 9:25). Or the person touched by God was healed of cancer. The doctor verified it. We give God all the praise.

We cannot redefine the good nature of God based on our experiences—good or bad. Even our experiences with God must be in agreement with His nature in order for us to consider them valid. They may be unusual and significantly out of our comfort zones, but still the good and loving Presence of the Father permeates every aspect of the encounter. This is key. Experience is never our measuring stick for the validity of God's work; God's unchanging character is.

Daily Scripture Reading

John 9:1-34

Prayer

God, I can't always explain what I see or don't see happen, but no matter what the outcome is, I choose to still believe You are good, You are all powerful, and You are for me. Help my mind to never falter in trusting You, no matter what.

April 17

You can't have Jesus healing a disease that the Father purposed for the person to have.

WHAT REALLY CAUSES people to stumble is if a person gets cancer or another disease after it looks like they had received healing. Too often people assume God brought it back because it was His will in the first place. God didn't cause it to come back any more than He gave it in the first place. Just because a sickness returns, this does not confirm that the sickness was willed by God. Through natural human perception, such a conclusion might make sense, but it is out of agreement with the truth of God's nature. God does not heal only to afflict. In the same way, God does not afflict someone with a disease to set them up for a healing moment. This is a confused understanding of how the Trinity operates.

This is a house divided against itself (see Luke 11:17). The Father and Son, two members of the Trinity, do not contradict one another by operating out of agreement. The Father does not ordain infirmity or affliction so that the Son can rush in to save the day. The Gospels reveal that Jesus only did what He saw the Father do. If the Father caused the disease, the Son would maintain it because the disease was given by the Father. The last thing Jesus would do is disobey the Father. There is no conflict of interest between God the Father and God the Son, with one specializing in afflicting while the other cleans up the mess through healing. Jesus clearly stated, "*I and My Father are one*" (John 10:30). If they were acting in contradiction with each other, this *oneness* would be compromised.

DAILY SCRIPTURE READING

JOHN 10:22-30 ▪ HEBREWS 1:1-4

PRAYER

Father, I will not believe that You would cause someone to be sick. You are not the healer and the afflicter. Your Word says that Jesus and the Father are one and that Jesus is the exact representation of the Father. I choose to believe what Your Word says—You are healer. You are everything that Jesus revealed You to be!

April 18

The lack is never on God's end of the equation.

REMEMBER, WE CANNOT judge the validity of the Holy Spirit's work based on man's response to it. For example, just because a Christian stumbles, makes a mistake, and commits a sin, this should not cause us to seriously question whether or not the Spirit was even working in their lives to begin with. Would we wish such a judgmental finger to be pointed in our direction?

Likewise, some attempt to invalidate certain moves of the Spirit because there were people who either stepped out of bounds into the flesh or those who received a touch from God and fell back into sin or some type of stronghold soon thereafter. We have a role of stewardship when it comes to the Spirit's activity in our lives. It would be foolish to question God because of a lack that squarely rests on the shoulders of people.

Daily Scripture Reading

1 Corinthians 10:12-13

Prayer

Lord, help me not to judge movements, organizations, or churches based on people's failures. Help me not to attribute failure on a person's end to failure on Your end. Give me wisdom and discernment when it comes to evaluating the Holy Spirit's work in other people's lives.

April 19

When God is serving wine, drink. When He's serving bread, eat.

OVER THE NEXT few days, we will look at another example: Gideon. God found Gideon hiding in a winepress, trying to thresh wheat. The Midianites had been stealing from the children of Israel for quite a while. Gideon no doubt was trying to get some provisions for his family without being robbed again. Regardless, threshing wheat in a winepress provides a fascinating picture. Wheat speaks of the *bread of the Word*—teaching. Wine represents the *felt experience of the Holy Spirit*—sometimes intoxicating encounters. They are never in conflict with each other from God's perspective. But they often are in ours. Each serves a purpose that the other can't address. The interesting picture is of Gideon trying to get the bread of His Word out of a place where wine is made. It won't work.

We saw this in the early days of the outpouring. People were angry because there wasn't as great an emphasis on teaching. We tried. It's just tough to get bread out of grapes. Most every time we did, we seemed to be working against God's heart for the moment. The opposite is also true. Many just want to sit around and sing or laugh when God wants to build our understanding through His Word.

Daily Scripture Reading

Judges 6:1-11 ▪ Matthew 9:14-16 ▪ Ecclesiastes 3:1-8

Prayer

Holy Spirit, help me to be sensitive to what You're serving at the moment. If You're serving wine, I want to drink. If You're serving bread I want to eat. If I'm in charge of leading a meeting, I want to follow Your lead and not my own agenda.

April 20

God doesn't cause the bad stuff, but instead equips us with the authority, power, and assignment to deal with the devil and his works. It is up to us to learn how to use the tools God gives us.

GOD SPEAKS THROUGH the angel of the Lord and calls Gideon a mighty man of valor (see Judg. 6:12). Gideon responds, *"O my lord, if the Lord is with us, why then has all this happened to us? And where are all His miracles which our fathers told us about?"* (Judg. 6:13). This seems so funny to me. An angel just spoke to him while he's hiding in a winepress, and almost without missing a beat he has a response to the angel. It shouldn't surprise us to know what Gideon was thinking about when the angel showed up. His guns were loaded.

If there were any verse in the Bible that seemed to describe the heart of people who often miss out on what God is doing, it's this one: *If God is with us, why has all this bad stuff happened?* And where are the miracles we have always heard about? God does not author the bad; He is the One who has empowered us with the tools that bring Heaven's solutions. It's time for us to learn how to use the tools He has given us, believing that they really are sufficient for the task at hand.

DAILY SCRIPTURE READING

JUDGES 6:12-40 ▪ EPHESIANS 6:10-18

PRAYER

God, thank You for the revelation that You are always with me and You will never leave me. Thanks for showing me that I have powerful tools to resist the enemy and release Heaven's solutions into the earth. Help me to courageously use the tools that You have given me.

April 21

Sometimes the best place to go to get encouraged is the enemy's camp.

NOTICE THE LORD said to Gideon, "If you're afraid, go down to the camp of the Midianites" (see Judg. 7:10-11). This was the enemy's base of operations! The next phrase says he went down to the camp. Again, that tells us he's still dealing with fear. Plus, the enemy's camp is a strange place to go to get encouragement. Moses once sent 12 spies out to get a good look at the Promised Land, which also happened to be an enemy's land. Ten spies brought back a bad report because of their fear and made the nation of Israel afraid (see Num. 13:25-33). Those ten spies just stayed together and fed one another's fears.

Sometimes the best place to go to get encouraged is the enemy's camp. That's where the two spies, Joshua and Caleb, got their encouragement, and they refused to allow the fearful ten to feed them their fear. And now this is where God sent Gideon, the fearful one. It almost seems like divine humor—if you're afraid, go to the one you're afraid of. As he did, he heard that one of them had a dream, which the other interpreted as being about Gideon wiping them out (see Judg. 7:13-14). That indeed encouraged him.

Daily Scripture Reading

Numbers 13 ▪ Judges 7

Prayer

God, You always have the most brilliant strategies to win and help me overcome the enemy. Help me to face my fears and not allow them to remain overwhelming. I know that with You on my side, anything is possible and victory is sure.

April 22

I can't think of any picture of the Spirit-filled life that more accurately describes my heart than this one: God put Gideon on like a glove.

THE STORY GOES on to report that Gideon and his men beat the Midianites and restored Israel to a place of strength and out from under the abuse of surrounding nations. It's a wonderful story. But in the middle of this miracle is a most unusual verse. *"But the Spirit of the Lord came upon Gideon"* (Judg. 6:34). That would be good enough just as it is. But it really says so much more.

The word for "came upon" actually means *to put on, wear, clothe, be clothed* (see the *New American Standard Exhaustive Concordance*). In the footnotes of my study Bible it says, "In Hebrew this literally means 'The Spirit of the Lord clothed Himself with Gideon'" (*The Spirit-Filled Life Bible*, page 357). Stunning! God is clothed with Gideon. What a glorious picture of the lifestyle that the Holy Spirit would bring all of us into because of Pentecost. God has chosen to clothe His Spirit using your body—and it's not just for a time or a task as was the Old Testament experience. The same Spirit Who clothed Himself with Gideon has come to clothe Himself with you!

Daily Scripture Reading

Judges 6:34 ▪ 1 Corinthians 3:16-17

Prayer

Holy Spirit, I am Your dwelling place. Fully possess my body, soul, and spirit. Move me, speak through me, bless people through me, overcome the enemy through me, and change atmospheres through me.

April 23

The Presence of God is hosted by a person so significantly that He actually lives through them.

WHEN THE PRESENCE of God lives through you, this does not cancel out who you are. It's capturing it to the fullest, immersed in divine influence. It is as though your personality, your gifts and demeanor are all being expressed through God living in you. Most importantly, here is another grace moment. With Gideon, he had received *favor that brought the enabling Presence of God into His life to empower him* to do what was impossible for him to do.

Gideon was a necessary part of God's plan being accomplished. Since the beginning of time, He has intentioned to partner with humanity to bring divine purposes to fruition in the planet. The only way humanity can accomplish the extraordinary is by receiving extraordinary ability. This comes through the empowerment of God's Spirit. In the same way that Gideon hosted God, you have been extended the same opportunity. What Gideon experienced for an assignment, you have been given as a lifestyle. He wants to *live* through you.

Daily Scripture Reading

1 Corinthians 12:7-11

Prayer

Thank You, Holy Spirit, for living inside of me and flowing through me to do the impossible. There is no way I could move in Your gifts or power without Your Presence living inside of me. Please do the impossible even more in and through me. It is my great joy to partner with You!

April 24

God had none of us before we were created. He didn't like it. That's why He made us.

I'VE HEARD SO many pray, "None of me, all of You!" It's a noble prayer. I'm sure it comes out of a desire to not have our selfishness exert any influence on the outcome of things. But shouldn't our righteousness have an effect on the outcome of things if God has in fact made us righteous in Christ?

It's not as though we don't matter and only Jesus matters. Remember, many believers mistakenly take John the Baptist's prayer as a model, *"He must increase, but I must decrease"* (John 3:30). That is actually not a legal prayer for us. John was closing out a season as the greatest Old Testament prophet. He was passing the baton on to Jesus who would initiate the existence of the Kingdom of God on earth. The focus was shifting from *John and the Law* to *Jesus and the Kingdom.* John had to decrease. Jesus had to increase. Because of this, Jesus now lives inside of you through the Holy Spirit. He made a choice to inhabit us and, yes, clothe Himself with us as He did Gideon. You matter in God's unfolding Kingdom plan. You have significance. This is not an invitation for pride; it is a call to place high value on the One who has come to live within us and rest upon us.

Daily Scripture Reading

John 3:22-36 ▪ Ephesians 2:10

Prayer

God, help me to see my humanity like You do. Help me not to despise what You call beautiful. Show me what true humility looks like and develop that in me.

April 25

When Jesus left the earth He didn't say we were to decrease. Instead He passed that same baton on to us with His name, power, and authority and commissioned us to continue in what He started.

SOME WOULD IMPLY that it's all Jesus and none of us. I don't believe that. There's no question that He is the determining factor in any significant situation. But we sometimes get an unhealthy view of our lives and our own place in His plan. John the Baptist's prayer in John 3:30, "*He must increase, but I must decrease*," does not give you and I the license to embrace an unhealthy self-image.

In context, John the Baptist was closing out an era. John's ministry *had* to decrease in order for Jesus' influence to increase. When we believe that it is a noble and holy thing to pray, "Lord, decrease me," we entertain a limited understanding of *Christ in me*. Jesus is not separate from us any longer. Remember, the Spirit of God has clothed Himself with you. He has commissioned *you* to represent Him in the earth. *You* are a vital part of Jesus being demonstrated to the world, because *you* are His representative!

Daily Scripture Reading

Galatians 2:20 ▪ 2 Corinthians 5:20

Prayer

Jesus, it is so amazing that I am in You and You are in me. Thank You, Holy Spirit, for making this possible. Please show me what it looks like for me to be Your ambassador. What can I do today to represent You well?

April 26

What is needed is not less of us and more of Him. What is needed is all of us covered and filled by all of Him!

GOD CREATED YOU uniquely to reveal His glory in a way that is absolutely exclusive to you. Scripture gives us an idea of how intricately God forms an individual person. Examples range from Psalm 139 to Jeremiah 1. He did not create robots. Humankind was not manufactured in some type of assembly line—the individuality of our fingerprints verifies this! You were fashioned with great purpose and intention. Nothing was arbitrary or accidental.

When you are covered by and filled with *all* of Him, then the unique person you were formed to be intersects with the glorious One living within you. This is what God desires for you. He does not want you to lay down your uniqueness. He is not asking you to crucify your God-given character traits and personality. Of course there is sanctification. Right now, we are not focusing on sin, failures, or mistakes. These must be placed in a completely separate category, otherwise we run the risk of evaluating our distinctness and branding it something that needs to be crucified. This is not discipleship. Your sin nature was crucified, not your personality. Your rebellion was dealt with on the Cross, not *who* you were created to be.

Daily Scripture Reading

Psalm 139

Prayer

I renounce the lie that I am not beautifully made and I declare that I am fearfully and wonderfully made. Thank You, Father, for the unique way You have made me. Continue to show me how the person You have formed and fashioned me to be reveals You to the world.

April 27

There's no question Jesus is the answer. But He won't do it without us. That has been His plan from the beginning.

GOD'S SOVEREIGNTY IS unquestionable. He created all things and, likewise, upholds all things by the "*Word of His power*" (Heb. 1:3). He is absolutely capable of overthrowing the powers of darkness using nothing beyond a breath or a syllable. In God's sovereignty, He made a decision to include you and me in this process. Such is a privilege only reserved for His intimates, created in His image and likeness. Your very design is absolute proof that God has ordained you to be a vessel through which He will carry out His plans on the earth. It reveals one fit for total compatibility with the Creator.

Paul makes this relationship clear when he writes, "*For we are labourers together with God*" (1 Cor. 3:9 KJV). We do not labor in our own strength, though. God gave us a commission but did not leave us empty-handed. He supplied us with the ultimate ability to complete the task: *Himself*. He did not simply give us power, although He does. He actually gave Himself to us by filling us with His Spirit.

Daily Scripture Reading

1 Corinthians 3:9-17

Prayer

God, thank You that You never give me an assignment that You don't equip me for. Thank You for Your endless wisdom, power, and love. It is by Your Spirit, not my own strength, that I can complete the commission You have given me to bring Heaven's divine solutions to this world.

April 28

We need to think consistently with God's ways, pray according to His promises, and live according to His provision and be put on like a glove again.

THE RENEWED MIND is essential if we are going to live like a people who are truly filled with God. This resurrected life demands a complete reorientation of how we perceive reality. No longer are we simply trying to make it through the day—surviving. We have been brought into a New Covenant. The New Testament is not simply a written record of what happened *then* or what God was able to do through *them*. There is no *then* and there is no special group of *them*. This is our common approach to a supernatural life—it made sense back then, either in the life of Jesus or through the apostles' ministry; however, for modern people living in an age of technology and sophistication, such an ancient power seems well beyond our ability to safely comprehend. The New Testament was not for *then*; it is for *now*! It is for you. The New Testament is *your* blueprint for normal, everyday Christianity.

God never called us to bring Him down to our level of intellectual processing. Sadly, theology void of the Spirit can have the tendency to do this. There is theology on fire with God's Presence, and then there is a theology of intellect. True theology pursues the renewed mind. The Spirit living within you enables you to think like God does. Only He can accomplish this. Remember, the One within you knows and searches the deep things of God (see 1 Cor. 2:10-11). There is none closer to a man than the spirit of that man. His very core, his essence. Likewise, there is none Who knows God better than His Spirit.

DAILY SCRIPTURE READING

1 CORINTHIANS 2:6-16

PRAYER

God, help my mind and body to submit to Your Holy Spirit. Rule and reign in every area of my life. Help me to start thinking like Jesus and not try to make sense of Your ways from human reasoning. Thank You that I have the mind of Christ. Let that truth match up with how I think.

April 29

We are looking at the privilege to host the Spirit of God, the great prize, and learn how He moves and works in and through people. This is the one assignment we were all born for.

YOU WERE BORN to be a dwelling place for God's Presence. Gideon was an Old Testament prototype of what all believers have access to today—the ability to be empowered by God's Presence to accomplish the impossible! Remember, God does not look at our weakness; He looks at our Presence-empowered potential and calls it forth.

Often, we are awaiting some sovereign solution to the madness and chaos in life, when in fact, God's Word to us is the same as it was to Gideon: *"Go in this might of yours.... Have I not sent you?"* (Judg. 6:14). Gideon was one of those Old Testament figures who was empowered by the Spirit for a task and a season. You and I have received the remaining Presence of the Holy Spirit. Our lives are His home and that positions us to always be ready to go in *"this strength"* (which is God's supernatural strength) and release whatever a situation, circumstance, or impossibility needs for transformation.

Daily Scripture Reading

Zechariah 4:6-7

Prayer

Holy Spirit, please renew my mind so that I don't see impossible situations based on what is possible in the natural. Remind me how You healed the sick, raised the dead, walked on water, and that the same Presence of God that empowered Jesus lives inside of me! Open my eyes and help me to see any impossible situations You want me to partner with You to change today.

April 30

As believers, we are filled with the most significant potential imaginable—the empowering Presence of God lives inside of us!

ALL OF HEAVEN has been assigned to ensure that we have everything we need to reach our God-designed destinies. What is the key? *Activity*. Not works or religious activity. Remember, we did nothing to earn or deserve the infilling of His Presence. This was released to us completely by grace. Too many are working for what they have already received by inheritance and thus live perpetually frustrated. This often positions believers to ask for things that are already theirs and then call it prayer. Rather than asking, we ought to be decreeing what the Lord has already declared as "so."

God is not looking for activity in the religious sense. We are not working for Him, but are rather co-laboring with Him. We recognize what activity we should be "doing" when we intimately confront the Jesus of the Gospels. Not the Jesus of religion, nor the Jesus of tradition. We need to have a deep, transformative encounter with Jesus, as He is, for He has sent us in the same manner that the Father sent Him in (see John 20:21).

Daily Scripture Reading

Matthew 21:18-22

Prayer

Jesus, I desire to have an encounter with You. Draw near, Holy Spirit. Teach me how to powerfully declare Your will over people and situations to see Heaven move on their behalf. This is exactly what You did and You have empowered me to do the same!

MAY

Sneak Previews

May 1

God, the master Producer and Orchestrator of life, has some surprises in store for us all.

GOD HAS ALWAYS loved to tell secrets to His own. This is the divine exchange that took place between Him and the prophets. There was a voice from Heaven that sought an ear on earth to reveal secrets to. Amos 3:7 tells us, "*Surely the Lord God does nothing unless He reveals His secret to His servants the prophets.*" Throughout history, He has given glimpses of what was to come. In the Old Covenant, He revealed these glimpses to His prophets. Now, we all have access to His voice.

The prophets served as forerunners for what you and I would come to know as normal. What was extraordinary in their day has become regular in ours. It should be regular, not common. It should be normal, never taken for granted. We are living in a day that truly would have surprised those of old. Even though they received glimpses, we have access to the fullness. What they saw in prophetic picture, the blood of Jesus has brought us *into*. The ancient cry of Old Covenant prophets has become the living reality of New Covenant believers.

DAILY SCRIPTURE READING

AMOS 3:7-8 ▪ JOHN 10:1-18

PRAYER

Jesus, thank You for being my good shepherd and always speaking to me. Thank You, Holy Spirit, that I cannot miss Your voice. Attune my spirit to all the ways You are speaking to me. Feel free to speak to me in new and different ways. May my heart always be postured to hear from You however You choose to speak.

May 2

As a people, we carry a sense of hope that things can and must be better than they presently are.

BECAUSE OF THE Master's design, everyone lives to make life better. Some serve the betterment of humankind, and others merely serve themselves.

This affects all areas of life—science, technology, entertainment, etc. Everything lives under the influence of this inner desire. It is in the nature of humans, the result of being made in the image of God. This is the way creative people function. We draw upon God-given abilities to come up with solutions to solve problems and answer whatever issue is in the way of progress.

God works with this instinct and draws us into our potential through promise and the wonder of possibility. Because of this, we live in the tension between what is and what is to come.

DAILY SCRIPTURE READING

ROMANS 8:18-23

PRAYER

God, thank You for making me creative, just like You are. Draw me into the purposes and promises You have for me and the world around me. Would You give me creative solutions to improve my home, school, workplace, and city?

May 3

God has given every human being a sense of hope for a better future.

SOME DROWN OUT this inner conviction through sarcasm, the defense mechanism of disappointment, while others silence that voice by a theology of unbelief. Still others have it stolen from them through abusive treatment by others. But it was planted there in the beginning and can be restored.

The very Author of Hope lives within us. In fact, the One Who lives within you has already gone into the future. As long as we are a people filled with God's Presence, we are a people filled with possibility. The question: *Will we draw hope from this possibility*, or attempt to suppress it due to its impossible and occasionally inconceivable nature? The possibility of a better future can significantly unnerve us. This is not because we have an aversion to experiencing good in our lives, but because our minds cannot comprehend a state of existence beyond our present conditions, be it horrible, mediocre, or outstanding. Remember, the same One Who provides hope for a better future also gives you the grace to start imagining it!

DAILY SCRIPTURE READING

JEREMIAH 29:11-13 ▪ ROMANS 5:1-5

PRAYER

God, thank You for hope—the positive and confident expectation of good. You know exactly where I am and exactly where I am going. You are taking me from glory to glory, day by day, bringing me into divine destiny. You are working everything out for my good and Your glory.

May 4

God is famous for giving sneak previews of His coming attractions.

THE OLD TESTAMENT is filled with teachings and revelations that were for the practical expressions of life and worship for Israel. Yet ultimately they were things that prophesied of and spoke to the future. It dealt with everything from the coming Messiah to the new nature given to His people to God's relationship to humankind. Each subject and promise was wonderful, but way beyond comprehension.

Paul refers to these prophetic previews as "*things which are a mere shadow of what is to come*" (Col. 2:17 NASB). It is easy for us to reflect back on the heroes of the Old Testament, longing to live in their day. Hebrews 11 is often responsible for stirring up this desire—and rightly so. We read about those "*who by faith conquered kingdoms, performed acts of righteousness, obtained promises, shut the mouths of lions, quenched the power of fire, escaped the edge of the sword, from weakness were made strong, became mighty in war, put foreign armies to flight*" (Heb. 11:33-34).

Even so, what took place under the Old is still a *shadow* of what you have received in substance through Christ. These testimonies will carry eternal weight, as they should. At the same time, the individuals written about in Hebrews 11 lived under an inferior covenant. God came upon them for a time, not with permanence. And to think, the men and women who wrote history actually longed for what you and I walk in. Truly incredible.

Daily Scripture Reading

Hebrews 11:39-40; 12:1-2 ▪ 1 Corinthians 10:11
Colossians 2:16-17

Prayer

I am grateful for the written records of men and women in the Old Testament. Thank You, Father, that I can learn from their victories and mistakes. It's amazing to think about the great things You enabled them to accomplish, and how I have even greater access to You than they did because of Jesus. Please give me grace to follow in their footsteps and step into even greater things.

May 5

God doesn't hide things from us. He hides things for us.

WHILE *"IT IS the glory of God to conceal a matter"* (Prov. 25:2), He loves to reveal things to His people. He hides for those who are humble and the hungry.

If God made His revelation widely accessible for just *anyone*, it would become possible for many under a wrong spirit to become puffed up with intellectual pride rather than brought low with humility. Humility is what qualifies us to discover the hidden things of God. It is where true hunger is birthed. By nature, the humble are hungry. They recognize that they are without. They are lacking in fullness. At the same time, they are not beggars. Humility in the Kingdom is not poor self-image or taking on the status of a lowly beggar, unworthy to receive anything from God.

Humility understands that the secrets of the Lord are reserved for His intimates. The humble are certain that, regardless of how deep they have gone in the Spirit, they have still only scratched the surface of what has been made available in Christ. This revelation will keep your heart postured to be one with whom God shares His secrets.

Daily Scripture Reading

Proverbs 25:2 ▪ Matthew 13:10-17

Prayer

God, thank You for entrusting Your secrets to me. What an honor to be called Your friend. Protect me from a prideful spirit and help me to live hungry to experience more of You. I want to remain humble and childlike, ever hearing, seeing, and understanding what You are revealing. You are truly great and there is always more of You to know, encounter and release to the world.

May 6

The New Covenant era is what the prophets looked ahead to see and spoke about.

WHAT YOU HAVE received because of Christ is the very era that the prophets of old looked toward with longing. The prophets were often called seers. The title wouldn't be necessary if all they saw was what already existed. The gift was to enable them to see the unseen of their day as well as to have a *knowing* of the coming days.

These men and women pointed to *our* moment in time—those living under the age of grace. They were serving Israel, for sure. But ultimately, they were serving both the *wild olive branch* as well as the *natural branch*—the Gentile and Jew who would make up that mysterious people called the body of Christ (see Rom. 11:17-24; Eph. 3:4-9). They were serving those who would be alive in the last days, which started at the resurrection of Christ.

And this is now 2,000 years later, the last of the last days! They saw the moment we have the honor of stewarding.

Daily Scripture Reading

Romans 11:17-24

Prayer

God, it is so exciting to be alive at this moment in history—a time that was foretold by the prophets. Help me to make the most of my time, abilities, and resources.

May 7

Make at least a mental list of the kings and prophets who are your heroes, the ones who actually dreamed of the day we live in—Solomon, David, Isaiah, and Daniel. The list goes on and on. And yet there's not one of them who saw what was coming and did not have an ache in their heart to be able to taste of that reality—a reality that we now enjoy.

THE PRIMARY FOCUS of their dream was twofold: 1) to have a new heart with a new nature, and 2) to have the Spirit of God live in and rest upon each believer. Those two ideas were beyond comprehension for everyone, even the 12 disciples.

Jesus had to instruct them that the Holy Spirit being here with and in them would even be better than having Him, the Son of God, with them in the flesh (see John 16:7). Yet there wasn't one of them who wouldn't have chosen to have Jesus remain in the flesh if the option had been given to them. Without knowing it, they were on the edge of something that had been the inner focus of many of the *greats* who had gone before them—a tipping point, as some would describe it.

> *For I say to you, that many prophets and kings wished to see the things which you see, and did not see them, and to hear the things which you hear, and did not hear them* (Luke 10:24 NASB).

Daily Scripture Reading

Luke 10:21-24

Prayer

Lord, I am so thankful that I live on the other side of the torn veil. Because of Jesus, I am able to see, hear, and experience things that prophets and kings in the Old Testament longed for. Help me to not take for granted what generations before me wanted to see.

May 8

Prophets and kings, the who's who of biblical days, had an awareness of a superior reality that was coming.

AS MUCH AS the forefathers of old longed to be a part of this superior reality, it was forbidden. That privilege was reserved for you. This should cause our hearts to live in perpetual gratitude, overwhelmed by the incomprehensible value of what God has brought us into because of His Son.

Now, the great history-makers stand in the cloud of witnesses watching with both excitement and wonder as the mystery of Christ unfolds before their eyes. Of course, we did nothing to earn the privilege of living in this hour, under a new and better covenant. It is the choice of the Sovereign One.

This brings us to a deep place of responsibility and accountability because we have access to something that these kings and prophets missed out on. Sobering indeed.

Daily Scripture Reading

Philippians 4:4-7 ▪ Colossians 3:15-17

Prayer

All I can say is thank You. Thank You, Father, for creating me, choosing me to be part of Your family, and allowing me to live under the New Covenant. Increase my capacity to be thankful every day by increasing my ability to see everything that Jesus has opened up to me through the New Covenant.

May 9

Kings and prophets, the ones most mindful of unseen realities, were given sneak previews of what was coming. And every one of them would give anything they had to taste of what we have been given.

LET'S ASSUME FOR a moment that Solomon is one of the kings of whom Jesus spoke in Luke 10:24—a safe assumption, I think, considering the nature of his wisdom and his prophetic insights.

Think about what it must have felt like for this uniquely privileged man to long for our day. He had all the possible wealth this world could offer, enough to make that of the wealthiest of this day pale in comparison. His impact on nations caused leaders who hated him to serve him. He was feared because of this wisdom that seemed to come with Presence, for wisdom is a person (see 1 Cor. 1:30). Enemies sat in silence because of it. Nations talked about him. Even kings and queens traveled great distances just to hear him speak. They would even try to trick him with life's most difficult questions, yet he would answer them all. His skeptics became fans.

There was nothing he could dream of that he couldn't have. That is, except for one thing—the future. His future is your present reality *in Christ.*

DAILY SCRIPTURE READING

1 CORINTHIANS 1:26-31

PRAYER

Holy Spirit, thank You for being who You are and for living inside of me. You are wisdom, righteousness, truth, and love. Fill my mouth with Your words of wisdom and love as I speak.

May 10

It's what prophets do. They see beyond their day and speak accordingly.

DAVID WAS NO doubt one of those that Jesus referred to in Luke 10:24. He was both king and prophet. *"Brethren, I may confidently say to you regarding the patriarch David...because he was a prophet...he looked ahead and spoke"* (Acts 2:29-31 NASB). The king and the prophet is the apostle/prophet combination of the Old Testament. To imply that apostles are kings only works when we see kings by God's design—highly favored to serve more effectively—the least of all.

Apostles receive prophetic insight into what God is doing. They look ahead and speak in agreement with what they see. This demonstration of New Testament kingship is not ruling as we commonly recognize it. To rule apostolically is to model our ultimate example, Christ the servant. When our eyes catch glimpses of prophetic realities and we are invited to bring them to pass in our day, it is not so we can boast in our spirituality. Boasting robs us of what prophetic vision releases—a picture of how to serve humankind more effectively. The prophets of old spoke to represent God and they spoke to serve humanity through the Word of God. Likewise, we have *all* received the Holy Spirit to both represent Jesus to the earth and serve humanity by following His example.

DAILY SCRIPTURE READING

ACTS 2:22-39 ▪ MATTHEW 20:25-28

PRAYER

Jesus, help me remember that all the authority You give me is for the purpose of serving people. Give me the heart of both a king and a servant, so I can represent You well. What is one way that I can serve someone today?

May 11

The Old Testament is filled with people who got to taste of things ahead of time.

THESE ARE THOSE sneak previews that stir up hunger for more. The prophets who received glimpses of the day we are living in were people who operated with tremendous conviction. They served God in obedience, desperate to take their unique position and sow into the superior realities that Heaven was screening before their eyes. Even though what they tasted has become our normal, they enjoy the fruit of their efforts. Surely looking upon our day from the great cloud of witnesses, they delight in watching what they experienced in part unfold in fullness...*before us.*

All of the Old Testament face-to-face encounters were ahead of their time in the sense that this level of intimacy was to become normal only after the blood of Jesus was shed. Even Gideon had to pinch himself to make sure he was still alive after his encounter with God (see Judg. 6:22-24). He seemed surprised to find out he actually was. How incredible to think that what these men and women experienced were just *tastes* and *previews* of what we have received in fullness through the Spirit.

Daily Scripture Reading

Ephesians 3:1-12

Prayer

Thank You, Lord, for making a way for me to have an intimate friendship with You. Help me to bring other people into Your Kingdom so they can also have a relationship with You.

May 12

God entices and draws us into faith for the impossible and then completely outdoes Himself.

Have you ever gone to see a movie because the advertisement made it look so funny, but when you saw it you noticed all the funny moments in the movie were already in the trailer? It's a great disappointment. The movie never got any better than that 60-second spot. God is not like that.

It's just the way He is. He gives a glimpse of something to come, knowing that even those who saw it coming would be surprised when it actually did. His coming works are represented in words and pictures but can never be fully contained in them. He surpasses all description and everyone's anticipation of good. He is extreme in all the right ways!

Daily Scripture Reading

Psalm 146

Prayer

God, thank You for all the times You have surprised me with things turning out better than I expected. I can trust in Your good nature and be confident that You will always work things out for my good. I invite You to surprise me with Your extreme goodness today!

May 13

We have been given one of the greatest privileges of all time—abounding with hope in a time of hopelessness.

THIS IS WHAT it looks like to be a *light on a hill*. Even so, many who have been given the honor to steward hope have allowed the pressures of this life to derail them from their purpose. And the one who is to be a fountain of hope actually mirrors the hopelessness of those without Christ. This is especially true as it pertains to the last days.

When these individuals consider the future, they can only really get happy about the fact that Heaven is near. And they should. That is to be the great hope for every believer. We also have the privilege of watching Heaven come near *now*. Take it a step further—you and I have been assigned to participate in this glorious ambush! This should elevate our hope considerably. It gives us renewed focus to approach every day, with its various trials and circumstances, with confidence of a positive outcome. This is true Bible hope. It is not wishing or thinking, all the while embracing the expectation of something *not* working out. True hope seizes God's promises, bringing that which was reserved for another day *into* today. This is the responsibility of all Kingdom citizens. We represent our true homeland by bringing its culture to our temporary abode—the earth.

DAILY SCRIPTURE READING

MATTHEW 5:14-16 ▪ HEBREWS 11:1

PRAYER

God, increase my hope and faith so that I can shine brightly for You no matter what is going on around me. Let people ask me why I am so hopeful and happy, so I can tell them about You. If there is any place in my belief system that is not aligned with Your truth, reveal that to me so no lies hinder me from shining brightly.

May 14

Our assignment should concern us more than our destination.

Heaven is your destination; *now* is your assignment. We must recognize the significance of the moment we have been placed in if we are going to be effective agents of Kingdom transformation. When we see the promises of God and the supernatural demonstrations of His power as exclusively reserved for the millennium, we will not place any demand upon our faith in this present hour. This keeps us looking forward to our day of destination rather than being effective stewards of our present assignment.

We must be known for hope for the day we live in, as the purposes of God are always great. He will do everything needed, according to His promises for His victorious bride. When Jesus said there would be "*wars and rumors of wars*" (Matt. 24:6)," He wasn't giving us a promise. He was describing the conditions into which He was releasing His last-days army of transformational people.

Daily Scripture Reading

Acts 1:9-11

Prayer

Heaven fills my heart with delight and excitement. But Lord, that is my destination. Help me to not focus on my destination in Heaven to the point where I start neglecting my assignment on earth. In fact, show me how I get to experience some of my destination now by releasing Your Kingdom on earth. Holy Spirit, You are the down payment of eternity. You have come from the age to come. I can experience some of the glory and joy of eternity right now because of Your Presence in my life.

May 15

When God shows us what's coming, it's not so we will strategize and plan. It's so we'll get hungry and draw into our day what was reserved for another day.

WHEN WE CATCH glimpses of what life is like in Heaven, it is not a summons to pursue or embrace escapism. Our exposure to heavenly realities should stir up a healthy desire for eternal life in our eternal destination. Absolutely. At the same time, we have a present stewardship over the future glimpses we receive. God shows us what is ahead to stir our hunger to draw what we see in one world into this one.

Each of us has received an assignment that was intentional and time specific. Think about it. You were not deposited into the days of Moses, Elijah, or Jesus. Likewise, there is a chance that you might not be stationed in the last of the last of the last days of civilization just prior to the Lord's return. Our times are in God's hands (see Ps. 31:15). Does this give us the right to long for the past or yearn for the future, all the while discounting where we are right now? Not at all.

Truth be told, you are living in the most glorious hour in history! God wants to show you what's ahead, not so you can get ready to check out, but so you are all the more stirred to be the gate He uses to release His Kingdom through.

Daily Scripture Reading

Hebrews 6:5

Prayer

It is possible for me to experience the powers of the age to come right now. Holy Spirit, You are the One who draws me in to taste of the culture and atmosphere of Heaven now, so that I know what I am called to represent and release here on earth. I am an ambassador of Heaven in this world. Even though Heaven will be my destination forever, it is also the world I am called to represent and release right now.

May 16

As long as we idolize another era, we'll be blind to the importance of our own.

I DO BELIEVE ONE of the primary works of the devil is to get us to discount the moment we live in. We discount our present moment by having a skewed perspective of the past and future. When we believe the past is unsurpassable and that the encounters with God enjoyed by those of yesteryear are the pinnacle and cannot be touched, we will memorialize a former day and spend the present looking back upon the "good ole days."

Likewise, when we place too much emphasis on the future, be it end-times speculation or a preoccupation with getting to Heaven one day, we can see how we start to devalue our unique moment in history. Surely, when we do this, it is poor stewardship of God's present assignment upon our lives.

Now is what we have been given stewardship over. All the proof we need is the Presence of the Holy Spirit living within us. He has not changed. Past, present, and future, He works and operates the same. The Spirit within you wants to do the same things in *your day* that He did through Jesus in His day.

Daily Scripture Reading

Acts 1:6-8

Prayer

Keep my vision set on the assignment You have called me to fulfill now. You have placed me in this unique moment in history for divine purpose. I do not want to be blind to it, Lord. I don't want to be like the disciples, who occasionally got so focused on another time, the events of Your return, that they were almost distracted from fulfilling their present calling. The times and seasons of history are in Your hands, Father. Help me to steward Your Presence and bring the Kingdom to my generation by co-laboring with Your Holy Spirit.

May 17

Whenever God gives us a promise, it's because He has gone into our future and brought back the word necessary to get us there.

GOD HAS GONE ahead of us, fully securing the future for us. Faithfulness keeps us in sync with His perfect plan. When we remain faithful to what He says, we are not simply expressing obedience. We obey Him because we live in awareness of how much He loves us. We also obey knowing that our God is a strategist. He knows the end from the beginning (see Isa. 46:10). Remember, the One Who lives within you has already seen the future. Likewise, He is the only One qualified to perfectly direct your footsteps in order to step into this future, I repeat, a future that He has *already* seen.

When God gives you a promise, He is basically giving you a glimpse of the future in the present. He may do this through a prophetic word, a vision, or a certain promise in Scripture that seems to ignite your heart when you review it. It goes without saying that God is eternally worthy of our complete obedience. However, if we need another reason to celebrate obedience to Him, it is simply this—when we say "Yes" to His direction, we are saying "Yes" to His glimpse into our future. He wants to escort you into the place that He has divinely planned. The key to doing this is wholly relying upon the Spirit's voice. Remember, He speaks based upon what He sees, and He sees *all.*

Daily Scripture Reading

Isaiah 46:8-10

Prayer

You know the end from the beginning, Lord. The One Who has already gone into the future lives inside me. Holy Spirit, You know and search the mind of the Father—and You reveal His thoughts to me. You share promises with me that were pulled out of my future and revealed to me now for encouragement. I trust You because You have already seen where I am going.

May 18

Throughout the Bible, God is creating a desire within the hearts of His people not only for Heaven as a location, but Heaven as the realm of His present rule.

THIS DESIRE, IN one respect, is a return to the Garden. Eden represented the perfect rule of God over all spheres of created order. He ruled over Heaven directly, and He ruled the earth through delegated authority—humanity. Even though sin corrupted this design for a season, Jesus came to seek and restore that which was lost. He restored man to God in the place of relationship. We are faithful to reinforce this truth, particularly when it comes to evangelism. This is essential. Jesus did not come to establish a religious system. In fact, His coming marked the end of a former system and the inauguration of an entirely new dimension of living—a people filled with Presence.

One of the high purposes of the Law was to position oneself, or a people, to stand worthy before God. Such was an impossibility. The Law was not imperfect; it was perfect—too perfect for our complete obedience. Humankind's condition made it problematic, as our own efforts could never work hard enough for us to qualify for worthy status before the Worthy God.

Now, the Spirit has come to live within us. He has brought us into the experience of righteousness that God purchased through the blood of Jesus Christ. Right standing is a theological reality to be grasped, but it is also a lifestyle to be experienced. On the other side of righteousness should be a man or woman taking full advantage of life in the Spirit and filled with the Spirit. It is only in this place, humanity redeemed and possessed by the Holy Spirit, that Heaven's present rule can be reestablished in our midst.

Daily Scripture Reading

2 Corinthians 5:21

Prayer

The blood of Jesus has put me in right standing with You, Father. Because of His blood, my sins have been forgiven and I have been filled with Your Holy Spirit.

May 19

God's job is to get me to Heaven. My job is not to go to Heaven; my job is to bring Heaven to earth through my prayers and obedience.

YOUR ETERNAL DESTINATION has already been taken care of through the work of Jesus. He did what you could *not* do in order to bring you to where you could not go. Our joy is the thought of Heaven eternal; our job is release of Heaven on earth.

God has already done His job upon the Cross. Not only did He secure you a place in Heaven, but He actually deposited the Presence and power of Heaven *into you*. This was released on the Day of Pentecost when the Spirit of God fell upon those gathered in the upper room. This group represented the firstfruits of a mighty global work of God that would culminate in *Heaven on earth*. Regardless of the different approaches we can take to the end times, the majority of us can gather around the climatic end result—two worlds fully merging.

This is certainly a glimpse of what is to come. Yet, the prayer of Jesus invites us to view what is to come *one day* as an availability reality for *today*. The American Standard Version of the Bible translates Jesus' words this way, "*Thy kingdom come. Thy will be done, as in heaven, so on earth*" (Matt. 6:10 ASV). This is your assignment for today: *As in Heaven, so on earth*.

Daily Scripture Reading

Matthew 6:10

Prayer

I want to see Your world transform this one through me. Holy Spirit, shape my prayers to reflect this assignment of bringing Heaven to earth. This is the birthplace of supernatural transformation. As my prayers start sounding like Jesus', I trust that I will start walking in His power.

May 20

One of the more meaningful principles of Bible interpretation is that the first mention of something in Scripture carries extra weight.

IN GENESIS 28, we see the first mention of the house of God in Scripture.

> *Then Jacob departed from Beersheba and went toward Haran. He came to a certain place and spent the night there, because the sun had set; and he took one of the stones of the place and put it under his head, and lay down in that place. He had a dream, and behold, a ladder was set on the earth with its top reaching to heaven; and behold, the angels of God were ascending and descending on it. Then Jacob awoke from his sleep and said, "Surely the Lord is in this place, and I did not know it." He was afraid and said, "How awesome is this place! This is none other than the house of God, and this is the gate of heaven." He called the name of that place Bethel* (Genesis 28:10-12,16-17,19 NASB).

It sets a standard for a subject that the rest of Scripture will support and add to. The rather strange part of this example of the house of God is that there is no building there. It's not a tabernacle or tent that is movable, neither is it a temple that is permanent. It is God with man on the side of a hill. It's a great picture of reality from God's perspective.

The house was not a building. It was not some type of structure built from bricks and mortar. From the very beginning, God's vision for His house was a place of divine intersection—two worlds colliding. In the New Testament, this prophetic picture of God's house finds substance in Christ (see John 1:51). Not only do Heaven and earth meet up again—they find their intersection in a Person. In John 1:51, it was Jesus. Now, because of His shed blood and work of atonement, the Church has become this place of divine intersection.

Daily Scripture Reading

Genesis 28:17a ▪ John 1:51

Prayer

Thank You, Father, that I am Your house!

May 21

The house of God is the gate of Heaven.

THE ELEMENTS OF the story in Genesis 28 are simple—open heaven, Father's voice, angels ascending and descending, and ladder on the earth reaching to Heaven. This in its entirety is a picture of the Church. But the most astonishing part is the conclusion Jacob made from this revelation. *This is none other than the house of God, the gate of Heaven.* Did you catch it? The house of God is the gate of Heaven on the earth.

You are God's house, which suggests that *you* are the gate of Heaven on the earth. From the outset, no physical structure was able to fulfill the heavy mandate attached to this concept—*God's house.* Tabernacles and temples were inferior glimpses of a superior reality that was to come through Christ. The curtain was torn down the middle, demonstrating God's desire to break out...and break in. He broke out of a structure that was altogether unsatisfactory for containing His Presence and, on Pentecost, broke in to the only structure that would truly be fit to become His Sprit's dwelling place—the frame of redeemed humankind.

DAILY SCRIPTURE READING

GENESIS 28:17B

PRAYER

Show me how to live as Your gate on the earth. May my life be a transition point that releases the Presence and power of Your world into this one.

May 22

A gate is a transition place that takes you from one realm or place to another.

GATES ARE SIMPLE but interesting items that are a part of our daily lives. Perhaps you have one that takes you from your front yard to the public sidewalk or your backyard to the driveway. They are transition points for both entry and exit. Gates provide access from one place to the next. In the same way, the Spirit-anointed body of Christ is the gate of Heaven's resource on the earth. While there are undoubtedly cases where God moves sovereignly and mysteriously, His general mode of operation is through His people. This is why God needed to grace us with the gift of His Spirit.

Until the coming of Christ, man—by and large—proved to be an unstable gate. While the Old Testament is filled with the stories of victory, there are also individuals who finished poorly, fell into sin, and proved unfit to stand under the weight of God's assignment. Jesus' blood made provision for humankind to be filled with the One Who sanctifies. The Perfect One resides within us, removing holiness from the realm of impossible.

Remember, the same One Who sanctifies also empowers. God looks upon His church as a fit "gate" through which to release His supernatural resources into this world. This is because God completely trusts Himself. If God trusts Himself, then He trusts those who are filled with Himself. The key to enjoying and sustaining the benefits of *being* a gate is stewarding this privilege with awe. Let's resolve to be the gate through which His Presence can flow without hindrance or restraint.

Daily Scripture Reading

Genesis 28:12

Prayer

As Your gate, I have a responsibility—to be a conduit through which Your Presence can freely move. I desire that the same Spirit Who has transformed my heart to rest powerfully upon me. May nothing restrain You from using my life as Your gate to transform this world.

May 23

The Church is the eternal dwelling place of God. And at this moment in time it is a building built on the edge of two worlds.

THE EMPOWERING PRESENCE of the Holy Spirit lives inside of you and me. *We are the Church.* The Spirit of God is the One Who positions us to live under an open heaven, just as He did for Jesus—the Son of Man. That title, *Son of Man*, is significant because it refers to Jesus' identification with humanity. He made it possible for you to be a building situated on the edge of two worlds. Our eternal position is "*seated...with him in the heavenly realms in Christ Jesus*" (Eph. 2:6 NIV), but our present location is in this world. Jesus lived the same way.

There is no greater model of One Who lived on the edge of two worlds than Jesus. He was ever watching His Father's movement and listening to the Father's voice, while unceasingly confronting the ills of humanity. It was His vital connection to the Father's world that was responsible for His level of effectiveness in this world. Jesus was, is, and ever will be God. At the same time, God wanted to give us a duplicate-able blueprint for living the normal Christian life. He decided to do this by laying aside His divine privileges and operated as a Man anointed by the same Holy Spirit that lives within us. By identity, position, nature, and in every other dimension, Jesus *was* God incarnate. He was the Word veiled in the flesh. At the same time, He was also 100 percent Man Who showed you and me what life could be like living on the edge of two worlds.

Daily Scripture Reading

Ephesians 2:1-10

Prayer

I live on earth but my citizenship is in Heaven. Show me how to live aware of both worlds so that I can serve as the most effective gate of Your Presence possible.

May 24

We are dual citizens of both Heaven and earth.

THE APOSTLE PAUL was aware of his dual citizenship in both Heaven and earth. One could say that he lived *from* Heaven *to* earth. This is what elevates one from being "too heavenly minded to be of any earthly good" to being an effective ambassador for God's Kingdom here on earth. The "too heavenly minded" description is profoundly misconstrued. The problem is not in the words being used. Rather, the defect is the definition we have assigned to the phrase.

For many, one who is "too heavenly minded" tends to ignore the realities of earthly life. This ignorance tends to be fostered by an often good-intentioned spiritual pursuit of higher realities. The disconnect is in the lack of demonstration. A heavenly mind *must* have an impact on the earth, otherwise it is not given opportunity for demonstration. It is the demonstration of a heavenly mind that actually gives God the glory He deserves. To think from Heaven to earth is *not* to ignore earthly realities. Rather, it is to upgrade our approach to everything that comes with living in the fallen world. We don't ignore circumstances, nor do we pretend problems away. Instead, we face life head on, thinking as citizens of Heaven who are bent on demonstrating the superior realities of His Kingdom in this world.

DAILY SCRIPTURE READING

PHILIPPIANS 3:20

PRAYER

My citizenship is in Heaven and my assignment is on earth. Show me how to live as a dual citizen, where my point of origin is in Your world and my place of temporary residence in this one. You love this world, Lord. You loved the world so much that You sent Your Son. He did not come to condemn, but to save and restore. As a citizen of Your world, help me to continue the same mission as Jesus—reconciling people to the Father and helping them become citizens of Heaven.

We are not only those who are to pray for God's Kingdom to come, we are the tools who are often used by God to release that reality into this one.

JESUS GAVE ASSIGNMENTS—AND then supplied His people with power to fulfill these assignments. In John 20, we see a perfect example of this. The resurrected Christ is interacting with His disciples. We enter the conversation where *"Jesus said to them again, 'Peace be with you; as the Father has sent Me, I also send you.' And when He had said this, He breathed on them and said to them, 'Receive the Holy Spirit'"* (John 20:21-22 NASB).

The disciples are given a truly extraordinary assignment. When Jesus told them, *"as the Father has sent Me, I also send you,"* they were well aware of what that implied. The same works, the same power, the same authority, the same mandate, and the same mission of reconciliation that God sent Jesus on was now being passed on to the disciples. Surely they branded themselves as ineligible for such a task. They had seen what Jesus did. In fact, they enjoyed unique seasons where Jesus conferred a measure of authority and power upon them to accomplish supernatural exploits. It was temporary, though, not abiding. Now, everything was changing. Their assignment had been upgraded and the only One able to give them power for the mission was departing.

It almost seems like Jesus did not give their minds too much time to consider the options. When He gave the extraordinary commission, He imparted extraordinary power. Perhaps even *as* He was giving the disciples their mission, He breathed upon them and they received the Holy Spirit. Remember, the breath of God's Spirit is always sufficient for the assignment He has given you!

Daily Scripture Reading

Acts 1:8

Prayer

Holy Spirit, You have given me power to be Your witness.

May 26

It's helpful to understand that our obedience always releases His world into this one in a way that is more substantial than we ever thought possible.

THERE IS POWER in saying "Yes," even when our minds cannot wrap around what we are signing up for. This is exactly what happened to Jacob during his prophetic encounter in Genesis 28. After witnessing angels ascending and descending upon the ladder, along with hearing the voice of God, his response was quite interesting: "*Surely the Lord is in this place, and I did not know it*" (Gen. 28:16).

Even though this moment was destiny-defining for Jacob, his natural mind could not fully process what was going on, hence his statement, "*I did not know it.*" Obedience is required to bring God's world into this one—full comprehension of every detail is not. It is quite common for God to call us into obedience before our minds catch up with what He is summoning us into. This demands absolute trust and confidence in His nature. Only God is worthy of our "Yes," even when our minds have no clue what is going on.

Abraham is a perfect example. God called him to sacrifice his child of promise, Isaac. There is no way this request made sense to Abraham. Nevertheless, he said "Yes" and the rest is history. Your "Yes," to God today could very well be a history-making step of obedience!

Daily Scripture Reading

Genesis 28:16

Prayer

Father, help me to say "Yes" to You, even when my mind cannot fully comprehend what You are doing. Give me spiritual eyes to recognize the move and work of Your Spirit, even when I do not completely know what is going on. It does not matter. I obey even if I do not fully know. Though I cannot see, I trust You completely. You see all things, and You are leading me along a good path!

May 27

It's the nature of humanity to crave, dream, and desire.

GOD HAD REVEALED so much to the prophets, not only through their prophetic words, but also in their heavenly experiences. I believe it was written in the hearts of prophets as well as the average person that there was more, much more than had ever been considered possible.

This *more* became personified at Jesus' baptism. What prophets had contended for in the past was being fulfilled in the Jordan River. Heaven broke open that day and responded to the deep desire of humanity. A Man had entered the world Who gave humanity license to crave, dream, and desire...with hope. In the Old Testament, this desire for more was met with tastes, glimpses, prophetic words, visions, and partial experiences. Under that former era, it was impossible for the Spirit's fullness to be released because no worthy Man had entered the scene who would be qualified to receive the *abiding* anointing. This all changed when Jesus came.

The fullness of Heaven's supply and resources flow through the Person, Presence, and power of the Holy Spirit. Remember, Jesus was and is the Eternal God, but He also lived as the Son of Man anointed by the Holy Spirit. This was to show you and me, the sons and daughters of man, how to live under an open heaven and release the resources of Heaven into the earth through the Spirit of God.

DAILY SCRIPTURE READING

COLOSSIANS 2:16-17

PRAYER

As I spend time reading the Old Testament and reflecting on what the heroes of the faith experienced, remind me, Holy Spirit, that what they tasted was a shadow of what I have received in Christ. The prophecies, the buildings, the elements of the tabernacle, the visions—all of these things stirred their hunger for a coming day. This is the day I get to live in! Show me how to truly honor and steward what I have received in the Spirit.

May 28

You can't crave for something sweet if something sweet doesn't exist.

C.S. LEWIS HAS rightly made the following observation:

> If I find in myself a desire which no experience in this world can satisfy, the most probable explanation is that I was made for another world (Lewis, *Mere Christianity*).

Our hearts are satisfied to the degree that we remain in communion with the representative of this other world, the Spirit of God. It is He Who grants us foretastes and glimpses of what this other world looks and operates like. Everything in Heaven is characterized by the Presence of the Glorious One, seated upon the throne. No glimpse is sufficient without Him. Any snapshot we receive of God exposes us to the One Who is infinitely beyond our ability to scratch the surface of in this lifetime. Should this fact discourage us? Didn't Jesus come so that we could *know God*? He sure did. We just need to be careful when it comes to defining what this *knowing God* looks like.

Some people assume they know God because they appear to know a lot of theological information. Sadly, information alone is very different from a personal, intimate, experiential knowledge of God. Information by itself puffs up the head, leaving the heart stale (see 1 Cor. 8:1). Pursuits that are sparked by a taste of His Presence and power, on the other hand, humble us. We realize how little we know about the great God we serve, and yet recognize how much we have access to in His Presence.

Daily Scripture Reading

Hebrews 11:8-10

Prayer

Thank You for the encounters in Your Presence that constantly remind me that so much more is available. More to experience. More to know. More to release. Every taste and every touch that I receive stirs me to press in for more of You!

May 29

The hunger for more in God testifies that more actually exists and is available.

IT WAS THIS craving for more that drove Abraham to look for the unseen. *"He was looking for the city which has foundations, whose architect and builder is God"* (Heb. 11:10 NASB). It was the inner conviction that something substantial, more real, eternal, and built by God Himself is available for all.

Hunger for more is evidence that *more* actually exists—*somewhere.* It may not exist right before our eyes. It is beyond the confines of our present experience. Think about it. If *more* was within the realm of our previous or current experience, by nature it would *not* be defined as "more." The quest for more is motivated by the vision that something exists that *passes, exceeds,* and *surpasses* our present dimension of experience.

Where we presently are in God is not the conclusion of where we *can* go in Him. To place religious limitations on how deep we can journey in God's Presence is to have an inaccurate picture of His greatness. Remember, He is God. We cannot assume that, at any point this side of eternity, we will even begin to scratch the surface of all that He is. Yet, He beckons us to pursue and press into His Presence.

Just because we will not be able to search Him out in entirety *now* should not restrain us from experiencing what *is* accessible.

Daily Scripture Reading

Ephesians 3:20

Prayer

Every encounter I have with You can be exceeded. Help me to celebrate every touch I receive of Your Presence, but never settle. Keep me from believing that what I have tasted, what I have touched, and what I have known is all there is. Constantly remind me that there is more, Lord. You use hungry people to establish cities. You delight in filling hungry hearts—keep my heart hungry, I pray!

May 30

Jesus is the Light that enlightens everyone who comes into the world.

EVERYONE HAS RECEIVED this enlightenment. Creation itself testifies to its reality (see Ps. 19:1-4; Rom. 1:20-21). But busyness, shame, and pride keep us from being in touch with the understanding of the unseen that God has put into the consciousness of every person born on this earth. What we do with this insight is up to us.

Jesus spoke to His disciples in a very strange way. He said, "*In My Father's house are many dwelling places; if it were not so, I would have told you; for I go to prepare a place for you*" (John 14:2 NASB). You'd think He would be saying, *If it were so, I would tell you*. Or, *Because it is so, I have told you*. Why was His approach so opposite to our thinking? He had no need to promise them what they had an inner awareness of. He is speaking to an assumed awareness of heavenly realms, which exists in the heart of every person. He is acknowledging that reality.

The awareness of these realities exists in your heart as well. When He comes near, words are unnecessary. His manifest Presence stirs the deep places in your heart, reminding you that they were created to be satisfied by the deep of God.

DAILY SCRIPTURE READING

JOHN 1:1-5

PRAYER

Jesus said that He was the light of the world. Before He left, He told us, through the disciples, that we were the light of the world. You have passed this assignment to us, Lord. May I shine brightly, not because of who I am—but because of who I am in Christ, and Christ in me. May I arise and shine His Light that brings true enlightening to everyone in the world.

May 31

Anointed prayer always has a prophetic nature to it.

I CAN ONLY IMAGINE the nature of the prophets' dreams. They not only had the inborn awareness of more, some of them had caught glimpses of what was coming. And some even saw Heaven, the throne of God, and the mysterious angelic realms. The overall hunger was for God's world to have an effect on this one. Isaiah even prayed, *"Rend the heavens and come down"* (Isa. 64:1 NASB). It was a prophetic word in the form of a prayer.

The cry for Heaven to influence earth had once again exploded from the heart. This time it was through the prophet. God had already set the stage to answer this and instructed Isaiah to pray and declare it. In the Old Covenant, hearts cried out for a *day* that would come. How glorious to know that we get to experience this day in our own!

Daily Scripture Reading

Matthew 13:17

Prayer

Lord, the day that the prophets of old longed to see is now. Jesus made this possible at the Cross and the Holy Spirit has actually brought me into the power of this day. Keep me from praying prayers that have already been fulfilled. Instead, show me how to live out these New Covenant realities. They are my inheritance in Christ!

JUNE

Answers to Ancient Cries

June 1

The cries for God, some from the righteous and some from the unrighteous, have sounded through the ages. I grew up hearing there was a God-shaped vacuum in the heart of every person. I believe it.

THIS LONGING FOR God is seen in so many ways, including the drive to make things better in life. I've traveled all over the world. And one thing that exists in every people group I've seen is the desire to discover new things and make what exists better. This passion is firmly rooted in everyone.

Such a desire finds its full expression under the influence of God's Presence. Even though we can see this desire within humanity to improve life, apart from Christ it remains unsatisfied and unfulfilled. The key is defining what it looks like to truly *make life better*. This takes place under the influence of the Kingdom, and the Kingdom is released in the Presence of the Holy Spirit. As we carry God's Presence into the world, serving humanity and representing Jesus, we expose longing hearts to the *One Thing* that completely satisfies...and yet leaves us ever hungry for more.

Daily Scripture Reading

Isaiah 61:4

Prayer

You have anointed me to help rebuild the ruined cities and restore the former desolations. You are not on a mission to condemn and destroy the world. It has already been harmed enough by the effects of sin. You desire to bring restoration, hope, and freedom to creation through Your people. Help me to be your son/daughter, filled with your Spirit, who has been purposed to answer the cry of creation.

June 2

God created us with desires and passions and the capacity to dream. All of these traits are necessary to truly make us like Him.

WITH THESE ABILITIES, we can discover more of God, our purpose in life, and the beauty and fullness of His Kingdom. When these abilities exist unharnessed by divine purpose, they take us to forbidden fruit. This was a risk God was willing to take in order to end up with His dream—those made in His image, who worship Him by choice, who carry His Presence into all the earth.

It is possible for us to live in a place where our free will is under God's governing influence. At first, this sounds like a contradiction. Perhaps to the natural mind, but I have to believe that it makes complete sense in the context of the Kingdom. How can one live in freedom and yet be under God's governing influence, all at once? This takes place when our dreams and desires actually reflect the nature of the Creator. They are not the fruit of God forcing Himself upon us, manipulating us to dream and desire like He does.

He did not create robots; He fashioned free agents. The Father experiences great joy when those He has given freedom to, dream *with* Him. They desire *in* His Presence, not separate from it. This is what it looks like for us to live in His likeness.

Daily Scripture Reading

John 15:1-8

Prayer

You created me to dream, Father. As I abide in You and You remain in me, we dream together. I do not dream independently of You. I dream in Your Presence. I create in Your glory. Passions are birthed in the secret place of our intimacy together.

June 3

It was known somehow that the realities of Heaven and earth must be closer to each other.

ISAIAH REPRESENTED THE cry of all humanity when he prayed, *"Rend the heavens and come down"* (Isa. 64:1 NASB). In this prayer, the cry for Heaven to influence earth had once again exploded from the heart. Earth was crying out for Heaven's invasion. This time it was from a prophet. God had already set the stage to answer and instructed Isaiah to make the prayerful declaration. It was a prophetic word in the form of a prayer.

Then, Heaven's answer came. The revelation and release of God's redemptive program is now unstoppable because of the Anointed One. Jesus came as our Redeemer and our template. He went to the Cross so that it would become possible for a company of anointed ones to overspread the earth with God's glory. During Jesus' public ministry, He gave us a glimpse of the lifestyle that would become available to every Christian, forgiven of sin and filled with the Spirit. Because of Jesus, the ancient cry was answered. Heaven had come close to earth—and because of Pentecost, its advancement would only continue!

DAILY SCRIPTURE READING

ISAIAH 64:1

PRAYER

You have answered this ancient cry, Lord! Instead of praying for You to rend the heavens and come down, show me how to cooperate with Your Spirit and release what You have already provided.

June 4

When John the Baptist said the Kingdom was near, he was prophesying about what Jesus would manifest and release.

THE WATER BAPTISM of John was known as a baptism of repentance. That made Jesus' request for John to baptize Him strange and quite difficult to process. Jesus had no sin to repent of. But John's baptism was also a part of his announcement of the Kingdom being near. John knew he wasn't worthy to baptize Jesus. In fact, he confessed his need for the baptism that Jesus would bring—in the Holy Spirit and fire (see Matt. 3:11). But Jesus insisted. Being willing to do what you are not qualified to do is sometimes what qualifies you.

Even through the act of baptism, Jesus was unveiling the nearness of the Kingdom. He was identifying with those He came to liberate from sin. As the spotless Son of God, Jesus was completely without sin. So why be baptized? This moment is what marked the beginning of His public ministry, a lifestyle that would become the template for future generations of believers to follow. He was intentional about identifying with us in every way. Surely Jesus foresaw a day coming when people, His people no less, would look upon His works and conclude that they were exclusive to Him because of His divinity. He was making a bold pronouncement through baptism, declaring to all generations: "What I am doing, you will also do."

Daily Scripture Reading

Matthew 3:1

Prayer

Your Kingdom was revealed in the Person of Jesus Christ. He has shown me what it looks like to carry and release Your Kingdom in my everyday life. Even though other voices try to distract me from this example, keep my eyes fixed upon Jesus, the Author and Finisher of my faith. He is my Messiah and He is also my model for living. Thank You, Lord, for the gift of Your Son—Jesus! He not only brought me into Your Kingdom, but has shown me how to live as a citizen of this Kingdom.

June 5

Nothing happens in the Kingdom until first there is a declaration.

JESUS ANSWERED JOHN'S objections to baptizing Him by saying, "*Permit it at this time; for in this way it is fitting for us to fulfill all righteousness*" (Matt. 3:15).

Righteousness was fulfilled in this act because here Jesus became the servant of all, identified with sinful humanity, and was now positioned to announce that the Kingdom of God is at hand. This announcement brought the release, because the Kingdom operates through declaration. Reality is born in the place of announcement. Before eyes witness the manifestation, the mouth releases the prophetic declaration.

Through Jesus' declaration, He was announcing the inauguration of a Kingdom lifestyle that would become accessible to all believers throughout history.

Daily Scripture Reading

Matthew 3:15

Prayer

Open my eyes to more clearly see and respond to the example of Jesus. He did not need to be baptized—He was without sin. Instead, He was baptized to identify with humanity, showing me everything that would become possible for a human being in right relationship with God. Because I am forgiven of sin and filled with the Spirit, the works of Jesus are now accessible to me. He did His miraculous works by the power of the Spirit. Thank You, Father, for giving me the same Spirit and the same power!

June 6

What had been promised through the ages had started. But no one expected this: Heaven invading earth through the humility of a man—the Son of God, the Son of Man.

WHEN JESUS WAS baptized in water, Heaven took notice. Here is an interesting description of this divine moment.

> *Immediately coming up out of the water, He saw the heavens opening, and the Spirit like a dove descending upon Him; and a voice came out of the heavens: "You are My beloved Son, in You I am well-pleased"* (Mark 1:10-11 NASB).

Jesus saw the *heavens opening.* The ancient cry of Isaiah was being fulfilled at this historic moment. In Isaiah 64:1, the prophet cries out for an open heaven and a release of Presence from God's world into this one. Specifically, Isaiah's prayer was for a Person. He was not just seeking the demonstrations or gifts or acts of power, though all are to be celebrated and earnestly desired. Nor was he seeking a temporary visitation or anointing, where the Spirit came upon someone for a specific task. This is what was known in Isaiah's day. This was the case throughout history. God would come down for a time, but at some point that time would come to an end. The task would be completed, the anointed man or woman would pass away, and that was it.

The cry for something *more* was fulfilled when Heaven opened over the Son of Man and released the Spirit of God. Perhaps Isaiah did not even fully grasp the object of his pursuit. All he knew was that there was more than what had been tasted in days past. This is what he wanted more than anything.

Daily Scripture Reading

Mark 1:10-11 ESV

Prayer

Your Son made it possible for me to live under an open heaven. He answered the cry of the prophets. Now, Heaven is opened and Your Presence has come to live inside of me.

June 7

The heavens opening at Jesus' baptism by John was not a simple parting of the clouds. It was a violent act.

THE VIOLENCE OF this act was not aimed at lost humanity. Rather, its target was the reign of darkness brought upon the earth through humankind's agreement with satan in Eden.

The word *opening* means to *cleave, split.* It is translated as *opening, split,* and *tears* one time each; *divided* and *tear* two times each; and *torn* four times. Interestingly, it is the same word used to describe both the veil in the temple being *torn* and the rocks *splitting* open at Jesus' death, as Heaven and earth shook as a witness to the injustice of that moment—One so perfect dying for those who deserve death.

> *Then, behold, the veil of the temple was torn in two from top to bottom; and the earth quaked, and the rocks were split* (Matthew 27:51).

In Isaiah 64:1, a cry of intercession was made on behalf of desperate humanity—*rend the heavens and come down.* At Jesus' baptism, God answered this prayer in Person.

Daily Scripture Reading

Matthew 27:51

Prayer

Your Presence empowers me to push back darkness in my life and this world. Just as Jesus was sent on a mission to destroy the works of the enemy, so You have given this same assignment to me. The Presence Who broke open the heavens and invaded earth when Jesus was baptized is the same Presence Who lives inside of me in the Holy Spirit.

June 8

Tearing the heavens was in itself an act of ultimate grace and glory, resulting in spiritual forces of darkness suffering serious consequences.

THE MAN, CHRIST Jesus, was now clothed with Heaven, thoroughly equipped for all His earthly purposes. And His equipping was a prophetic foretaste of what would soon be made available to all.

Darkness could not grasp the implications of this moment. If it did, satan would never have proceeded with the crucifixion plan (see 1 Cor. 2:8). Jesus' blood actually invited you and me into the open heaven that He walked under. Up until Jesus received the Holy Spirit, no human being was fit to receive the abiding or remaining Presence of God. Sin made this impossible. Jesus reversed this through His death on the Cross.

This reversal spells absolute destruction for the enemy and his tyranny on the earth—in multiple dimensions. Jesus by Himself brought great devastation to the powers of darkness as He walked the earth. He healed the sick. Cast out devils. Jesus was constantly undoing the enemy's influence over people and cities. If that was not enough, His redemptive work brought *utter* ruin to the devil and his kingdom. Now, because of Jesus' blood, believers everywhere have received the same Spirit that anointed the Son of God to destroy the works of the devil (see 1 John 3:8). Darkness does not stand a chance.

Daily Scripture Reading

1 Corinthians 2:8

Prayer

The Cross made it possible for me to experience Your anointing. The powers of darkness would have never crucified Jesus if they knew what His sacrifice would make available! I am not filled for a season or for a task—I am anointed and filled with Your Spirit for all the days of my life.

June 9

The veil in the temple, the rocks around Jerusalem, and the heavens all experience the same act of violence. They give witness that the King with a superior Kingdom has just come onto the scene.

AT JESUS' DEATH, everything was shaken. Each expression of shaking and breaking revealed that full provision had been made for the open heaven that Jesus walked under to become *our reality.*

Consider the testimony of the veil, the rocks, and the heavens at Jesus' death:

- The veil—God was not tied to an Old Covenant anymore as the requirements had been met through Jesus' death. It was torn top to bottom, as it was His doing.
- The rocks—the hardest places on earth were responding to the change in seasons, splitting open to signify that Jesus, the King of glory, was welcome to rule here.
- The heavens—the prince of the power of the air had no authority over Jesus, who would be the prototype of every believer who would walk the earth after His death, resurrection, and ascension into Heaven.

Daily Scripture Reading

Hebrews 12:28-29

Prayer

I belong to an unshakeable Kingdom. Even though things in the world are shaking all around me, I carry what is eternal, unshakeable, and steadfast. Help me to release the power of Your Kingdom into every shaking circumstance in life.

June 10

Jesus paved the way for His experience to become our experience.

AS WE START to live out of our baptism in the Holy Spirit, it is necessary for us to have an accurate understanding of what took place at Jesus' baptism. He is our model and template for the Christian life. In a sense, His baptism is our baptism, not concerning sin, but the Spirit.

In Mark 1, we read the following account of Jesus' baptism in the Spirit: "*And when he came up out of the water, immediately he saw the heavens being torn open and the Spirit descending on him like a dove*" (Mark 1:10 ESV). God was responding to those ancient cries for the heavens to be torn open (*rend the heavens*). This had been His desire all along. It was only when Jesus came into the picture that Isaiah's prayer could be fully answered. For the earth to be filled with God's glory, its inhabitants needed to be first filled with His Spirit. Jesus' experience had to become our experience in order for us to complete this task.

So then, what happened when the heavens were torn open in this act of violence? The Spirit of God came down. This is the answer to Isaiah's prayer. This is in response to the cries of the kings and prophets who all ached for this day.

Daily Scripture Reading

John 14:12

Prayer

Because of the Holy Spirit living inside of me, I am able to do the very works that Jesus did. His experience is an example for what I should expect from my Christian life. Thank You, Lord, that I can do all things because of Your Presence living within me!

June 11

To look for another open heaven is to incorrectly steward the one we've been given.

THE HOLY SPIRIT, the treasure of Heaven that Jesus and the Father spoke so reverently about, has been released on earth. When it comes to the topic of revival or outpouring, we need to be careful to identify what we are asking for. Too many believers are crying out for what God has already faithfully sent into the earth. Powerlessness is not the result of God's unwillingness to give, but humankind's inability to steward what it has already been given. This is the key to enjoying Jesus' experience as our own. It is living before God as a son or daughter, not a beggar.

When we beg, we automatically assume unwillingness from the other end. The act of begging hopes that the perseverance coupled with desperation will elicit a response. It is one thing to be desperate and to persevere for breakthrough; but to beg is to believe that the one we are begging of prefers for us to remain in a state of lack. This is not our Father. The problem is that we are begging for an inheritance that has already been freely released to us. We are crying out for an outpouring from Heaven that has already come to the earth. With good intentions and hungry hearts, we ask God to open the heavens. I have to wonder if He is looking down at the Church, hoping that we would respond to the open heaven by living as an open gate.

Daily Scripture Reading

Acts 2:1-4

Prayer

Your Holy Spirit has already been poured out! I press in for fresh fillings and encounters, which Scripture tells me are available. However, I do not look for another Holy Spirit. I don't look for a new open heaven. He has already come and He lives inside of me. I don't cry out for another Spirit; rather, I desire to experience the One Who lives inside of me in even greater measure!

June 12

For the believer, most closed heavens are between the ears.

WHETHER OR NOT we believe that Heaven is open does not negate the truth that it is. Our thoughts do not alter the open heaven over our lives; instead, they determine whether or not we partake of this reality. Jesus Christ secured an open heaven for every single Spirit-indwelt believer. This is a fact. The question is: *Do our minds agree with this fact or do they entertain a lie?*

No doubt we are familiar with Paul's words to the church in Rome, "*Do not be conformed to this world, but be transformed by the renewing of your mind*" (Rom. 12:2). One of the practical ways that we live out of a renewed mind is by maintaining awareness of what we *have*, not what we think we lack. When we live under the influence of what we perceive we lack, we are always fighting to pursue these items which seem ever evasive and just out of reach. To reorient our minds and become focused on what we possess *in Christ*, as those anointed by the Spirit, we posture ourselves to draw from the resources of His world and release them into ours. We believe the resources of the Kingdom are readily accessible because the blood of a better covenant has secured them for us.

Daily Scripture Reading

Romans 12:2

Prayer

Shape my thoughts to agree with every provision that Your blood made available. Because of Jesus' blood, I am filled with the Holy Spirit. I was qualified to be filled because I was cleansed. Because I am filled, I walk under an open heaven. Unlimited supernatural resources flow from Your world to this one through me. Show me how to walk in this identity and steward Your Presence well.

June 13

Living as though the heavens were brass over us actually plays into the devil's hands as it puts us in a defensive posture.

THIS PERSPECTIVE VIOLATES what Jesus accomplished. He put us on offense with His commission, "Go!" The enemy keeps believers on the defensive by trying to maintain a state of deception in those who have received power. He wants us to believe that we are beggars, when in fact we are royal children with a mighty inheritance.

This certainly doesn't mean that darkness isn't able to cast a long shadow over a person, or even a city or a nation. We often find ourselves in spiritually dark environments. I can take you places where just being there could cause you to tremble, as the realm of darkness is so prevalent, destructive, and dominant. Darkness is a reality and its agenda is to secure your agreement. When we believe that darkness is more powerful than it really is, we position ourselves on the defense.

We play into the enemy's deception when we view the realm of darkness as superior to what it actually is. It is foolish to consider a desolated kingdom as powerful, let alone superior to a conquering kingdom. We cannot entertain this deception if we long to see God's superior Kingdom transform the landscape of this world.

Daily Scripture Reading

Matthew 28:18

Prayer

Continue to renew my mind to agree with Your thoughts, Father. Position me to live on the offense, not the defense. I am not fighting for victory, but fighting from victory. Jesus already won the victory and commissioned me to "Go," not simply defend and fight the devil. Show me how to agree with what He has already done, live out of His finished work, and boldly fulfill the assignment You have given me!

June 14

Believing a lie empowers the liar.

THE ONLY WAY that the enemy becomes big to us is when we believe that he is. This is one of the key tactics he has aimed at the Spirit-empowered body of Christ. He shudders because of Who lives within you. He knows your potential, because He saw Jesus' works.

Jesus did not bring deliverance to demonized people because He was God. Jesus Himself reveals the supernatural Source of His chain-breaking power by explaining "*if I cast out demons by the Spirit of God, surely the kingdom of God has come upon you*" (Matt. 12:28). It was the anointing of the Holy Spirit that gave Jesus the ability to set the captives free (see Luke 4:18). Likewise, it is the anointing upon you that empowers you to bring freedom to captives. As long as you believe the devil is bigger than he really is and that the darkness is so thick, so strong, and so powerful, it will become difficult for you to confidently draw from the Spirit of God within you and release deliverance to those in need.

DAILY SCRIPTURE READING

MATTHEW 12:28

PRAYER

Your Spirit empowers me to heal the sick and deliver the oppressed. I have no power in and of myself—I am completely dependent on Your Presence within me to accomplish the supernatural. The works of darkness are no match for the Greater One Who lives inside of me!

June 15

Darkness is an inferior power, one I cannot afford to be impressed with.

OUR ATTENTION MUST be on the provisions and promises of Christ and the open heaven over each one of us. I believe that keeping my focus on those things describes at least in part what it means to abide in Christ (see John 15:4). This is what Paul means when he encourages us to set our thoughts upon things that are *above* (see Col. 3:1-2).

To believe darkness is superior is to buy into a lie that ultimately empowers the liar. The devil's days are numbered. He is utterly powerless. He is desperately searching for open doors of agreement where he can plant and cultivate his lies. Scripture tells us that the enemy, "*your adversary, the devil, prowls around like a roaring lion, seeking someone to devour*" (1 Pet. 5:8 NASB). It is worth noting that the devil is *not* a roaring lion. His aim is to masquerade *like* a roaring lion. He can initiate the devouring process when someone starts to believe he actually is a roaring lion. Let's cease being impressed with this one whose charade is as old as time itself.

Daily Scripture Reading

1 Peter 5:8

Prayer

Help me to remember that the devil is not a roaring lion—even though he tries to convince me that he is. He is unimpressive and inferior when measured beside the Risen Christ. He is a defeated foe and I have been given authority to tread upon his works of darkness. Keep me from agreeing with his lies, Lord. This denies him the right of access and keeps him from infiltrating my life through my thoughts!

June 16

Our refusal to fear reminds the devil that he is finished!

TO FEAR, IN one sense, is to agree with a lie and empower the liar. The enemy operates using fear. We are either operating out of fear or out of faith—the two cannot peacefully coexist. Naturally, darkness would prefer you to live under the cloak of fear. This restrains us from using the currency of faith, which gives materiality to God's promises. Faith unlocks and releases our full provisions in Christ. Such a lifestyle consistently reminds the devil of his defeat. He has no hold over the one who says "no" to his invitation to embrace fear.

When we fear, darkness has become elevated. Our perspective of Kingdom solutions has decreased. To deny fear is to deny the enemy the place of power he so desperately craves. To embrace faith is to agree with God's perspective on reality: The devil is finished and His Kingdom is ever-increasing!

Daily Scripture Reading

2 Timothy 1:7

Prayer

I have not been given a spirit of fear, but of love, power, and a sound mind! Fear gives the enemy access to my thought life—access that he does not deserve. Keep my eyes fixed on Your goodness and love, Father. It is Your love that casts out all fear. I am loved by You. You are with me. You have thoughts and plans of good toward me.

June 17

When in doubt, always worship.

If for some reason you can't seem to sense what to do in a given environment, *worship*. This is always the right perspective. In one sense, to worship is to magnify. To magnify God through worship does not imply that our actions have the ability to make Him bigger or smaller than He really is. He is God. Yet, when we choose to magnify God, we are coming into agreement with Who He is. To magnify is to make larger. The wonderful thing about magnifying the Lord through worship is that no matter how big our praises make Him, we never run the risk of exaggeration or embellishment. It is quite impossible for our mortal words, as beautiful and wonderful as they can be, to fully capture the greatness of God *as He is*.

In the same way that there is always more of God for us to experience, there is always more of Him to celebrate through our praise!

Daily Scripture Reading

Acts 16:22-30

Prayer

I magnify You, Lord. Greater is He Who is living within me than any circumstance, any impossibility, any fear, or any mountain I come up against. The Presence of the Greater One is not only with me, but in me. Keep my eyes fixed on this truth—and help me to live a life of worship, responding to this. I respond to Who You are and live mindful that the God I worship has made a covenant to live inside of me forever.

June 18

We cannot let darkness shape our awareness of the heavenly atmosphere that dwells upon us.

ONE DIMENSION OF living out of a renewed mind is awareness. Are we more aware of the darkness around us or are we more aware of the Spirit resting upon us? The One Who rests upon us is the solution to the darkness around us. This would suggest that the person who lives aware of the Holy Spirit's empowering Presence is a constant threat to darkness.

Perhaps our greatest threat to the advancement of darkness is our ability to shut it down by simply saying, "No, you do not deserve my attention and my awareness." This is where victory begins. It is not a call to pretend like darkness does not exist. Instead, it is to treat darkness appropriately—as space that is destined to be transformed by the light we carry.

DAILY SCRIPTURE READING

1 JOHN 4:4

PRAYER

Increase my awareness of Your Great Presence living within me. Help me not to become overly aware of the darkness around me, but to constantly look within and remember that the One Who trampled the powers of darkness lives inside of me!

Greater are You, Holy Spirit—the One living in me—than the forces of darkness in this world. Help me to live mindful and aware of Your greatness.

June 19

Mature believers carry Heaven's atmosphere in such a way that others are able to stand under their shade and receive protection.

THE *SIZE* OF the open heaven over us is affected in some measure by our maturity and yieldedness to the Holy Spirit. Think of the open heaven as a big oak tree. The bigger and more stable the tree is, the more people can stand under its shade. To use another analogy, others can *draft* on our breakthroughs and become changed.

For those of us who are filled with the Holy Spirit and live yielded to His indwelling Presence, we have the privilege of bringing others into a taste of what we enjoy continuously. This is not meant to be sustained. Sooner or later, the one who enjoys the shade of what we carry must become a shade tree themselves. By providing shade, we give a foretaste of what is available to all who would say "Yes" to Jesus.

Daily Scripture Reading

Acts 2:5-6

Prayer

Just as an entire city felt the impact of the outpouring of Your Spirit, I ask that You would use my life to release Your Presence. I ask that those who may not even know You yet would experience the powerful impact of Your Presence resting upon me.

June 20

To live unaware of the open heaven over us is to contribute to the war over our hearts and minds as it pertains to the truth of Scripture.

TO LIVE UNAWARE of the open heaven over us keeps us focused on what hasn't happened instead of living from what has happened. What *has* happened is that the Son of God was also the anointed Son of Man. God came to earth and, for the purpose of showing us how to live like Him, became a Man anointed by the Holy Spirit. Only God could pull that off successfully. God remained God, but became a Man—Who was filled with the Spirit of God. The One qualified to live under open heavens made provision for His reality to become yours. This is what we must learn to live aware of.

The language of *open heavens* points to an unrestricted flow of supernatural resources from God's world to this one. The catalyst is always an anointed individual. Jesus was the model for what it looked like to live under an open heaven. He never intended for His experience to be unparalleled or unreachable, as Jesus' earthly ministry is an invitation to us to rise higher in our Christian lives.

DAILY SCRIPTURE READING

MATTHEW 3:16-17

PRAYER

The heavens were opened to Jesus at His baptism when He received the Holy Spirit. In the same way, the heavens are opened to me because I have received the abiding Presence of Your Spirit in my life. Jesus paid the price so that Heaven would remain over me all the days of my life.

June 21

We owe it to God to live aware of what He has done and draw from the reality He has made available.

JESUS PAID A debt that we could *never* pay back. In fact, our minds are utterly incapable of conceiving of how such a debt could even be repaid.

To "owe" God is not to try and pay Him back for the debt He paid. No. It means to become aware of everything Jesus purchased at the Cross and start drawing from what He has made readily available. We cannot afford to pray from the place of lack anymore. To pray from lack when the answer has already been provided through the Cross keeps us perpetually trapped in a spiritual state of limbo.

We tend to ask for what has already been freely given. There is a time for petition and there is a time for declaration. There is a time to ask and there is a time to release. Jesus always knew what to do by following the Father's example. In like manner, Jesus has given us His example as our model and His Spirit as our Source of instruction. He will always show us the correct posture to take.

Daily Scripture Reading

Mark 16:15-18

Prayer

Help me to live a lifestyle that takes advantage of everything that Jesus paid for. There is no way I can ever repay Him for what He did for me on the Cross. My sin debt was beyond comprehension—and He paid it in full! Instead, help me to live out of the inheritance purchased at Calvary. This is truly the only way I can repay Jesus. This is the best way I can say "Thank You" to Him—by accessing everything that His purchase made available to me!

June 22

The heavens were torn open, and there is no demonic power that is able to sew them back together.

THE FATHER LONGS for the Spirit Who lives in us. What power of darkness exists that could block their fellowship? But when we live with a primary awareness of the enemy and his plans, we instinctively live in reaction to darkness. Again, if I do, then the enemy has had a role in influencing my agenda. And he isn't worthy. My life must be lived in response to what the Father is doing. That is the life that Jesus modeled for us.

This means that you are a significant threat to darkness. The key is not allowing the darkness around you to shape your awareness of the Kingdom atmosphere that dwells upon you. Remember, greater is He and the Presence living in you. Now take that revelation to the next level. The greater Presence inside of you was always intended to be released to transform the environment around you!

DAILY SCRIPTURE READING

JAMES 4:5

PRAYER

Thank You, Father, for the glorious fellowship and communion that You have brought me into with Your Spirit. Show me how to live out of this place of intimacy. By doing so, I automatically am walking in victory over the powers of darkness, for there is nothing they can do to block this glorious fellowship!

June 23

We always reflect the nature of the world we are most aware of.

WE REFLECT OUR citizenship in Heaven when we become more aware of those realities than the ones we are presently facing. Heaven is filled with perfect confidence and peace, while this world is filled with chaos and mistrust in God. Living aware of open heavens has incalculable results. An open heaven suggests that the currency of that world is continuously pouring into ours. We are those gates—the catalysts through which divine resource flows through. The confidence, peace, rest, joy, and wholeness of God's world flows through us to the degree we are aware of these heavenly realities.

This is why the enemy is strategic about sidetracking our focus. If we are always mindful of demonic strategies and the tactics of darkness, we will live on the defensive. Our daily goal becomes to make it until the end of the day...alive and well. Such a posture leaves a victorious Church unnecessarily battle-scarred. When we are more aware of the conquering, unshakeable Kingdom that we have been purchased into, our approach to darkness will be directed otherwise. It will not be from a place of struggle, but from a position of guaranteed victory. The wrestling match is not on our end; if there is any, it should always be on the enemy's. Any efforts displayed from his end simply try to deceive us into believing he is something other than totally defeated!

DAILY SCRIPTURE READING

COLOSSIANS 3:1-4

PRAYER

Keep my mind set on things that are above, not beneath. Help me to be more aware of heavenly realities than present circumstances on earth. Show me how to navigate this thought process, Father. I don't want to be detached from what is going on here—at the same time, I don't want to be moved by what I see. Show me how to partner with You to release the realities of Heaven into situations on earth that need Your solutions.

June 24

When God is here, there is always more to come.

SOME ARE BOTHERED when we talk about God coming into a situation, His Spirit falling upon us, or the Holy Spirit moving in a meeting, etc. Often, as we get ready to minister to people we will invite the Holy Spirit to come, in the John Wimber fashion. The question is, "Why invite God to come when He is already here?" It's a good question. It makes no sense whatsoever to pray that way unless we understand that there are different measures and dimensions of God's Presence.

It's important to hunger for and invite that increase. Isaiah had a perception of this reality, saying, *"I saw the Lord sitting on a throne, lofty and exalted, with the train of His robe filling the temple"* (Isa. 6:1 NASB). The word *filling* implies that His robe filled the temple, but then continued to fill it. He came, but He kept coming. There is always more!

DAILY SCRIPTURE READING

ISAIAH 6:1

PRAYER

It is always legal for me to cry out for more of Your Presence, Lord. Even though I am already filled with Your Spirit, there is so much more of You for me to experience. I don't ask for another Pentecost; I ask for a fresh filling of what has already been given to me through grace. I pray for a deeper knowledge and intimacy with You, Spirit of God. Fall upon me afresh!

June 25

Reformation and revival history shows us what's available. The responsibility for the measure of God's Presence that we carry lies with us. We always have what we earnestly want.

HERE IS AT least a partial list of the measures of His Presence; each one is an increase of the previous:

- God first inhabits everything and holds all things together (see Col. 1:17). He is everywhere, the glue that holds His creation in place.
- A second dimension of God's Presence is His indwelling Holy Spirit in the lives of those who have been born again. He specifically comes to make us His tabernacle.
- A third dimension is seen when believers gather in His name. As He promised, He is *"there in the midst of them"* (Matt. 18:20). This is where the principle of exponential increase comes into play.
- A fourth measure or dimension occurs when God's people praise Him, for He says He inhabits the praises of His people (see Ps. 22:3 KJV). He is already in our midst but has chosen to manifest Himself upon us more powerfully in that atmosphere.
- A fifth measure is seen when the Temple of Solomon was dedicated: God came so profoundly that priests were incapacitated (see 1 Kings 8:10-11). No one could even stand, let alone play instruments or sing. They were completely undone at that measure of Presence.

It's always biblical to ask God for *more* because there is always more of Him to be known and experienced!

Daily Scripture Reading

See passages listed above.

Prayer

Lead me from glory to glory, God. There is so much more.

June 26

We are here to grow into the maturity of Jesus, bring as many converts to Him as possible, and transform everywhere we have authority and influence.

WHAT WE SOMETIMES fail to realize is that all of these assignments are impossible. Every one of them. But strangely, they are possible if they are the fruit of something else. And this is *something* we can actually do. Let me explain.

We are called into fellowship with God. In this process, He has made it possible for us not only to come to know Him, but also to have Him live inside of us and even rest upon us. Everything we could ever want out of life flows from that one privilege. King David understood this concept better than most New Testament believers. He referred to it as the *one thing* (see Ps. 27:4).

God's Presence is our *one thing*. Apart from vital union and connectedness with Him, we can do nothing (see John 15:5). With Him and drawing from His life within us, we can do all things (see Phil. 4:13). Disconnected from the revelation of His Presence within us, our assignments sound impossible. When we step into an increased awareness that God Himself is living within us, the same assignments that once sounded beyond belief become well within our grasp. True, they would be impossible to those operating in mere human ability. This is not our reality, though. We may be weak, naturally speaking, but our weakness gives the Greater One all the more opportunity to reveal Himself through us!

DAILY SCRIPTURE READING

PSALM 27:4

PRAYER

Help me to keep Your Presence as my one desire. Above everything else—every task, every assignment, every vision, every dream and every desire—may the Presence and Person of Jesus be the great quest that defines my life.

June 27

Stewarding the Presence of God, hosting the Presence, is the only way impossible dreams can be accomplished.

All of life gets reduced to one thing—how we steward the Presence of God.

The fulfillment of these dreams is actually the byproduct of hosting Him well. Jesus affirmed this principle for life when He taught, *"But seek first the kingdom of God and His righteousness, and all these things shall be added to you"* (Matt. 6:33). The Kingdom of God is not something separate from His actual Presence. The Kingdom has a King.

In reality, the Kingdom of God is within the Presence of the Spirit of God. *"For the kingdom of God is...in the Holy Spirit"* (Rom. 14:17). This command by Jesus is to prioritize our lives down to the *one thing* which is eventually evidenced by righteous living. This approach ensures that the first thing always remains first. Beyond principles, formulas, and assignments, God Himself must remain our focal point.

Daily Scripture Reading

Romans 14:17

Prayer

I seek first Your Kingdom above all else, Father. It is my driving pursuit. Show me how this is practically understood and experienced on an everyday basis. I pray that You would bring me into a deeper understanding of the relationship between Your Spirit and Your Kingdom. Show me how to demonstrate the Kingdom in even a greater measure as I enjoy deeper intimacy with the One sent to be my Helper and Comforter.

June 28

God watches over the watch of those who watch the Lord.

I ONCE HAD THE Lord wake me in the night with His voice, making that statement. It's been a number of years since that encounter. Thinking of that moment still excites and yet puzzles me all at the same time.

The "watch" represents God-given responsibilities. It's what a watchman does—he looks over his responsibility to make sure things are safe and properly taken care of. God was essentially telling me that He would watch over my watch (responsibilities) if I would make "watching Him" my only responsibility.

It was His invitation for me to become Presence-centered.

Daily Scripture Reading

Hebrews 12:2

Prayer

Holy Spirit, I ask You to keep my eyes fixed upon Jesus. Fill my eyes with His glory, His goodness, His wonder, and His character. Open the Scriptures afresh to me to behold the Son of God like never before. Awe me. Stir my hunger to walk in everything that Jesus made accessible to those who would follow after Him. Watching You, Lord, is my great responsibility. I trust everything else in my life to Your faithful and most capable hands.

June 29

When we discuss our responsibilities in life, many good things come to our minds. But for me now it always boils down to the one thing—His Presence.

EVEN THOUGH WE live filled with the Holy Spirit's Presence, there is more Presence available to us, not for receipt, but for experience and release. You and I received the same Holy Spirit as Jesus Christ. This Spirit is not inferior, nor is He a downgrade from the original model. Although it sounds humorous, there are many believers convinced that they are unable to access what Jesus had because, after all, *that was Jesus!*

Jesus is forever unparalleled and unique in His role as Messiah, but He never intended to be unique when it came to His earthly works (unique as in the *only* one who healed the sick, performed the miraculous, set people free from torment, etc.). The same Spirit belongs to you and me; and when we experience powerful encounters in His Presence, it awakens us to what we possess and gives us the supernatural ability to release it to the world around us.

Daily Scripture Reading

Romans 8:11

Prayer

May I see the Holy Spirit as He truly is—the same One Who raised Jesus Christ from the dead. Father, this truth alone tells me me that there is so much more of Your Presence to draw from and experience in my life.

June 30

The Holy Spirit lives inside of every believer but does not rest upon every believer.

HOW CAN THE Spirit Who lives within *not* rest upon? Is it possible for us to house the most glorious treasure imaginable and yet not host His Presence well? The matter of salvation is settled through the regenerative work of the Holy Spirit. Empowerment is another topic. We can be saved and on our way to Heaven without enjoying the benefits of salvation, which involve bringing Heaven to earth.

Going to Heaven benefits me, while bringing Heaven to earth benefits the world around me. When we become overly consumed with getting people into Heaven, we help them secure eternity without providing them with a vision for today. Getting the matter of eternity settled is beyond priceless. In no way do I wish to devalue the purpose of evangelism and our commitment to see as many people enter the Kingdom of Heaven as possible.

However, for many who enter the Kingdom, the next question is, *now what*? The "now what" is helping believers walk with the power of the Spirit resting upon them. This means that the One Who set us up for eternity has been given control and influence over our lives to such a degree that every arena is impacted by His Presence. This is what we are moving toward. This is discipleship and sanctification—the influence of the One dwelling within now coming upon us and transforming every part of us to more accurately represent the image of Christ.

Daily Scripture Reading

Luke 4:18

Prayer

Just as the Spirit was upon Jesus and anointed Him to do supernatural works, I desire for His Presence to rest upon me in the same manner. I know, Holy Spirit, that You live inside of me. I am a child of God and it is You Who constantly reminds me that I am saved—that I am in the Father's family.

JULY

Your Inheritance of Outpouring

July 1

The promise of the Father, the coming of the Holy Spirit, reintroduces us to the original purpose for humanity—a people suited to carry the fullness of God on earth.

AS HIGHLY REGARDED as Pentecost is in our hearts, I'm not sure we really see the significance. On the day of Pentecost, the baptism in the Holy Spirit was given. This baptism in the Holy Spirit is called the Father's Promise.

The Father, the One Who only gives good gifts, has given us this gift. All life flows only from Him. He is the One Who is the orchestrator and conductor of life, and He has given a promise. And this is it. This is His special gift. He has actually given us *Himself.* Such a gift calls us to an equally glorious stewardship.

Jesus made it possible for humanity to host the fullness of God on the earth. The Holy Spirit has empowered us to carry out this purpose.

Daily Scripture Reading

Acts 1:4-5

Prayer

Holy Spirit, You constantly remind me that the Father Who promised is faithful. You are the promise of the Father, sent to empower me to carry His fullness into the earth.

July 2

Without question, the most dramatic invasion of Heaven to earth happened in this moment—the Day of Pentecost.

And suddenly there came from heaven a noise like a violent rushing wind, and it filled the whole house where they were sitting (Acts 2:2 NASB).

A NOISE CAME FROM Heaven. Two worlds met. It was like a violent rushing wind. The word for *rushing* is *phero*. Out of the 67 times that word is translated in the New Testament, it is *rushing* only once. The other times it has the meaning *to carry, to bear,* or *to bring forth.*

It would be foolish for me to suggest changing how it's translated. But I would like to suggest adding the *bring forth* aspect to our understanding of its meaning. So then, could the word *rushing* imply that this was a noise, a violent wind, that *carried* or *brought forth* something from its place of origin to its destiny—from Heaven to earth?

I think so.

Daily Scripture Reading

Acts 2:1-2

Prayer

Holy Spirit, You have come to bring Heaven's invasion to earth. Thank You for choosing me to participate in this incredible assignment—releasing God's world into this one through serving humanity.

July 3

This sound did in fact carry a reality from that world into this one.

THIS HEAVENLY SOUND transformed the atmosphere over the city of Jerusalem. In one moment it was changed from the city that crucified Jesus to a city that wanted to know what to do to be saved. How did that happen? Through sound—a sound from Heaven.

Both sound and light are vibrations. And on this day it was the vibration of Heaven that introduced a different drumbeat to a city that was unaware of whose drumbeat they were marching to. For the first time they could really see.

Daily Scripture Reading

Acts 2:3-7

Prayer

Holy Spirit, I give myself to You afresh today. May the world see Your Presence increase upon my life as I learn to host You in a greater way. May they be amazed and astonished—not because of who I am, but because of Who You are in me!

July 4

The roar of Heaven summoned this city to its purpose and call.

THE HOUSE OF God is the gate of Heaven on earth. Remember, it's the house built on the edge of two worlds. And right there, on the Day of Pentecost, we see the effect on its surroundings when the people became open to what God was doing. There was a literal release of something from that world, *through the gate* into this one. And a city was positioned to experience unfathomable change.

Gates were opened. The heavenly sound was heard and experienced on earth. This is what brought a city to attention. Could it be that we too are assigned to bring cities to a posture of attention by carrying the sound of Heaven?

Daily Scripture Reading

Acts 2:8-13

Prayer

Holy Spirit, You have filled and empowered me to declare the mighty works of God. May I constantly share testimony of how the Father is working and moving so that others would discover how good He truly is.

July 5

We have the unique privilege of carrying God's Presence. In doing so, we cause this kind of conflict so that these two realities, called Heaven and earth, could dance together in perfect harmony.

BECAUSE OF PENTECOST, Heaven and earth would be able to enjoy increased collision. Jesus was one Man anointed. There was only so much Heaven that even Jesus, God Himself, could bring to earth as one man indwelt by the Presence of God. Even though in a moment Jesus could have chosen to flood every dimension of space with His manifest glory, He had another plan in mind.

To bring two worlds together, He was going to use humanity. Those He had created in His image and likeness to extend the borders of Eden would be responsible, once again, for extending borders.

Daily Scripture Reading

Acts 2:14-21

Prayer

Holy Spirit, You have come to bring two worlds together. As I host Your Presence, I am fulfilling what was written in the prophet Joel. Your Spirit is being poured out upon all flesh. Use me to participate in this great outpouring, that every eye would see and every heart would know that You are at work in the earth.

July 6

It's important to note that violence in the spiritual realm is always a peace-filled moment for His people.

THIS PICTURE OF Pentecost is similar to the picture given at Jesus' baptism in that it was a violent activity from Heaven. It upset the powers that were accustomed to occupying the space over that city. And in Acts 2, the Holy Spirit was released in the same way as at Jesus' baptism—this time upon an entire company of people instead of exclusively upon Jesus.

Pentecost brought an increased fulfillment to the prophetic dream Jacob had. Jesus was the model of what the gate of Heaven looked like. He was the only Man in history who lived under an open heaven, where angels ascended and descended upon Him. Now, something significant was taking place. What Jesus experienced as one Man was now being *poured out* on an entire people group. This is what the prophets yearned for with great hunger and expectation: "*It will come about after this that I will pour out My Spirit on all mankind*" (Joel 2:28).

The end goal was for "*all mankind*" to receive the Spirit. Pentecost marked the beginning of this fulfillment!

Daily Scripture Reading

Joel 2:28

Prayer

Holy Spirit, You desire to encounter all of humanity. May Your vision fuel my assignment in life—to bring every single person into an encounter with Your Presence. Rest upon me even more, Spirit of God, so that I can bring a lost and orphaned planet into an encounter with You. You are the One who draws us to the Father through the Son.

July 7

Every peace-filled moment you experience brings terror to the powers of darkness.

THAT'S HOW THE Prince of Peace can crush satan under our feet (see Rom. 16:20). Only in the Kingdom of God is peace a military tool. A violent act in the heavens is what released supernatural peace over the city on the day of Pentecost.

It is the Presence of peace that undoes the works of darkness. In an atmosphere of peace, darkness cannot prevail. Its mission is thwarted, for peace invades the places that darkness mistakenly assumes it owns. The enemy wants to fill our lives with fear. He wants to own the thought lives of humanity. He wants to set the atmosphere and climate in regions throughout the earth. Peace prevents darkness from having the upper hand. We do not yield to the strategies of the enemy, for peace comes by ushering in the Prince of Peace and His Kingdom.

Remember, this Kingdom comes through the Presence and Person of the Holy Spirit. Where His Presence is, there is peace.

Daily Scripture Reading

Romans 14:17

Prayer

Holy Spirit, You bring the Kingdom of God through releasing supernatural peace! Your Kingdom is righteousness, peace, and joy in the Holy Spirit. Help me to see that as I bring Your peace, I am releasing Your Kingdom and pushing back darkness.

July 8

Imagine an atmospheric shift over an entire city.

WHEN THAT MYSTERIOUS sound was released at Pentecost, thousands of people began to gather to the one hundred and twenty at the upper room. It was nine o'clock in the morning. People were still preparing for the day. But they dropped everything. Men laid down their tools, women had their children put down their toys. A sound filled the air that also filled their hearts.

This is the full scope of what took place on the Day of Pentecost. It is important for us to increase our level of clarity concerning this landmark moment in history. When we reduce what took place at Pentecost, it becomes easy, if not automatic, to reduce the gift and power of Pentecost—the indwelling Presence of God.

DAILY SCRIPTURE READING

ACTS 2:37

PRAYER

Holy Spirit, help me to partner in Your agenda to transform cities. You desire to bring entire regions into the Kingdom. You desire to shift atmospheres over geographical landscapes. Show me how to do my part and participate in Your destiny for my city today! Use me to release the sound of Heaven where I live.

July 9

A sound was released over them that cleared the air for the first time in their lives.

THIS IS THE very city that rose up to crucify Jesus. His Presence among them was the one good thing they had, and they destroyed it by responding to the spirit of murder, the one thing civilized people pride themselves on resisting.

Yet what erupted out of the heart of God, the sound that was released through that open heaven, erupted over an entire city. No one knows why the crowd gathered in front of the upper room. No handbills or posters were distributed. No announcements were made.

Their thoughts were clear. They could reason. They sensed divine purpose. It seemed as though God was summoning people. And that's exactly what happened.

DAILY SCRIPTURE READING

ACTS 2:6

PRAYER

Holy Spirit, use me to release the sound of Heaven in my life and over my city today. May Your Presence upon me clear the air over those living in torment and bondage.

July 10

They gathered to a sound, an indistinguishable sound, one that reached deep into the hearts of people.

GROWING UP, I always thought the people gathered on Pentecost because the one hundred and twenty were speaking in tongues, which was in the people's native languages. But that doesn't make sense, especially for an international city where foreign visitors are common.

Apart from an act of God, it would be nearly impossible to cause people to leave their businesses, homes, and activity centers to gather for no known reason. This sound called to something deep within the heart of this city, calling to restore it to its original purpose. This city was to be known as a city of His Presence. King David made that dedication many years earlier in the tabernacle he built within that city which was dedicated to 24/7 worship.

Deep was truly calling unto deep as the sound of Heaven was drawing out hunger in the hearts of man.

Daily Scripture Reading

Psalm 42:7

Prayer

Holy Spirit, cause Your sound upon my life to awaken the deep longing in people for Your Presence. You alone satisfy the deep cries of the human heart.

July 11

When you change an atmosphere, you change a destiny.

TO ILLUSTRATE THE nature of this heavenly sound, I like to compare it to that of a musical instrument. A gifted musician can get an almost magical sound out of the saxophone as they skillfully breathe across the reed properly placed in the mouthpiece of the instrument. Now in the same way, consider the breath of God blowing across the reed of the hearts of one hundred and twenty people releasing a sound over a city that changed its atmosphere.

That's what people heard. A *harmonic* sound that came because one hundred and twenty were together in *unity*, not only with each other, but with the Spirit of the resurrected Christ. That is the sound that was heard some 2,000 years ago. It was a sound that initiated the ushering in of 3,000 people in one day. A momentum was created through this open heaven that made it so people were *added* to their numbers daily (see Acts 2:47). That continued until it opened even more and they moved from *addition* to *multiplication* (see Acts 9:31).

Daily Scripture Reading

Acts 9:31

Prayer

Holy Spirit, I ask You to change the atmosphere over my city. I declare multiplication over the community of believers—that supernatural growth would take place, people would be ushered into Your Kingdom, and that those who are born again would become mature disciples, walking in Your fullness.

July 12

Often what we think drives the world away from the Gospel actually brings them to it. It only drives away those who have been taught against it.

When Peter saw the crowds gather, he had an uncontrollable urge to preach. This man, who was a coward only days ago when questioned by a servant girl (see Mark 14:69), now stood heroically before thousands to proclaim the good news. Remember, it wasn't just the fact that he had to give witness to a large crowd. It was before a crowd that was now mocking what they saw once they were drawn to that place. This sermon came in the midst of the most unusual manifestations by God's chosen people. The crowd thought the hundred and twenty people were drunk.

Many would brand a context like this as "disorderly." Our natural minds start to reason, *How can God move and transform people when such unusual things are going on*? The unusual actually invites the lost, for they are, at some level, deeply discontented with the usual. When the body of Christ repackages the world and presents it as the Gospel, we are not doing any favors. This is not being harsh or irrelevant. The goal is relevance, just in the deepest, most transformative place.

Daily Scripture Reading

Acts 2:13

Prayer

Holy Spirit, help me to welcome the unusual and supernatural. These are the very things that the world longs for. Show me how to carry Your Presence boldly, not trying to reduce Your truth in fear of offending people.

Cowards are only one touch from God away from becoming courageous preachers with great power.

"WHAT MUST WE *do to be saved?"*

That's quite a response from the people who crucified Jesus only weeks earlier. Was it Peter's sermon? While I don't want to take away from the moment of profound bravery, Peter preached under an open heaven.

This atmosphere carried the sound of Heaven that changed the mindset of an entire city in moments. His message was quite brief. But it was filled with power, and it brought understanding so that the nervous mockery stopped and the real issues of the heart could be seen. In this one message, 3,000 people were saved.

This became the devil's worst possible nightmare. And it would only continue as generations of other men and women have preached under that same open heaven.

Daily Scripture Reading

Acts 2:14

Prayer

Holy Spirit, thank You for empowering ordinary people—yes, even people who have made mistakes and failed—to preach Your Gospel and see supernatural transformation take place. You are the one who takes cowards and changes them into courageous preachers of Your Word. I ask You to exchange fear and timidity in my life for Your boldness. When I am weak, You are strong!

July 14

Suddenly, things progressed from the anointing/open heaven existing over one Man, Jesus, to the one hundred and twenty, and now imparted to 3,000 new believers.

THE POTENTIAL OF this movement is unlimited, until the whole earth is filled with His glory! And that is God's intention through those who host Him well, all while yielding to the wonderful Holy Spirit.

Pentecost signified an exponential increase of the open heaven that was previously over Jesus. Jesus remains both our model and our Messiah. He modeled what life under an open heaven would look like and was the Messiah who redeemed us out of sin and brought us into the very reality that He walked under. He showed us what life should look like and, through His shed blood, brought us into that very experience. No longer would the anointing be reserved for one man, one priest, one prophet, or one king. No more would supernatural empowerment be seasonal or task-driven.

At Pentecost, the 3,000 brought into the Kingdom were a glorious firstfruit of the masses throughout history who would become responsible for filling the earth with Heaven's sound.

Daily Scripture Reading

Acts 2:41

Prayer

Holy Spirit, give me eyes to see like You do. You see individuals, but You also see cities, regions, and nations. Keep me mindful of how You see so that I can effectively pray Your will and Your purposes into being. Increase my expectation for what You want to do in my life, in my city, and in my nation!

July 15

This Holy Spirit baptism is not for tongues; it's for power.

I HAVE A PENTECOSTAL background, for which I am very thankful. My forefathers paid quite a price to preach and defend that the baptism in the Spirit and speaking in tongues is still for today. I owe it to them to do nothing to take away from their accomplishments, but to add all I can. Having said that, I have seen that many have come to the wrong conclusions about this Holy Spirit baptism.

It is not about simply receiving the ability to speak or pray in tongues. I believe this is absolutely important and available to everyone. However, tongues should never be equated with this baptism. It is a gift and a byproduct. Even the power that the baptism in the Holy Spirit gives us must be treated appropriately. The baptism is not just about receiving power for miracles. It's so that the power-charged atmosphere of Heaven can rest upon a person, which forces a shift in the atmosphere over a home, business, or city.

Daily Scripture Reading

Acts 2:4

Prayer

Holy Spirit, I celebrate every blessing that Your baptism has released in my life. Prevent me from being narrow-minded about it, associating it with only one gift or one manifestation. The same Spirit who gives utterance to speak in tongues empowers me to operate in every supernatural gift as You will.

Use me however You want, Spirit of God. Flow through me as You so chose! I am hungry and I am willing. I ask, confident that I will receive. Your baptism has given me power to do the impossible. May I never limit it to what I have personally experienced or seen—there is so much more!

July 16

The baptism in the Spirit is to make us living witnesses and examples of the resurrection of Jesus—the ultimate display of Heaven's power.

THE SPIRIT OF the resurrected Christ is what filled the air on the day of Pentecost. Christianity is *not* the Cross; it is the resurrected life. There is no access to the resurrected life or the power of Pentecost beside the Cross. There is only one way and it cannot be bypassed nor should it ever be downplayed.

Even still, the Cross is our essential gateway into the resurrected life of Christ. His resurrection power lives within us in the Person of the Holy Spirit. The Spirit was responsible for bringing Jesus out of the grave, and He is also responsible for displaying resurrection power through our lives today.

Daily Scripture Reading

Acts 1:4-8

Prayer

Holy Spirit, remind me of Who I have been empowered to be a witness of. Help my life to give clear expression and accurate witness to the risen Christ because of Your Presence upon me.

July 17

The understanding of God that existed in that heavenly realm actually influenced the language of the one hundred and twenty here on earth.

I CAN ONLY IMAGINE that after ten days of praying together the one hundred and twenty were tired and had probably exhausted everything they could think of to pray about. Suddenly, their affection for Jesus was taken to a level they had never known or experienced before.

Their spirits became empowered by the Holy Spirit in that *suddenly* moment. They were alive, really alive for the first time in their lives. They spoke of things they didn't understand. Two worlds collided and they spoke of the mysterious ways and the mighty deeds of God.

Daily Scripture Reading

Acts 2:2

Prayer

Holy Spirit, You not only give gifts and empowerment—You release greater understanding of Who God is.

This baptism is likened to wine and not water. Water refreshes while wine influences.

WHEN GOD CALLS a particular baptism a *baptism of fire*, it is obviously not one of mere refreshing. Heaven has come to influence earth in this baptism. But when that rushing mighty wind came and the language of Heaven poured forth from their lips, they also were refreshed by what influenced them.

Paul would later point out that praying in tongues edifies us. There's little doubt about that happening to this small group. To top it off, they were speaking something so completely satisfying, so accurate and powerful, that it was like experiencing a completely new day. And they were. This heavenly language came as an eruption from their hearts. But for the first time in their lives, and actually in all of history, they said what needed to be said perfectly without missing it or falling short in one way or another.

This is because they were operating under the intoxicating influence of the Holy One, now dwelling within them.

DAILY SCRIPTURE READING

ACTS 2:13

PRAYER

Holy Spirit, Your Presence influences me. It supernaturally transforms who I am. You don't come in and change my personality. Instead, my personality is brought under Your divine influence. Anything that prevents me from being the person You have designed me to be is brought beneath Your influence and I am free to fully radiate Your nature through my life.

July 19

The intention of the Lord is that this baptism of fire would ignite every heart.

THIS WOULD BE best expressed by a people who were Presence-driven instead of ministry-driven. It's not about what I can accomplish for God. It's all about Who goes with me and my doing all I can to protect that most valuable connection.

When it comes to living out the experience of our baptism in the Holy Spirit and immersion into His Presence, we must be careful not to get swept up into spiritual professionalism. Many people experience this glorious gift, and instead of embracing it as an invitation to greater intimacy and friendship with the Lord, it becomes a ministry job promotion. Evangelist Reinhard Bonnke refers to this as the mistake of wearing our experience with the Holy Spirit as some type of spiritual "badge of honor."

DAILY SCRIPTURE READING

LUKE 3:16

PRAYER

Holy Spirit, come and ignite my heart with Your fire. Help me burn brightly for Jesus and passionately pursue Your Presence no matter what the cost. You are worth it all.

July 20

We always need more.

A **FEW YEARS AFTER** this great outpouring of the Spirit at Pentecost, things were still going quite well. In fact, the numbers were increasing daily, and miracles would shake an entire city. Peter and John released a miracle to a lame man that seemed to shake up everyone (see Acts 3:1-10). They were credited as having great boldness. As a result, they were arrested, interrogated, persecuted, and finally released. Upon their release they went to a prayer meeting and prayed for more boldness.

> *And now, Lord, take note of their threats, and grant that Your bond-servants may speak Your word with all confidence, while You extend Your hand to heal, and signs and wonders take place through the name of Your holy servant Jesus* (Acts 4:29-30 NASB).

And the Spirit of God came in...again. They had already been filled with the Spirit's power, so what was happening on this occasion? They were experiencing a new dimension of what they were already filled with.

The Spirit came in power and literally shook the building where they were assembled. These powerful manifestations of the Holy Spirit are purposed to equip us with an encounter. Notice I used the word *equip*. People often talk about "having" an encounter. The encounter is great, so long as we steward it well.

Daily Scripture Reading

Acts 4:23-31

Prayer

Holy Spirit, I cry out for more of Your Presence. Just as the disciples experienced a fresh touch of Your power, I ask for the same thing—a fresh filling—that I might declare Your Word with fresh boldness.

July 21

Being full of Holy Spirit is not evidenced in tongues; it is evidenced by being full.

HOW DO YOU know when a glass is completely full? It runs over. Peter, on the day of Pentecost, is filled with Holy Spirit.

In Acts 4, Peter joins many others in a prayer meeting. Their overwhelming expression was to cry out for more. Peter prayed for more. He did not pray for relief in the midst of persecution, but instead for more boldness, that expression that sometimes offends, so that he could go deeper into the realms of darkness and pull out more victims.

And the Bible says:

> *And when they had prayed, the place where they had gathered together was shaken, and they were all filled with the Holy Spirit and began to speak the word of God with boldness* (Acts 4:31 NASB).

We must understand that we are equipped with encounters with the *more* of God, just like the apostles were in Acts 4, for a purpose. For them, it was to declare the Word of God with even greater boldness and effectiveness. For you and me, it is to impact whatever sphere of life the Lord has placed us in with His Kingdom purposes.

Daily Scripture Reading

Acts 4:31

Prayer

Holy Spirit, show me the true evidence of being filled of Your Spirit—being full. Help me to be overflowing with Your Presence to such a degree that I must keep crying out for more. You fill me up in order to release overflow to the world around me.

July 22

If you are doing this right, you must get filled often.

IN EPHESIANS 5:18, Paul instructs believers, *"And do not be drunk with wine, in which is dissipation; but be filled with the Spirit"*. Again, to be filled with the Holy Spirit is compared to living under a controlling influence. This is not a one-time only experience. To believe that to be filled with the Holy Spirit is something that happens only once and, eventually, we graduate on to the "next thing" is incorrect. Even though we *receive* the Spirit once, Paul talks of a continuous filling. There is a distinct moment when He comes to take up residence within us, true. However, the process of the Spirit taking complete possession of is a lifelong, from glory to glory transformation.

More accurately translated, this text in Ephesians 5 would read something like: *Be continually filled* or *be being filled*. It is ongoing. It is continuous. It is necessary. There is always more of Him to be filled with. Keep in mind that Heaven is open over you. You are not asking for the Holy Spirit to come down and inhabit you again. Remember, that is the one-time experience. You are inviting Him to increase the reign of His habitation within you. For the Kingdom's government to increase in the earth, it must first increase in us. This takes place as we live *ever* filled with the Spirit's empowering Presence.

Daily Scripture Reading

Ephesians 5:18

Prayer

Holy Spirit, I desire to be continually filled with Your Presence. I never want this to become limited to an experience or a past event; help it to be my lifestyle! There is always more. I can always go deeper. There is always increase available because of Who You are.

July 23

We are to live in such a way that we give away all we get, while our capacity for Him increases.

WE ARE CALLED to freely give what we freely receive. Jesus Himself instructed the disciples to "*heal the sick, raise the dead, cleanse the lepers, cast out demons. Freely you received, freely give*" (Matt. 10:8, NASB).

As we continue to freely give, we create space to continually receive. This is the ultimate setup for our increased filling: *Giving away what we have already been entrusted with.* We might be crying out for *more* while the Lord is evaluating what we did with the last *more* that He poured out upon us.

There is always room for increase where there is good stewardship of what has already been received.

Daily Scripture Reading

Matthew 10:8

Prayer

Holy Spirit, I desire to release everything that You have given me. As You have given me Your Presence and power, show me how to give these things away in my everyday life. I desire to see others experience the healing, transformation, and fullness that You have brought to my life.

July 24

When we live full of the Holy Spirit, experiencing overflow, only more of Him will do.

MORE IS A perpetual availability to every Spirit-filled believer. To be *refilled* is not to receive another Holy Spirit; it is to experience the One we have already received in an increased measure. Even though the language of "more" can unnerve some, we must approach it logically. Logically, you have God living inside of you. Paul could not have presented this more clearly when he reminded the Corinthians "*your body is the temple of the Holy Spirit who is in you, whom you have from God*" (1 Cor. 6:19).

God is the Uncreated One. He knows the end from the beginning (see Isa. 46:10). This is the One Who spoke worlds into being (see Gen. 1:1-3). He has named every star and has numbered every single hair on your head (see Isa. 40:26; Luke 12:7). This God without limits and boundaries has come to make you His temple. If the Spirit within you truly is this great, then it stands to reason that we, being finite human beings, have yet to mine the depths of this Infinite One. This is what makes it completely legal for us to cry out for more—because there is *always* more of the Infinite One to experience.

DAILY SCRIPTURE READING

1 CORINTHIANS 6:19

PRAYER

Holy Spirit, I don't need to beg You for more. I don't need to cry out for a new outpouring from Heaven. There is always more available, and I praise You that the One Who offers more is the One Who lives inside of me. I am Your temple, Lord. The One Who fills the temple with His Presence and continues to fill it with more is the same Spirit Who lives within me.

Needing to be refilled is not a sign of something gone wrong. Continual dependence on more is a good thing.

THE LIFELONG PURSUIT of more is evidenced by humility. Humility is the gateway to true hunger and there is an incredible promise reserved for those who live hungry for God:

> *Blessed are those who hunger and thirst for righteousness, for they shall be filled* (Matthew 5:6).

There is no doubt as to whether or not those who hunger and thirst shall be satisfied. It is settled. To live in this measure of hunger demands a walk of corresponding humility.

Is it possible to be hungry for God and not humble? Yes, but these individuals cannot be trusted with the increase. Humility is demonstrated by the end goal of the individual.

Our challenge: Do we want to experience more so God can be expressed more clearly through our lives, or so that His expression draws more attention *to* our lives? It sounds like the difference is slight, but I can assure you, our bent of heart determines everything in positioning ourselves for greater increase.

DAILY SCRIPTURE READING

MATTHEW 5:6

PRAYER

Holy Spirit, You satisfy my hunger and thirst. Because there is more of You available, help me to constantly draw from Your Presence. Show me how to be continually dependent on Your filling and refilling in order to fulfill the assignment You have given me.

July 26

There are parts of our walk with Christ that should never be reduced to a list of goals and accomplishments.

IT IS SO easy to assume that something like the baptism in the Holy Spirit is primarily to make us more useful in ministry. That makes us *top heavy* in the sense that we become *professionals* in areas of life that were really reserved for *romantics.*

The moment we reduce God to a list of goals, principles, and ministry accomplishments, we have stepped outside the boundaries that position us to experience more. It is stunning to consider that there are actually "boundaries" that keep us positioned to experience an increase of His Presence in our lives. Boundaries and increase don't tend to go together. It almost sounds contradictory, but the paradigm works in the Kingdom. These boundary lines are hunger and humility. They are love and intimacy, commodities that cannot be measured by external ministry successes or accomplishments. Such boundary lines are matters of the heart. Either we burn with Him, or we do not.

To try and reduce God in any way is a dangerous road for us to travel. The reasoning is simple. When we "reduce" God, we are doing absolutely nothing to God Himself. We are ultimately doing ourselves the most significant disservice. How we see Him shapes every aspect of our lives. Let's behold Him *as He is.* It is not through formula that we step into our purpose; it is through intimacy, "*because as He is, so are we in this world*" (1 John 4:17).

DAILY SCRIPTURE READING

1 JOHN 4:17

PRAYER

Holy Spirit, fill me afresh so that I can give a greater picture of Jesus to the world through my life. Help me to show people what Jesus truly looks like so they get an accurate representation of Who the Father really is.

July 27

While it is one of my highest privileges to serve Him completely, my labor is the byproduct of my love.

THIS UNIMAGINABLE PRIVILEGE of carrying God's Presence should never reduce me to a laborer for God. The decision of being a servant or a friend is still being made by people around us every day. Friendship does not cancel our service; it brings substance to it. We serve *from* relationship, not for it. We are not trying to work into God's good graces. Grace has positioned us to labor out of desire, not duty. We are willing to do anything for Him because He is our one desire.

There is always a *because* to our service. He is God Almighty. His sheer identity demands unquestionable obedience and lifelong service, no question. Yet, the Holy One made it possible to actually invite you and me into the process of being servants who are also friends. We serve and we enjoy closeness with the One we are serving. The Lord wants us to have a vision for what we are doing when we say "Yes" to Him. He is eternally worthy of our submission regardless of whether or not He gives us an explanation. Yet, Jesus clarified, "*I have called you friends, for all things that I heard from My Father I have made known to you*" (John 15:15).

Mike Bickle has been quoted, saying, "Lovers will always outwork the workers." *This is absolutely true.* Closeness with the One Who has invited us into deep friendship is what produces a desire to co-labor with Him. We say "Yes" to serve Him and to receive revelation of how the Father wants to use our service.

Daily Scripture Reading

John 15:15

Prayer

Holy Spirit, You have brought me into divine friendship with God. Help me to live as both a servant and a friend. I hear what the Father is saying, I feel what He is feeling, and I say "Yes" to whatever He asks me to do.

July 28

In the outpouring of the Holy Spirit is the revelation of the face of God.

THE HEART OF God is clearly seen in this amazing prophecy from Ezekiel. *"I will not hide my face from them anymore; for I shall have poured out my Spirit"* (Ezek. 39:29). There is nothing greater than beholding His face.

"In the light of the king's face is life, and his favor is like a cloud of the latter rain" (Prov. 16:15). Rain is a biblical metaphor for the move of the Holy Spirit, thus the term *outpouring*. This verse also links God's face, His favor, with the outpouring of His Spirit. The Spirit demonstrates to reveal.

He moves in power to show us a Person.

DAILY SCRIPTURE READING

EZEKIEL 39:29

PRAYER

Holy Spirit, show me the Father's face in every outpouring and revival. He is my pursuit. I praise You for the great manifestations, signs, and wonders that revival brings. I am thankful for the freedom and deliverance that Your power releases. In all of it, keep my eyes looking for the Father. Help me to grow in my knowledge and understanding of Your ways, Lord, as I study Your works in the Spirit's outpouring.

July 29

The outpouring of the Spirit is the fulfillment of the quest for God's face.

MOSES EXPERIENCED THE transforming Presence of God on his own face (see Exod. 34:29-35). It was the result of his own face-to-face encounter with God. The outpouring brings us to His face again. And believe it or not, Moses' experience pales by comparison. "*How will the ministry of the Spirit fail to be even more with glory?*" (2 Cor. 3:8 NASB).

So then, as we prioritize hosting His Presence, we learn to release His face of favor into the earth. That is what people of great favor do. Moses enjoyed one level of favor, being one who carried the radiance of God's face for a time. You and I have been ushered into an even greater expression of favor. Moses enjoyed a season of shining the light of God, while you are called to *be* the "*light of the world*" (Matt. 5:14). Under the Old Covenant, the people could not truly *be* light. In fact, they would barely gaze upon the light radiating from Moses' face.

Now, because of Jesus' blood, the One Who unveils the light of God actually lives within you. The Holy Spirit makes it possible for you to assume your position as one who carries and shines glory in a measure that Moses could not even step into.

Jesus' words set us up to anticipate a greater experience of favor than any human being had enjoyed in times previous. Under the Old, a man's face radiated with glory for a season, but then it faded. In the New, a company of people are filled with the One Who causes the redeemed to *arise and shine* (see Isa. 60:1).

DAILY SCRIPTURE READING

EXODUS 34:29-35

PRAYER

Holy Spirit, You have made it possible for me to experience and exceed what Moses had under the Old Covenant. His encounters with You caused His face to shine for a time. Now, because You live inside of me, You have made it possible for me to actually be a light. I am the light of the world. I am a city on a hill, filled with Your Presence to shine Your light to the world around me!

July 30

Where we go in revival, we can't go past His face.

THE ONLY DIRECTION to go is to cry out for a greater measure of His Presence in the outpouring. Psalm 80 continuously links the favor of His face with the work of His hand. It is easy to become distracted with the wonderful demonstrations of power and manifestations. If we are not careful, signs and wonders can even become the end-all of revival. These things are truly our treasure and delight, not as an end in themselves, but because they all release greater glimpses of the Father's face and His divine nature.

Israel witnessed incredible miracles, but the people's hearts remained hard. They watched time and time again as God met their needs in supernatural ways. Breakthrough did not guarantee their devotion to God. Likewise, miracles do not automatically produce intimacy with the Father; they are invitational in nature. This is why hosting God's Presence is of the utmost importance. He desires to move in our midst; the key is, will we steward His move accordingly?

We cannot go on claiming that the move of God was ineffective because of how the people responded. Truly, we must reorient our minds to properly accommodate the Spirit's outpouring in our midst. What man does with God's divine invitation is his privilege and responsibility. Let's continually be looking for His face in every miracle, every sign, and every wonder. God's outpouring is nothing short of His unveiling. He is faithful to show us Who He is through how He works!

Daily Scripture Reading

Psalm 67:1-2

Prayer

Holy Spirit, cause the Father's face to shine upon me and reveal Who You are to the nations. This starts with me—in my life, in my family, among my friends, in my circle of influence. As You shine Your face upon me, help me to make Your ways clearly known.

July 31

The righteous who seek His face in intimacy are those who can be used to do great exploits.

HEROES OF THE faith became men and women *"of* [God's] *right hand"* (Ps. 80:17). He put them on like a glove and used them to display His signs and wonders. We must be those who see what's available and contend for a greater measure of His favor to be upon us.

Those who have gone before us and have shaped history all share a common characteristic: They had hearts that hungered for more than their present reality. This hunger launched them upon quests to not only experience the *more*, but also bring others into the same measure of breakthrough. Whether it was William Seymour during the Azusa Street Revival or Evan Roberts of the Welsh Revival, these pioneers tasted something of another world. This created a relentless stirring within them to see that taste transform *this world*.

We are still riding the momentum of these history makers today. They paid a significant price for many of the realities we enjoy freely. What they tasted in part, you and I can enjoy in *greater* measure. It is not full by any means, but there is increased momentum because these men and women sought God's face. In turn, He put them on as gloves to do mighty works in their generations that would ultimately shape the day in which we live.

Daily Scripture Reading

Psalm 80:17

Prayer

Holy Spirit, I long to be a person of God's right hand. I desire to live hungry for more than my current experience. Ruin me for formalism. Protect me from leveling out, believing that I have arrived. Bring me into new tastes of Your Presence. Give me glimpses of what is available, but not yet encountered. Cause my heart to burn as I read Your Word and see examples of those who walked with You in powerful ways.

AUGUST

Your Ultimate Prototype for the Normal Christian Life

August 1

Sometimes we don't know what we have in us until it's required of us to serve.

SOMEWHERE AROUND TEN years after the day of Pentecost, the church was experiencing growing pains again. It happened at least once before in Acts 6 when some of the widows were not having their basic needs met. It became apparent that to take care of people correctly they needed people who could give themselves to practical service while the apostles were able to commit themselves to prayer and the study of Scriptures. The new team of servants was called *deacons*. But now there was a much bigger problem. Gentiles were getting saved in great numbers, and they were affecting the culture and nature of this new organism called the Church. Some might say that the tail was now wagging the dog.

As a result of persecution, the Church then spread around the known world while the apostles stayed behind. People who were not thought to be leaders found themselves in a place where leadership was required. They stepped into a greater anointing and found out rather quickly what they had.

When we step into a position of service, this role places a demand on the grace within us. Power comes with purpose, and one expression of this purpose is to serve others more effectively.

Daily Scripture Reading

Acts 6:1-6

Prayer

Father, help me to step out and serve wherever and however You need me. As I do, reveal Your power and grant me a fresh revelation of the gifts, talents, and abilities You have placed within me.

August 2

Priorities get refined automatically when children are around.

I'VE SEEN THIS happen in our day. Church members get quite comfortable, and then revival hits. Those who reject it of course won't call it an actual move of God. But there's always a great influx of people who have "not paid the light bills" all these years who come into the church excited, wondering why people just sit there.

When you add to the mix a great number of converts, things really get exciting. New believers are known to bring all kinds of issues to the surface. My uncle used to say, "Every household needs a two-year-old." He was speaking naturally. But the same is true spiritually. New converts always present these "issues," which should be welcomed. It takes a Kingdom perspective to joy in these so-called issues because they signify an increase of new children being brought into the family of God. We provide discipleship, teaching, and instruction, absolutely. But we cannot place unrealistic demands on those who are in a place of early development, spiritually speaking.

DAILY SCRIPTURE READING

ACTS 6:7

PRAYER

Show me how to disciple Your people, Lord. Reveal someone in my life who I can come alongside to mentor and encourage. As new believers are brought into the Kingdom, may I help develop them into followers of Christ who are growing up and maturing in Your ways.

August 3

When you have a need to justify criticism you have to find a spiritual term to make it OK.

HOLINESS* OR *DISCERNMENT is often used for such moments. It amazes me how many people who have prayed for revival for years will leave a church once they get it.

I think of how Chuck Smith of Calvary Chapel in Costa Mesa made such a choice when confronted with this problem at the beginning of the Jesus People Movement. The members were concerned about their new carpet being soiled by the barefoot hippies. Pastor Chuck told them that he would tear out the carpet then. Priorities. Simple but profound.

We must go beyond mere toleration when it comes to new believers being radically touched in the place of outpouring. This should be cause for great celebration, regardless of the cost and discomfort.

Daily Scripture Reading

Acts 2:47

Prayer

Father, help me to rejoice over the work of Your Spirit as He brings people into the Kingdom. Help me not to judge them or criticize them if they are not growing the way I think they should. This is Your work, not mine. Show me how to collaborate with You to see more and more lives changed by the Gospel.

August 4

Great moves of God upset everything.

NOTHING IS LEFT untouched when His Presence comes. This should be unsurprising, because our God is described as a "*consuming fire*" (Heb. 12:29).

The apostles had many concerns. Most of these dealt with issues of holiness, which is a very legitimate issue. They had to settle on what salvation by grace really looked like. These new believers were challenging things that might have never been questioned by the Jewish believers. When you add to the mix the fact that there were those with unhealthy attachments to the old way of doing things, as in Mosaic Law, there was a real uncertainty about it all. I'm sure each apostle had their convictions as to how things should be.

We must be open to reconsider what we have been doing if revival seems to *upset* it. This is not proposing that we disregard scriptural truth. There is a difference between truth and the vehicle through which truth is communicated in our modern context. We must live in a place of continual yieldedness before the Lord, ever willing to adjust anything in our lives that His Presence disrupts.

DAILY SCRIPTURE READING

HEBREWS 12:29

PRAYER

Father, You are an all-consuming fire. I give You permission to disrupt the way I do things when You come like fire. Help me to be flexible and discern what You are doing so that I can move out of the way and let You work freely.

August 5

As fishers of men our job is to catch them and let Him clean them.

THE HOLY SPIRIT is responsible for sanctification. He is the agent of our maturity. There is responsibility from our end, but the empowerment always comes from His. We have been called to go into all nations. The Holy Spirit has commissioned us to go into the world and bring in the lost. What an unparalleled privilege to be an ambassador of God and an agent of reconciliation, uniting orphans with a perfect Father.

However, we must recognize the boundary lines of our ability when it comes to discipleship. The desire to help young believers grow and mature is certainly noble; the problems come when well-meaning people mistakenly assume the role of the Holy Spirit. We cannot water down truth. At the same time, we cannot *make* someone adhere to it.

Daily Scripture Reading

1 Corinthians 6:9-11 ▪ Titus 3:3-6

Prayer

Holy Spirit, You are the best teacher. Remind me that it is not my job to try to convince people they should be holy. In fact, it is not my job to make myself holy. You are the One Who makes that possible and I thank You for that empowering grace. Thank You for the work You have done in my life, and I invite You to continue refining me.

August 6

I've never heard of anyone studying their way into a revival.

THE FIRST LEADERS' conference was called for this elite group of apostles. They convened in Jerusalem, the God-chosen headquarters for the Church. As they met, they presented the issues. But the way they came to a conclusion is quite fascinating. They shared testimonies. They each had stories to tell pertaining to God's outpouring among the Gentiles. As they heard the stories they began to recognize a theme: God poured out His Spirit upon Gentiles before they knew enough to get themselves acquainted with Jewish traditions. In fact, He seemed to move among them with little regard for their own readiness for an authentic Holy Spirit outpouring.

What moves me in this part of the story is that they actually developed their theology around what they saw God do. They didn't approach the issue with an exegetical study of Jesus' sermons to find out what to do. That kind of study is noble and good. But you usually need the move of God to be happening before you get insight about what it is that is happening.

Daily Scripture Reading

Acts 15:1-29

Prayer

Lord, I know that Your Word is truth—I need Your help to apply it. I also need Your help to know what to do in situations that are not specifically outlined in Scripture. Please give me a healthy balance between studying and applying Your Word to situations, as well as recognizing and following along with how Your Spirit is moving.

August 7

We limit God to our present understanding of how God moves, all while praying that God would do a new thing among us.

I REALIZE THAT THIS seems to be treading in dangerous territory for so many, but to me the risk is worth it. Why do you think new moves of God almost always start with people who don't know what they're doing? Because when we have been *around* for a while, it is easy to embrace a mindset that assumes familiarity with the move of God. This familiarity is what prevented Jesus' hometown from giving Him the honor He deserved. In Mark 6:3, we see the people asking, "*Is this not the carpenter, the son of Mary, and brother of James, Joses, Judas, and Simon? And are not His sisters here with us*?"

Because of familiarity, a town missed its opportunity for significant breakthrough. Because of familiarity in our own lives, we can miss the very thing we cry out for because we don't recognize it when it comes. We don't recognize it because we think we know what it *should* look like.

Here's an interesting proposal: Let's approach Him like we don't know what we are doing. It's in this place of total surrender to His ways that we position ourselves to experience *His move*, regardless of whether or not it meets our specifications. It meets His and that is of supreme importance.

Daily Scripture Reading

Mark 6:1-6

Prayer

God, You are so much bigger than I can imagine. Your ways are beyond my comprehension sometimes. Help me not to miss what You are doing because of my own reasoning. Help me to remain open to new ways of seeing You move. I want to keep relying on You, Holy Spirit, and not just my own thoughts.

August 8

What we know can keep us from what we need to know if we don't remain a novice.

BIBLE KNOWLEDGE WITHOUT Bible experience can keep us trapped in a place of assumed satisfaction. We assume that knowing information about God is sufficient, when in fact such a place causes our momentum in God to plateau. This is not by His choice. God is not One to sovereignly arrange our stagnancy.

The way to Kingdom increase is living to learn. It is utterly impossible for one to claim any measure of expertise in the ways of God, primarily because it is impossible for the finite to wrap around the infinite. This is not to say that we are unable to access the infinite. Far from it. The One Who mortal minds cannot begin to wrap around actually makes us His dwelling place. While this is confounding, it is also encouraging. The same Paul who reminds us that our bodies are the temple of the Holy Spirit builds upon that truth by writing, "*Eye has not seen, nor ear heard, nor have entered into the heart of man the things which God has prepared for those who love Him*" (1 Cor. 2:9).

This reality concerning God, making reference to Isaiah 64:4, is what keeps us novices. Undoubtedly, Paul walked aware of the same magnificent truth concerning the vast superiority of the One Whom he served. But Paul did not end there. He continued, "*But God has revealed them to us through His Spirit*" (1 Cor. 2:10). Our New Covenant inheritance is a life of increasing access to the unknown. However, we cannot access these *things* through our own efforts; it is the Holy Spirit Who unveils them to us.

DAILY SCRIPTURE READING

1 CORINTHIANS 2:9-12

PRAYER

Holy Spirit, thank You for continually unveiling the inheritance I have access to through the New Covenant. I want to remain teachable. There is always more to discover and always more to learn when it comes to knowing You.

August 9

He still requires that primary advancements in the Kingdom be made through childlikeness.

CHILDREN DON'T KNOW everything. Even though this statement may seem overly simplified, the fact remains that many believers—particularly those who have been saved for a long period of time—can fall prey to thinking they know enough. To believe we know *enough* is the telltale sign that we do *not* know enough concerning the operation of God's Kingdom.

The prerequisite to life in the Kingdom is becoming *born again*. Is it any wonder that Jesus confronts Nicodemus, a thoroughly learned religious man, with the dire need to be *reborn* in order to enter this Kingdom? From the beginning, Jesus was emphasizing the need for childlikeness, down to the act of actually being reborn and re-entering childhood. Of all people, Nicodemus especially needed to hear this due to the amount of theological knowledge he surely had acquired over the years.

In knowing everything, one can sufficiently know nothing. In coming before God as a child, hungry and ready to receive, we posture ourselves to receive from Him without limit.

Daily Scripture Reading

John 3:1-9 ▪ Matthew 18:1-4

Prayer

Holy Spirit, I want to be as teachable as a child. Make me humble and help me come to You hungry and ready to receive. Help me never to get to a place where I think I know enough and don't need You to keep teaching me and leading me into more.

August 10

When we become experts we have chosen where we level off in our maturity.

ASSUMED EXPERTISE IN matters of the Spirit can blind us to receiving the very truth that God wants us to understand. Often, revelation strikes the heart before hitting our minds. It begins at a spirit level, not a thought level—although the byproduct is always a transformation of thinking. This is why there are times where you experience or see before you understand. The Holy Spirit moves before our minds are able to comprehend what is going on. The apostles dealt with this in Acts as the Holy Spirit supernaturally ushered Gentiles into the Kingdom. This presented some problems and raised some questions, specifically of how the Gentile believers should interact with Jewish custom or law. Many operating out of an "expert perspective" assumed that for these new converts to be legitimized, they needed to go through the same ritual processes as Jewish believers. They had a difficult time processing this new work of the Spirit and actually yielding their minds to the new thing God was doing in their midst—which, most likely, meant some significant change to how things had always been done.

It was only as they experienced the miraculous work of the Spirit in their midst that James *"stood and said, 'Brothers, listen to me. Peter has told you about the time God first visited the Gentiles to take from them a people for himself. And this conversion of Gentiles is exactly what the prophets predicted.'"* (Acts 15:13-15 NLT).

Scripture agreed with what they were seeing. They were willing to embrace a "see first" paradigm rather than the "expert approach" that claims total understanding of *how* God's Word operates. Sometimes we need to see the Bible in action before we truly understand the fullness of what the Holy Spirit was trying to communicate through the written Word.

DAILY SCRIPTURE READING

ISAIAH 9:6-7

PRAYER

God, I want to have encounters with You that lead me into greater understanding of You.

August 11

Experience gives understanding.

AS THE GENTILES were being brought into the Kingdom, naturally there were issues that needed to be addressed. The apostles were witnessing a move of God unlike anything ever seen previously. A people who were previously *not* a people were becoming born again into God's family. James, the apostle at Jerusalem, brought the testimony time to a biblical conclusion. He said, *"With this the words of the prophets agree"* (Acts 15:15). What he shared in the following moments was possibly new to him, as there's no record of this revelation being commonplace before this moment.

It appears to me that God actually dropped this Scripture into James' heart as the Jerusalem Council was taking place and the apostles were talking. In other words, God gave Scripture to James to back up the legitimacy of the stories being told. Biblical backing is vital. But I doubt there has ever been a great move of God where everything that happened was preceded by revelation—they understood it before it happened. Biblical backing came *after* the move of God. Again, the ability to measure an experience with Scripture is essential. The problem is, God often moves first and then invites us into His Word to discover that, just perhaps, our understanding of what we thought we knew needed to be upgraded. Our experience actually gives us a fuller understanding of what we read in Scripture.

DAILY SCRIPTURE READING

HEBREWS 1-2

PRAYER

Lord, I ask You to come and upgrade my understanding with experiences in Your Presence. I pray that I won't put You in a box according to my understanding of who You are in Scripture. Expand how I see you, Father. You are truly great and limitless.

August 12

David's tabernacle became the backdrop for life as we know it today in the New Testament Church.

TO ME DAVID is the greatest example of life under grace in the Old Testament. King, priest, and prophet—a complete prophetic picture of the Christ to come. His example also portrayed the coming New Testament believer. David's tabernacle existed for close to 40 years. It was a completely new approach to God—the priests worshiped God for 24 hours a day, 7 days a week, without a blood sacrifice.

This picture is absolutely stunning, considering that under the Old Covenant blood was of paramount importance for entrance into the Presence of God. It is not beyond God to draw one age into the prophetic foretaste of another. The very mandate of the New Testament believer is *on earth as it is in Heaven*. God has resourced us to draw the life and culture of one age, Heaven, into our present day. Likewise, God granted David the ability to construct a prophetic template for what New Testament life would look like, where the sacrifice was one of praise, not the blood of animals. He foresaw a day when a sacrifice would be offered and blood would be shed that satisfied the requirements of the Law. Only a sacrifice of such incomparable purity could open a door to the reality the tabernacle of David pictured.

The very One Who David looked forward to is the One Whose blood has made provision for us to "*draw near with a sincere heart in full assurance of faith, having our hearts sprinkled clean from an evil conscience and our bodies washed with pure water*" (Heb. 10:22 NASB).

DAILY SCRIPTURE READING

1 CHRONICLES 23:1-5 ▪ HEBREWS 10:19-25

PRAYER

Thank You for the privilege of worshiping You anytime I want because of the provision Jesus made on the Cross. I give You all the praise and glory right now in Jesus' Name.

August 13

There were several houses of God in the Old Testament, each a prophetic picture for what was to come.

THE FIRST WAS in the Genesis 28 story of Jacob meeting with God on the side of the mountain. It was called *Bethel*, which means the house of God. There was actually no building. God was there. That's what made it His house.

The *Tabernacle of Moses* gave us a picture of Jesus. Every piece of furniture spoke of something about the coming Messiah. It was built according the specific details that God gave Moses on the mountain in a face-to-face meeting.

The *Temple of Solomon* was more glorious and beautiful than anything ever built on earth. It was humanity's best effort to give God something to dwell in that was consistent with His worth. It was built according very precise plans, representing the permanent dwelling of God.

The *restored temple of Solomon* was built to twice the size of the original. When God restores, He restores to a place greater than before restoration was needed. It did not contain the beauty of the previous temple. Those who saw the former glory wept at the sight of the restored house. Those who didn't see the former house rejoiced at this one.

The *Tabernacle of David* was built for worship. No description of building materials was ever mentioned and no size is ever given. The Ark of the Covenant was there. The Presence of God rested upon the Ark. Priests worshiped 24 hours a day—different shifts were taken so this could be accomplished continually. The two outstanding factors are God was there in His glory and priests ministered to God nonstop.

Daily Scripture Reading

Genesis 28:10-22

Prayer

Thank You, Father, for the prophetic pictures in the Old Testament that reveal what was to come in Jesus. His blood made it possible for me to live in Your Presence—filled with Your Presence. Thank You for the glorious privilege of being Your house on the Earth.

August 14

The Church is the house that houses a priesthood—a worshiping community that offers spiritual sacrifices to God.

THIS PRIESTHOOD OF worshipers is God's restoration project. It is the fulfillment of the tabernacle of David, where all would be able to minister unto God. His design from the start was a "*kingdom of priests*" (Exod. 19:6). What was pictured in an elite few under the Old Covenant has now been fulfilled in a company of people. The blood of Jesus promotes every believer into the position of a priest.

> *You also, as living stones, are being built up a spiritual house, a holy priesthood, to offer up spiritual sacrifices acceptable to God through Jesus Christ* (1 Peter 2:5).

No longer is there need for a *physical* sacrificial system to make humanity acceptable before the Holy God. Blood sacrifices of bulls, goats, and sheep simply could not transition from the Old to the New, for it was impossible for them to remove the stain of our sin (see Heb. 10:4). An exchange has been made to where, now, the acceptable sacrifice is one of praise (see Heb. 13:15). Man no longer owed a debt to produce right standing before God. Jesus paid this in full. Now, the sacrifice is responsive, not redemptive. We *respond* to the work of redemption through spiritual sacrifices of praise rather than trying to *receive* redemption through physical sacrifices of blood.

Daily Scripture Reading

Hebrews 13:7-16

Prayer

God, may Your praise always be on my lips. I worship and adore You for Your great love and the sacrifice You made for me. You've bought me with a price, and I want to worship You with every part of my being. You are worthy.

August 15

We are the community of worshipers whose primary focus is ministering to God Himself.

SO WHAT IS being rebuilt? The Church, with its unique Davidic anointing for the Presence, is the fulfillment of the prophecy from Amos. We read:

> *In that day I will raise up the fallen booth of David, and wall up its breaches; I will also raise up its ruins and rebuild it as in the days of old* (Amos 9:11 NASB).

This prophecy spoke of a day when the tabernacle of David would be restored. When we consider the context, it is important to note that with raising up this *fallen booth* or *tabernacle of God*, there would also be the need for a corresponding priestly order. What we see pictured in the era of David had a company of priests ministering before the Lord night and day.

The significance for this prophecy lies in this one fact—only priests could carry God's Presence. God seems insistent upon that requirement. Because of Jesus, you and I are able to assume our position among such a priestly order. David prophesied this present reality through his Old Testament tabernacle, giving us a glimpse of what life would look like in a new day. Now, a community of worshipers could come before God's Presence and minister before Him without barriers.

Daily Scripture Reading

Amos 9:11-15

Prayer

God, it is such an honor to be able to come before You and minister to You. You have brought me into Your very Presence and have made me Your priest. Thank You for making me righteous through Jesus so that there would be no barriers between us.

August 16

Some of God's best lessons can't be learned in a class, they can only be learned on a journey.

SAUL WAS THE king before David. As King Saul had little regard for the Presence of God (Ark of the Covenant), David became king of Judah and then Israel. He was acquainted with the Presence of God from his time on the backside of the desert, caring for his father's sheep. In the journey of watching Saul's failure, David's desire for God's Presence was surely intensified. He recognized the value of stewarding the Presence at all costs. This is expressed in Psalm 51. David is responding to his sin with Bathsheba after being confronted by Nathan the prophet:

> *Create in me a clean heart, O God, and renew a steadfast spirit within me. Do not cast me away from Your presence, and do not take Your Holy Spirit from me* (Psalm 51:10-11).

Even though both David and Saul had sinned, it is notable to contrast their responses. While Saul plummets into an increased deluge of rebellion and darkness, David responds in broken repentance. He could not follow Saul's path—a man from whom the Spirit of God departed (see 1 Sam. 16:14). By journeying alongside Saul for a significant part of this process, David took a firm stand, refusing to allow his journey to mirror Saul's. What he learned by watching Saul's fall surely reminded him of the priceless treasure that is the Presence.

DAILY SCRIPTURE READING

PSALM 51

PRAYER

Holy Spirit, I desire to steward Your Presence at all costs. Show me how to protect this relationship, valuing Your Presence in my life as my supreme treasure.

August 17

God's Presence cannot be manhandled.

DAVID HAD MADE arrangements to bring the Ark into Jerusalem and place it in the tent that he pitched for that purpose (see 2 Sam. 6:17). It was David's number-one priority. There was nothing even close to the priority of God's Presence being with David, being with Israel. The story is exciting, intriguing, and deadly.

The nation of Israel planned for this day. They lined the streets to witness the ceremony of worship orchestrated to bring the Presence of God into the city of David, Jerusalem. Those who could play instruments brought them in a sacrificial celebration to honor God as He came. The finest ox cart was obtained for the event. Priests took their places as they ushered in the Holy One. But one of the oxen stumbled and nearly upset the cart that carried the Ark. Uzzah reached out his hand to steady the Ark out of his concern for the Presence. The anger of the Lord burned against him for his irreverence. God killed him.

This story alone should sober the hearts and minds of those who would tend to use the anointing for personal gain. God will not be commandeered by man.

DAILY SCRIPTURE READING

2 SAMUEL 6:1-11

PRAYER

I desire Your Presence because I love You. Help me to never pursue You just to get something from You. You supply every need and are happy to provide for me in every way possible. Even still, Your Presence is more precious than any provision that You could ever give. I celebrate the blessing and am truly grateful for all of it—but I don't pursue the blessing, I pursue Your Presence.

Sincerity alone will not save anyone.

TO SAY THAT David was scared of God is a great understatement. He was so sure this was the thing to do. His hunger for God was sincere and legitimate. Yet, the process that he set up led to this terrifying scenario: *"And the anger of the Lord burned against Uzzah, and God struck him down there for his irreverence; and he died there by the ark of God"* (2 Sam. 6:7 NASB). Even though David was sincere in his worship for God, he did not follow God's biblical order for carrying the Presence. One can be sincere but miss out on a lifestyle of encounter because of an incorrect approach to God's Presence.

In the New Testament, we have a blueprint in blood. Jesus opened a new and living way for us enter God's Presence. Further still, He made it possible for the Presence to actually take up habitation in a priestly people. This is the Church, those who have been redeemed by the blood of Jesus. To assume that God has any other plan to carry His Presence into the earth, apart from using His eternal priestly order, is to approach Him in the manner that Uzzah did. Scripture calls Uzzah's error *irreverence*. Perhaps he was sincere, but his irreverence was costly.

Drinking strychnine sincerely thinking that it's a fruit juice doesn't make it any less poisonous. We need to cease looking beyond God's designated order to carrying His Presence in the earth. Priests. People. Redeemed men and women are the ones designated to carry God in this planet. Any other method simply will not do.

DAILY SCRIPTURE READING

HEBREWS 12:25-29

PRAYER

Thank You so much for Your grace, Lord. Would You please help me find the balance between having a healthy reverence toward You and enjoying friendship? You are loving, compassionate and gracious, but You are also a consuming fire. Help me to walk in a revelation of our intimacy, but also, the true fear of the Lord.

August 19

Only priests can carry His Presence. Period.

When David heard that the household of Obed-Edom was prospering in all ways (because of the presence of the Ark), he became more diligent to find out what went wrong the day Uzzah died. He apparently turned to the Scriptures for insight.

> *Then David said, "No one may carry the ark of God but the Levites, for the Lord has chosen them to carry the ark of God and to minister before Him forever"* (1 Chronicles 15:2).

I love whenever I find a command or promise that has the word *forever* in it. It automatically means there's a principle involved that will carry over into this lifestyle of grace as well as our heavenly existence.

The priestly function was not abolished at the Cross; it has only changed forms. Whereas under the Old Covenant only certain individuals could assume the role of priest, the blood of Jesus has made all believers a "*royal priesthood*" (1 Pet. 2:9). Scripture reminds us that Jesus "*has made us kings and priests to His God and Father*" (Rev. 1:6). What was reserved for the few under the Old has become available to *whosoever will* under the New.

Daily Scripture Reading

2 Samuel 6:11-12 ▪ 1 Chronicles 15:1-15

Prayer

God, thank You for making me a royal priest who can carry Your Presence. I praise You for inviting me into this incredible priviliege.

August 20

Yielded people have the privilege of carrying (hosting) God into life's situations.

GOD WILL NOT ride on ox carts, even though the Philistines seemed to get away with it (see 1 Sam. 4–6). The Presence of God will not rest on anything we make. He rests on us. I believe that applies to organizations, buildings, etc.

People will often look at institutions that have been created to facilitate great ministries. But no matter how great the organization, the by-laws, or the reputation, God doesn't rest upon those things. It's people He has chosen to make His resting place.

Daily Scripture Reading

1 Samuel 4-6 ▪ Romans 8:9-11

Prayer

I invite You, Holy Spirit, to rest upon my life in an even greater way. Increase the measure of Your Presence released through my life as I live in daily surrender to You.

August 21

David was not a normal king. He would become known as the man after God's heart—the man of God's Presence.

DAVID ANNOUNCED THE new plan to usher God's Presence into his city. The people were ready. The priests were ready. The priestly musicians trained for the day. Those assigned to carry the ark of His Presence probably wondered about the fearfully exciting privilege involved in their job. After all, the last guy to get that close to the Ark died. But this time they had the will of God revealed in Scripture to support the process. This story is one of the greatest stories in the Bible. It should be known forward and backward by every believer, as it is key to clearly fulfill our role in this day. It is our story, ahead of time.

The day came. King David stripped himself of his kingly garments and put on a priest's tunic, basically a priest's undergarment. This was not something a king would be seen in normally. This all represents a heart motivated by sincerity and truth. David previously sought to host God's Presence, but his sincerity needed truth. He needed to accommodate God's blueprint. Here, we watch David extravagantly honor the One he loved. Truly a sneak preview of worship in *spirit and truth.*

Daily Scripture Reading

2 Samuel 6:12-15

Prayer

God, I want to worship You in spirit and truth just like David did. Help me not to be concerned with what anyone else thinks of my worship toward You. What matters most is worshiping You in the way You deserve to be worshiped!

August 22

Many respond to God once His Presence is realized. But some respond before He actually comes. They are the ones who usher in the Presence of the King of Glory.

IT IS WORTH noting that the Ark of the Covenant (the Presence of God) followed David into Jerusalem. Wherever David danced, God followed. He responds to our offerings. In this story, it's an offering of thanksgiving and praise expressed in the dance.

Another way of looking at it is God showed up wherever King David danced in an undignified fashion.

It might surprise us to find out what is attractive to Him.

DAILY SCRIPTURE READING

2 SAMUEL 6:16-19

PRAYER

God, I want to usher in Your Presence wherever I am. Help me to respond to You and honor Your Presence whether I see or feel You moving. I want to celebrate who You are and what You are going to do before anything actually happens.

August 23

Extreme worship always looks to be extreme foolishness to those who stand at a distance.

DURING THE PROCESSION of the Ark, there was one notable absentee. Michal, the daughter of Saul and wife of David, looked at the event through the palace window. Michal was appalled at David's lack of regard for how people perceived his passion, his humility in attire, and his complete lack of public decorum.

Instead of greeting him with honor, she tried to shame him.

> *But when David returned to bless his household, Michal the daughter of Saul came out to meet David and said, "How the king of Israel distinguished himself today! He uncovered himself today in the eyes of his servants' maids as one of the foolish ones shamelessly uncovers himself!"* (2 Samuel 6:20 NASB)

Some things can only be understood from within. Such is the case with authentic worship.

DAILY SCRIPTURE READING

2 SAMUEL 6:20

PRAYER

God, I want to express myself extravagantly in worship to You without shame... just like David did. Honoring Your Presence is more important than anyone's opinion of me. Please give me the grace to live a life of extravagant worship before You, the extravagant God.

Dumbing down our emphasis on the Presence should never be to accommodate the Michals in the house.

DAVID'S RESPONSE TO Michal was very bold in many ways.

> *So David said to Michal, "It was before the Lord, who chose me above your father and above all his house, to appoint me ruler over the people of the Lord, over Israel; therefore I will celebrate before the Lord. I will be more lightly esteemed than this and will be humble in my own eyes, but with the maids of whom you have spoken, with them I will be distinguished"* (2 Samuel 6:21-22 NASB).

The shepherd/king made it clear that God chose him above her father. This was a biting comment to say the least. Her disregard for the Presence of God revealed that she carried some of the same *lack of value* for the Presence that her father Saul had lived by during his reign. David goes on to say that she basically hadn't seen anything yet. In other words, if that embarrassed her, her future was not too bright. David was just getting warmed up.

Michal's criticism actually incited David to go to the next level in his worship. If she thought what David did was undignified, she'd better get ready for what was coming next. The devil actually doesn't mind worship that is tame. It is extreme worship that exposes religion and threatens darkness.

Daily Scripture Reading

2 Samuel 6:21-22

Prayer

Father, in response to Who You are and what You have done in my life, I cannot help but give You the highest praise. I continually bring before my mind the great things You have done. Every miracle, breakthrough, and blessing reveals Who You are. I give thanks for Your works, for they show me Your nature and Your character. You are truly worthy of all the praise!

Barrenness is the natural result of despising worship.

WHENEVER SOMEONE DESPISES extravagant worship, they put themselves in an extremely dangerous position. In doing so they are rejecting the reason why we're alive. Barrenness and the absence of worship go hand in hand. The Michal scene happened again during Jesus' ministry. It was when the costly ointment was poured over Jesus. All the disciples were upset, asking, "*Why this waste?*" (Matt. 26:8). An act that made the disciples uneasy was celebrated by the Savior (see Matt. 26:13).

Sounds very similar to Michal's response to David as she exclaimed, "*How the king of Israel distinguished himself today! He uncovered himself today in the eyes of his servants' maids as one of the foolish ones shamelessly uncovers himself!*" (2 Sam. 6:20 NASB).

Both wasteful expressions of worship created discomfort with religious perspectives and have been memorialized in Heaven's records forever.

DAILY SCRIPTURE READING

MATTHEW 26:6-13

PRAYER

God, You take great joy in extravagant, wasteful worship. Help me to pour out my love to You without fear or restraint.

Anyone can get happy after the miracle has come. Show me someone who celebrates before the answer, and I'll show you someone who is about to experience the answer.

THERE IS A wonderful verse that speaks to the effect of extreme worship on barrenness itself.

> *"Shout for joy, O barren one, you who have borne no child; break forth into joyful shouting and cry aloud, you who have not travailed; for the sons of the desolate one will be more numerous than the sons of the married woman," says the Lord* (Isaiah 54:1 NASB).

What a promise. In this chapter we find a barren woman who is exhorted to shout for joy *before* she becomes pregnant. The end result is that she will have more children than the one who has been having children all along. This provides quite the prophetic picture. The people who are people of worship, regardless of circumstances, will become fruitful in ways beyond reason.

This is the nature of faith—it looks ahead and lives accordingly.

Daily Scripture Reading

Isaiah 54:1-3

Prayer

My worship releases life where there is barrenness. In every circumstance—where there is hopelessness, impossibility, fear, or anxiety—keep me from agreeing with the problem and help me to release Your solutions.

May every solution begin with a posture of praise. I don't deny the problem; I just deny the problem of its power over my life (or over the life of the person it is afflicting). I declare Your praises. I exalt Your Name, King Jesus. I remember Your promises. Your Name is higher than any measure of barrenness. Even before my eyes see the miracle come to pass, I celebrate Who You are and what you are doing. You are the answer.

August 27

Jesus came to defeat the devil, expose his works, and reverse their effects.

IT WOULD BE appropriate to reintroduce the Genesis 1:28 passage here, as worshipers truly will *"be fruitful and multiply; fill the earth and subdue it."*

Are the examples of Michal and the Isaiah 54 woman really that significant? I believe they are. In David's tabernacle we are connected to our original purpose as worshipers to be carriers of the glory and restore fruitfulness to the barren places in the lives of those who have suffered at the enemy's hands.

We have inherited that privileged assignment of enforcing the victory of Christ in those same ways. Worshipers just do that by nature.

Daily Scripture Reading

Genesis 1:28

Prayer

You subdue darkness through our worship and praise. Your Presence brings life to the barren places. I don't need to enter into some special kind of "warfare worship" in order to defeat the works of the enemy. All worship is warfare. All true worship enforces the victory of Christ. This is who I am and this is what I carry as Your priest and as Your worshiper!

August 28

I believe it was David's hunger for God that enabled him to pull this experience into his day, even though it was reserved for another day.

WHEN DAVID BECAME king, he sensed that God was looking for something else—priests who offer the sacrifices of thanksgiving and praise through the yielded and broken heart.

This was done even though the Law he lived under forbade it. It was offered with musical instruments as well as the voices of the singers. In this context, every priest could come daily before God without having to bring a blood offering. This order of worship was done 24 hours a day, 7 days a week. This of course spoke of the day when every believer, a priest according to First Peter 2:9, would come to God in boldness because of what Jesus accomplished on our behalf. This is what was referred to when James said David's booth was being rebuilt.

David was the man after God's heart. He had a perception of God that would not be fully realized until Jesus would come and shed His blood for all. David's experience was a prophetic foretaste of something to come.

DAILY SCRIPTURE READING

1 PETER 2:9

PRAYER

As Your priest, I stand as one who ministers directly before Your Presence—day and night. You gave me a glimpse of what this looks like in the tabernacle of David. I take my place as Your minister, offering up a life of fragrant praise and worship.

August 29

Significance is always more important than visibility.

THIS TENT OR tabernacle that David built for the Ark was placed on Mount Zion. I live in northern California. When we speak of a mountain, we are speaking of a significant piece of our geography. Mount Shasta is over 14,000 feet in elevation. Mount Zion, on the other hand, is a simple rise in the earth and is contained within the city of Jerusalem. Zion means "sunny place," as it is where the sun shines first. What it lacked in elevation, it more than made up for in significance.

Some of the statements about Mount Zion are quite amazing to consider.

"Beautiful in elevation, the joy of the whole earth, is Mount Zion on the sides of the north, the city of the great King" (Ps. 48:2). Mount Zion is to be the joy of the whole earth.

"Out of Zion, the perfection of beauty, God will shine forth" (Ps. 50:2). Zion is perfect beauty. It is from there God shines forth.

"So the Lord will reign over them in Mount Zion from now on, even forever" (Mic. 4:7). All the other mountains are envious of Mount Zion. It is where God has chosen to dwell. And because it says "forever," it carries a New Testament application. It is referring to the worshiping community as His Mount Zion.

Daily Scripture Reading

Review Scriptures above.

Prayer

I am part of Your eternal worshiping community, Father. This is my identity and my great honor. May my life and my worship shine forth Your beauty for all to see.

August 30

Worshipers are in a place to call nations into their purpose, into their God-given destiny. It is the sacred privilege of those who worship.

PSALMS IS THE great book of worship. Songs were written to exalt God. But something unique happened in a few of these psalms. The writer would start to make declarations about the nations rising up to give God glory.

Decrees were made about every nation worshiping the one true God. Now, regardless of where you think this fits into God's plan for the nations, worshipers first declare it.

Below are a few verses that lend themselves to that thought.

> *All the ends of the earth shall remember and turn to the Lord, and all the families of the nations shall worship before You* (Psalm 22:27).

> *Let the nations be glad and sing for joy; for You will judge the peoples with uprightness and guide the nations on the earth* (Psalm 67:4 NASB).

> *May his name endure forever; may his name increase as long as the sun shines; and let men bless themselves by him; let all nations call him blessed* (Psalm 72:17 NASB).

Daily Scripture Reading

Review Scriptures above.

Prayer

All the ends of the earth shall worship You, Father. You desire for the earth to be filled with Your glory. I agree with the psalmist—nations will rise up to bless Your great and glorious Name. You desire for nations to be brought into the Kingdom. May our worship increase the open heaven that exists over the nations and usher them into their true destinies.

August 31

Worship affects the destiny of nations.

THERE'S A PROPHECY declared both by Isaiah and Micah that has spoken to my heart now for many years. It speaks of the mountain of God's house. This can be none other than Mount Zion. This is prophetically fulfilled in the last days. I believe that it is referring to the rebuilding of the tabernacle of David—the New Testament combining of believers from all nations into one company of people called worshipers.

> *Now it will come about that in the last days the mountain of the house of the Lord will be established as the chief of the mountains, and will be raised above the hills; and all the nations will stream to it* (Isaiah 2:2; see also Micah 4:1).

Look at the effect of this house being established as chief of all mountains. *Chief* means *head*. This government will be the head of all governments. As a result, all nations will stream to it, asking for the word of the Lord. I believe this is referring to the massive harvest that will take place before the end comes. It is brought about by worshipers. It is the rebuilding of the tabernacle of David.

Daily Scripture Reading

Micah 4:1-2

Prayer

Give me eyes to see how worship shifts the spiritual climate over entire nations! Even as I worship You, Lord, I pray that I would be aware of what is taking place in the spirit realm.

SEPTEMBER

Red Letter Revival

September 1

Jesus Christ is perfect theology.

JESUS IS THE visible image of the invisible God (see Col. 1:15). He came to show the world what the Father was like. Who better to represent God than God Himself? He came in the form of Jesus to accomplish the work of eternal salvation, but also to show humankind the loving Father that redemption would introduce them to.

During Jesus' final moments on earth, He explains to the disciples "*If you had known Me, you would have known My Father also; from now on you know Him and have seen Him*" (John 14:7). This apparently went over Philip's head because he said to Jesus, "*Lord, show us the Father, and it is sufficient for us*" (John 14:8). Philip basically responded by asking Jesus to do what He had *already been doing* throughout His life and ministry.

> *Jesus said to him, "Have I been so long with you, and yet you have not come to know Me, Philip? He who has seen Me has seen the Father; how can you say, 'Show us the Father'? Do you not believe that I am in the Father, and the Father is in Me? The words that I say to you I do not speak on My own initiative, but the Father abiding in Me does His works"* (John 14:9-10 NASB).

Everything that Jesus said and did was intentional. He was on mission to reveal the Father. We should not be expecting a different revelation of Who God is other than what has been entrusted to us in the Person of Jesus. He is truly perfect theology.

Daily Scripture Reading

Colossians 1:15

Prayer

Jesus reveals exactly Who You are, Father. He is the visible image of You—the invisible God. He has made it possible for me to know Who You are and understand what You are like. He reveals Your will. He shows me how You think.

Lord, cause my hurt to burn afresh to study the life and ministry of Jesus. There is no greater revelation of Who You are than Your glorious Son.

September 2

What you think you know about God that cannot be found in the person of Jesus, you have reason to question.

JESUS IS *THE* standard—the only standard given for us to follow. As simple as that thought is, I never cease to be amazed at how many people try to improve on the example Jesus gave us and create a new standard—one that is more relevant.

There appear to be two extremes in this regard—today I want us to consider just one of them. This is the Old Testament prophet-type ministry, whose view of God and man are accurate for their time, but very incomplete in regard to this hour that we live in. It is missing one significant ingredient—Jesus, the Reconciler. He fulfilled the demands of the Law and made reconciliation with God possible. He would not allow James and John to minister under that anointing when they asked for permission (see Luke 9:54).

That season is over! (See Luke 16:16.)

Daily Scripture Reading

Hebrews 1:1-3

Prayer

Jesus shows me exactly Who You are, Father. My eyes are fixed on His example, His model, His works, and His words. Anything that disagrees with Who Jesus was and what Jesus did, I bring before You to question. Jesus is the only standard I will follow!

September 3

If we water down Jesus' message and get converts, whose converts are they? If they did not hear the same gospel of abandonment of all to Jesus, then whose message did they hear?

THESE ARE THE ones who take great efforts not to offend anyone with the gospel. Honestly, that did not seem to be a value that Jesus carried. The heart is good in the sense that they want everyone included in the family.

Do we honestly think that the people who were unwilling to sell all in Jesus' day would be any more converted in ours?

Daily Scripture Reading

Luke 18:22

Prayer

You are worthy of my everything, Father. I will not give Jesus pieces and parts of my life. I refuse to give Him partial surrender. You can have it all, as You are the only One Who deserves it all.

September 4

So many want the "Old Time Religion" so much that they try to preserve a day that no longer exists in the heart of God.

THERE HAS BEEN a struggle in the Church for millennia about two contrasting challenges—maintaining the standards that Jesus set without going backward. In Matthew 11:12, Jesus uses language that describes the most significant shift to ever take place. Up until the *days of John the Baptist,* a former system had been enacted. This was the Old Covenant. The Kingdom was inaccessible to everyday people. Every now and then, an individual would rise up who God anointed for a special task. They lived under this anointing for a season, but it was not abiding. Jesus came and changed everything.

During Jesus' earthly ministry, the disciples did do miraculous works under the anointing—but like the heroes of the Old Testament, they walked in the Spirit for a season. However, they had access to something—or Someone—the Old Testament individuals did not. Jesus, the Anointed One, was giving them lessons in how to host the Holy Spirit Who would, ultimately, come to live within them *and* rest upon them. Although they have their place in church life, systems and structures can never substitute for the Presence. The spirit of religion is what keeps us tied to a day that no longer exists in the heart of God. It is even true that systems being used in a New Covenant context can become Old Covenant in nature if they are used to substitute for the Presence of the Holy Spirit in our lives and midst.

Pentecost did not birth a new system—it birthed a community of people filled with a Person to fill the earth with His glory.

Daily Scripture Reading

Matthew 11:12

Prayer

Your Presence is my great treasure, Holy Spirit. There are no substitutes or replacements for Your glory in my life. Structures, organizations, and systems to accomplish Your purposes are good—and at times very effective. Just help me to never see them as substitutes for the Anointing of Your Spirit.

September 5

Jesus is always contemporary, current, and relevant, more so than anything going on anywhere around us. The Father, Son, and Holy Spirit are ageless. They are relevance at its best.

CULTURE IS ALWAYS shifting. What we consider relevant in one season can quickly become outdated in the next. The most relevant truth is not what changes when seasons come and go, but the One who remains the same regardless of what continues to shift around us. The author of Hebrews reminds us of the timelessness of Jesus: "*Jesus Christ is the same yesterday, today, and forever*" (Heb. 13:8).

In this Scripture, we receive the strategy for always remaining relevant—regardless of the changes that will constantly take place around us. The key is standing upon and drawing strength from the unchanging. Hungry hearts will never be fully satisfied by that which offers substance for only a time or a season. The only One Who can keep us steadfast and grounded is the One Who remains forever steadfast Himself. *This is Jesus.*

DAILY SCRIPTURE READING

HEBREWS 13:8

PRAYER

Jesus, You are the same yesterday, today, and forever! You never change. You are always current and Your example is always relevant. I do not look for another blueprint on how to live the Christian life. Jesus, Your example is timeless and the only model worth following.

September 6

Greek and Hebrew are important, but not more important than learning to recognize His voice and release the miracle of healing to someone.

Bible schools and seminaries prioritize teaching instead of doing. While these institutions are instrumental in helping us establish strong theological foundations, what happens when a demand is placed on what we have been taught? I celebrate good theology, but I am not satisfied with it. If my theology does not yield a supernatural lifestyle, my priorities are imbalanced. Information about Jesus has become a distraction, preventing me from representing Jesus.

Leadership courses are important, but not more important than being able to lead someone to Christ or through deliverance. Management of finances is a big emphasis, and should be, considering how many failures there are. But Jesus taught the importance of managing our tongues and our families as well as our money. These are only hard classes to teach when the professors have no experience. Therein lies the problem. It is one thing to deliver information as theoretical concept; it is another to share from the well of personal experience. These are the individuals who have seen their theology produce fruit and are some of the best people to learn from.

Daily Scripture Reading

Matthew 22:23-29

Prayer

Lord, keep me from believing the lie that good information is enough. The religious leaders back in Jesus' time had information, but they missed the very point of Scripture. I am not satisfied with studying good theology; I want to see theology come alive before my eyes.

I pray that the One all true theology points to, King Jesus, would bring the Word to life. Your Word was not given just for study; it is a blueprint for living. As I read its pages, show me the realities that You have made freely available to me as one redeemed by Your blood and filled with Your Spirit.

September 7

People with theories are raising up a generation who are satisfied with theories.

WE CAN ATTEND one of the many fine Bible schools and seminaries across our land and take many courses on the study of Scripture, on leadership, music, administration, how to debate with other religions, etc. These courses have their place. And I'm only choosing from the schools that are true Bible-believing, born-again preaching schools.

Examine the courses. How many teach how to heal the sick or raise the dead? How many have classes on prayer and fasting, or casting out demons, or interceding for the nations until there's a change? The courses taught are good and valuable. But can they be more important than what Jesus commanded us to learn and do? Perhaps the reason they are not taught is that those who do the teaching don't know how. Many have pursued theological information at the expense of demonstration.

A solid theology is stunning—when it is accompanied by demonstration that backs it up. Everything we believe about God has the ability to produce simply because of Who He is. Even information about Him brims with the possibility of transformative power. It all depends on how we approach Him. If Jesus becomes a theological concept to be dialogued and debated, we will never witness transformation outside the confines of that conversation. However, if He is a Person to be followed and His experience can be *our* experience, theories will not suffice. If Jesus gives us an example that can be followed, we are hungry to lean in, behold the Son, and model His movements.

Daily Scripture Reading

Mark 12:24

Prayer

Jesus never gave His disciples theories; He gave them instructions and empowerment. Holy Spirit, You are the Person and power of God sent to live inside of me! I don't simply want to study information about You; I desire to intimately know You, see how You are moving, and carry Your Presence into the world, just like Jesus did.

Many stop short of a divine encounter because they are satisfied with good theology.

ONE IS TO lead us to the other. The religious leaders of Jesus' era missed their encounter with God because they were not willing to rethink their *understanding* of the Scriptures. It was limited and restrictive. It gave no room for the personification of the Word to enter the scene and reveal the Author of Scripture. This does not give us the allowance to adjust timeless truth to accommodate the popular opinion or perspective of the time.

Rather, it is a call for us to live increasingly yielded to the Spirit of God when it comes to understanding the Word of God. He inspired it and, as Jesus explained, He is the only One qualified to "*guide you into all the truth; for He will not speak on His own authority, but whatever He hears He will speak*" (John 16:13). True theology is always an invitation to encounter a Person, not just add more facts to our knowledge base. This begs the question, *What is the end goal of your theology*? Is it to increase our level of information and religiously follow all of the rules, or is it to encounter a Person and be transformed into His likeness from glory to glory?

Daily Scripture Reading

John 16:12-15

Prayer

Father, You did not send me a theology or doctrine—You gave me Your very Spirit. Holy Spirit, You are not a concept. You are not an "it." You are a divine Person. You are God Almighty, working in my life and moving in the earth. Help me to never reduce or lower my understanding of Who You are. I pray that I would always walk mindful of Who lives inside of me, drawing from Your endless well of strength, power, and Presence.

Massive efforts are made to do church in a timely fashion so we can continue with the rest of our lives. Apparently, many have not yet discovered that we really don't have a life outside of Christ.

THERE IS NO life outside of Christ. Paul expressed this as he wrote, "*For to me, to live is Christ, and to die is gain*" (Phil. 1:21). Whether he was laboring on earth for the sake of the Gospel or residing in Heaven with Christ, Paul made little distinction between the two. He was either with Christ in life or with Him in death. He had no concept of a compartmentalized life, where he was able to "do church" for a certain period of time and then move on with "business as usual."

Paul is one who stepped into the dimension of *extraordinary* or "*unusual miracles*" (Acts 19:11 NLT) because of this understanding. There was no division between the spiritual or secular for him. In the same measure that Paul experienced the Presence of God in a religious setting, he likewise walked in this same anointing while he made tents (see Acts 18:3). Remember, it was the sweat bands and cloths that were upon Paul's body *while he worked*, walking through everyday life, that were laid upon those who needed healing and deliverance (see Acts 19:12). This is what we are being called into. A people who recognizes that the same anointing that releases transformation in a corporate church gathering is responsible for working the extraordinary in the marketplace.

DAILY SCRIPTURE READING

ACTS 19:11-12

PRAYER

You have made the extraordinary possible, Father, by giving me Your Presence. You have given me the Holy Spirit, Whose Presence desires to saturate every area of my life. Everything I do, I do it as one filled with Your Spirit. I simply remind myself that, no matter where I am or what I am doing, I am not alone. I am not only anointed when I feel spiritual—I am anointed, period. Your Presence is always with me wherever I go.

We are never relevant because we mirror the culture of the world around us. We are relevant when we have become what the world longs for.

SOME BELIEVE THAT in order to change culture, we need to first mirror it. We need to be what we assume the world is longing for. This is false advertising. To manipulate and, in turn, market a "Gospel" to the world based on what we assume it wants is to present a false Gospel—and ultimately, we leave those we are trying to help with little hope.

Remember, Jesus is the Desire of All Nations (see Hag. 2:7). He is the One nations would pursue *if they recognized that they needed Him.* Our job is not to give the world what culture dictates; we have the privilege of delivering a relevance that transcends this. We have the ability to live a lifestyle that every human being on the planet longs for—they just don't know it yet. All of humanity was created to enjoy fellowship with God and to function in His image and likeness. When we, through the empowerment of the Holy Spirit, begin to model Christ, we show the world Who the Father is (see 2 Cor. 4:6). As we represent God, we become what the world longs for. This has the ability to break off the scales that prevent eyes from beholding the Desire of All Nations (see 2 Cor. 4:4).

DAILY SCRIPTURE READING

2 CORINTHIANS 4:1-6

PRAYER

Holy Spirit, You empower me to represent Jesus accurately with my life and through my words. Thank You for this amazing purpose!

September 11

We are His body on earth, the only Jesus many will see. The representation of Him must be accurate.

NO MAN MODELED hosting the Presence of God more effectively than the Son of Man. His very title, Jesus the *Christ*, points to His identity as the Anointed One. Because of the Holy Spirit, we all have the joy and privilege to partake of the anointing He modeled. This also means that we have been empowered to represent Him *accurately*. This goes far beyond asking "What Would Jesus Do?" The weight of this mission is sobering, yet supremely rewarding. Jesus has decided to continue His work in the earth through us. It is vital that we learn how to walk as He walked, following His example.

I'm jealous for what was upon and released through this Man, Jesus. Since I discovered that Jesus lived life in a way that we could actually follow, I have found myself burning for the many things that came naturally to Him. They came naturally not because He was God, but because He was anointed by the Spirit. It is important that when we read the Gospels, we pay close attention to His works. Why? John 14:12—what He did we are expected to do, because we received the same Spirit! This is what shows the world Who Jesus is.

Daily Scripture Reading

1 Corinthians 3:16

Prayer

Holy Spirit, saturate every part of my life. You are the One Who makes extraordinary and unusual miracles possible. You are the One Who has given me the ability to do the "greater works" that Jesus spoke about. I am Your house—Your temple. Overflow out of my life as I learn how to host Your Presence every day.

September 12

Since I discovered Jesus lived His life in a way that we could follow, I have found myself jealous for many things that were so natural to Him.

Of all the things that Jesus taught that challenge me to my inner core, I am even more stunned by the things unsaid. He carried the person of the Holy Spirit into the earth. He illustrated a lifestyle that is within reach but must be reached for. It will not come to us. Much of what we need in life will be brought to us, but most of what we want we will have to go get. It's just the way of the Kingdom.

My beginning years in ministry were filled with teaching from the Old Testament. I don't mean I taught Mosaic Law. I just loved the stories and learned to make New Testament applications. Those were important years—years I would not trade. But something has happened to me in recent years that I also would not trade. Jesus has come alive to me in ways I never understood before. His example is the inspiration for this devotional. Looking at how He lived has provoked me to jealousy—He successfully carried the "dove that remained."

Daily Scripture Reading

Matthew 4:18-22

Prayer

Just as Jesus called the disciples to follow Him, Lord, You have called me to follow His example. You have given me the Holy Spirit so that I would be able to model Jesus' life in both purity and power—in integrity of character and demonstration of the supernatural.

September 13

It's important to understand that power in the Kingdom of God is in the form of a Person.

PICTURE THIS WELL-KNOWN story in Jesus' life: The streets are crowded with people who are hungry for more. Some are in pursuit of God; others just want to be close to this Man who has become so famous for wonderful things. He has raised the dead, healed the sick, and has become the single subject of a whole town. People followed Jesus anywhere and everywhere. As this throng of people are walking down the road, a woman, a very desperate woman, sees her chance for a miracle. She has carried her affliction for many years without any hope of recovery. She presses into the crowd until Jesus is within reach. But she is way too embarrassed to talk to Him or even get His attention. She merely reaches out to touch the edge of His clothing.

> *Now a woman, having a flow of blood for twelve years, who had spent all her livelihood on physicians and could not be healed by any, came from behind and touched the border of His garment. And immediately her flow of blood stopped. And Jesus said, "Who touched Me?" When all denied it, Peter and those with him said, "Master, the multitudes throng and press You, and You say, 'Who touched Me?'" But Jesus said, "Somebody touched Me, for I perceived power going out from Me." Now when the woman saw that she was not hidden, she came trembling; and falling down before Him, she declared to Him in the presence of all the people the reason she had touched Him and how she was healed immediately. And He said to her, "Daughter, be of good cheer; your faith has made you well. Go in peace"* (Luke 8:43-48).

A withdrawal was made from the One who has been given the Spirit without measure.

DAILY SCRIPTURE READING

LUKE 8:43-48

PRAYER

Father, You are the One Who gives the Spirit without measure!

September 14

It's one thing to become aware of the Presence of God in worship, and quite another to realize when the Holy Spirit is released from us in ministry.

ON OCCASION, I have felt the anointing of the Holy Spirit released from my hands when I've prayed for someone for healing. It's so encouraging. But it is a whole new level to be so aware of the Holy Spirit who rests upon us that we notice when someone else's faith has put a demand on what we carry.

It could be said that the woman with the issue of blood made a withdrawal from Jesus' account. How aware of the Person of the Holy Spirit do we have to be to notice such a release of power when it flows from us? Add to this equation that Jesus was walking and talking with others when this happened. To me, this is astonishing. He is conscious of the Presence even when He is talking to others or listening to their comments and questions. It is for this that I am most jealous.

Daily Scripture Reading

Mark 5:29-30

Prayer

Father, I desire to remain conscious of Your Presence upon my life. There are people who need what I carry. Give me eyes to see these people and their needs as I go about my everyday routine. Help me never to become so overly conscious of what I am doing that I miss how Your Spirit might be moving upon others. Help me to carry Your Presence into these situation and release what Your Spirit provides. You bring healing, wholeness, and freedom to those You touch.

September 15

The Old Testament prophets showed the impact of the Presence of God upon a person for a specific task. But it was Jesus who revealed this as a lifestyle.

ONE OF MY favorite stories in the Bible is of Jesus' water baptism. We've already looked at it in part. But there's one more part of the story that is central to this book. It is recorded in John's Gospel.

> *John testified saying, "I have seen the Spirit descending as a dove out of heaven, and He remained upon Him. I did not recognize Him, but He who sent me to baptize in water said to me, 'He upon whom you see the Spirit descending and remaining upon Him, this is the One who baptizes in the Holy Spirit.' I myself have seen, and have testified that this is the Son of God"* (John 1:32-34 NASB).

Jesus sets the stage for a whole new season. The Old Testament prophets modeled this possibility amazingly, especially for their day. Because of this event, what the prophets modeled, you and I can step into as a lifestyle. The abiding anointing is now the inheritance of every believer because of Christ.

Daily Scripture Reading

John 1:32-34

Prayer

Thank You, Lord, for making a way for me to live filled with Your Spirit! I don't need to worry about Him leaving or forsaking me. He has been sent from Heaven to live and remain with me forever. I praise You for such a glorious inheritance.

September 16

We know that the Holy Spirit lives in us as born-again believers; the sad reality is that the Holy Spirit doesn't rest upon every believer.

I OFTEN ASK PEOPLE what they would do if an actual dove landed on their shoulders. How would they walk around a room or even go about their day if they didn't want the dove to fly away. The most common answer is carefully. It's a good answer. But it's not enough.

It is this—every step must be with the dove in mind. This is what I believe to be the key to the Spirit Who remains. He is the single greatest reference point, not only for direction and power in ministry, but actually for life itself. We've been chosen to carry the Presence of God. Amazing.

Daily Scripture Reading

Galatians 5:25 NIV

Prayer

Increase my awareness of Your Presence within and upon me, Lord. I pray that every part of me would move in greater step with You, Holy Spirit!

The Holy Spirit is in me for my sake, but He is upon me for yours.

I REMEMBER AS A young man hearing someone talk about being full of the Spirit. Having strong Pentecostal roots, I didn't consider this a new subject. But what I heard taught that day was new. The man of God simply spoke of two verses, neither of which referred to the baptism in the Spirit. It's not as much in my heart to make a doctrinal statement right now as it is to make a relational statement. These two verses are guidelines.

Do not grieve the Holy Spirit of God (Ephesians 4:30).

Do not quench the Spirit (1 Thessalonians 5:19).

This simple insight took my focus from the expressions of the Spirit (gifts, etc.) and shifted them to what the Holy Spirit actually felt because of me. And the more I walk with the Holy Spirit, the more my priorities shift to contribute to this relationship. This opens up new realms in walking with God that I had not considered.

Daily Scripture Reading

Ephesians 4:30

Prayer

May my life bring honor to You, Holy Spirit. You have chosen me to be Your house—Your temple on the earth. I pray that everything about how I live would host Your move in and upon my life. You live inside of me, and I am forever grateful for this! But, Lord—I desire for Your Presence to rest upon me and for You to release Your power to those who desperately need Your touch.

September 18

When the Holy Spirit rests upon a person without withdrawing, it is because He has been made welcome in a most honorable way.

TWO ESSENTIAL KEYS to hosting the Holy Spirit are not grieving Him and not quenching Him.

Do not grieve the Holy Spirit of God (Ephesians 4:30)

To not grieve the Holy Spirit is a command focused on the issue of sin—in thought, attitude, or action. *Grieve* is a word that means to cause sorrow or distress. It describes the pain the heart of the Holy Spirit can feel because of something we would do or allow in our lives. It is character centered. This is a boundary that must have the attention of anyone who is interested in hosting His Presence more powerfully.

Do not quench the Spirit (1 Thessalonians 5:19).

To not quench the Holy Spirit is a command that zeroes in on the co-laboring aspect of our relationship. The word *quench* means "to stop the flow of." The original language defines it as "to extinguish or put out." This word brilliantly uses two metaphors to illustrate this connection with God. "To stop the flow" could be illustrated by bending a garden hose in half until water no longer flows from it, while "extinguish" portrays the passion part of our walk with God. To lose passion for God always affects our ability to allow the Holy Spirit to flow from us to change circumstances around us. This verse is power centered.

Daily Scripture Reading

1 Thessalonians 5:19

Prayer

Protect me from grieving You, Lord, or quenching Your supernatural work in my life. Holy Spirit, flow freely through me. Move without restraint!

September 19

God always honors His Word, regardless of the vessel in question.

I DON'T UNDERSTAND THOSE who consider sin to be a lighthearted matter. It is especially disturbing when those individuals seem to be gifted in power ministry. This reality causes some to reject the gifts of the Spirit altogether. For them, it seems to be evidence enough that the gifts can't be from God because God would never use people walking in sin.

Others go to the other extreme and are offended at God for allowing people who live in sin to still function in some measure of anointing. I agree; it is a great mystery. Nevertheless, God desires to confirm His Word, not the vessels who carry it. This is the problem with believing that signs and wonders authenticate the *person* declaring truth. Truth is truth, regardless of whose lips declare it. The disconnect comes when the person speaking truth is not living in alignment with the Gospel he or she claims to uphold as supreme. This is why we must have eyes set on what God *is* doing, even if He is moving in the midst of significant human weakness.

His Word reveals His character, not ours. And to not respond to His Word is to violate the covenant He created. The key is pressing in for the balance. We need to be a people of purity and power, character and demonstration, not content to elevate one at the expense of devaluing the other.

Daily Scripture Reading

Psalm 138:1-2

Prayer

Father, You honor and confirm Your Word. Thank You that, in spite of my weaknesses and shortcomings, You still chose me to carry Your Presence. And Lord, help me never to be content staying where I am. You change and transform me from glory to glory as I am doing Your work.

September 20

Sometimes true character can only be formed in the trenches of warfare and life.

I SURE HOPE WE will soon come to a day when this nonsense of tolerating sin stops for us. To make up for this weakness in the body, many have taught that character is more important than power. I taught this myself for many years. We have devastating stories to prove our point. Our stories are missing one minor detail: Jesus didn't teach or practice it that way. In fact, when Jesus gave power and authority to His disciples in Luke 9, it was immediately followed by some of their biggest blunders.

Right after the disciples received this impartation, they are found rejecting other followers of Jesus—exclusivity had poisoned their hearts. Previous to this, they spent considerable time arguing who was better than the other. They had just returned from ministry to their hometowns. It stands to reason that their success in power ministry had given each of them all the evidence needed to prove their points—they were the greatest! James and John topped it off by wanting to kill an entire city of Samaritans by calling down fire on them. The spirit of murder was unrecognized by them, all in the name of ministry and discernment. All of these huge blemishes came to light after the glorious moment when Jesus entrusted them with power and authority. Their character was seriously flawed. The greatest part of this mystery is that He followed what we might call a failed experiment in chapter 9 by releasing the same anointing over 70 others in Luke chapter 10. He entrusted power to people who were far from qualified to walk in extraordinary anointing. And yet, sometimes the stewardship of His power is the very thing that forms the character we need to sustain it.

Daily Scripture Reading

Luke 9:46-56

Prayer

You are developing me every day to more accurately reflect the character of Jesus. I never want to elevate power above character. At the same time, You are not calling me to wait for perfection in order to release Your power. I pursue both!

September 21

It is true that power is not more important than character. But it is equally true that character is not more important than power.

WHEN WE MAKE the mistake of elevating character above power, the gifts of the Spirit become rewards and are no longer gifts. This emphasis has actually damaged our effectiveness in the gifts of the Spirit. In fact, this approach has caused as much damage in the area of supernatural gifting as flawed character has damaged our witness to the world. Both are essential. Character and power are the two legs we stand on, equal in importance.

For every gifted person without character, I can show you many people with character who have little power. That has been the focus of the Church in my generation in most parts of the world. A lifestyle without power has been considered normal. As a result, they are making little difference in the world around them. We must stop grading on the curve, where our approval comes from fitting in to the accepted standard. We must return to Jesus Christ—perfect theology, the ultimate example of the gifts of the Spirit working in the context of the fruit of the Spirit: character and power together.

Daily Scripture Reading

1 Corinthians 14:1

Prayer

I desire both the gifts and fruit of the Spirit. Help me not to pursue one while neglecting the other. May my life demonstrate both power and purity, bringing a full representation of Jesus to the world.

September 22

When the Church discovers who she is, she no longer wants to be rescued. There's a big difference between being rescued from the big bad devil and being taken up for a wedding. And only one is acceptable for a believing believer.

IT IS INTERESTING to note that the groups of people who walk in little power are much more inclined to believe that the Church is going to get weaker and weaker before the end of time comes. They are prone to a view of the last days where very few will actually endure to the end. This perspective seems to legitimize their powerlessness, giving it a purpose. It's ridiculous.

On the other hand, those who walk in power see the desperate condition of the world, but also see the world's openness to God when the impossibilities of their lives yield to the Name of Jesus through our lips. Instead of waiting to be rescued, this Church assumes her position as the rescuing, transformative agent in the world.

Daily Scripture Reading

Ephesians 3:1-13

Prayer

Your Word says that the Church has been called to make known Your manifold wisdom to the rulers and authorities in heavenly places. We are called to represent You in this world, revealing Your wisdom before the powers of darkness and causes them to retreat.

I am not waiting around to be rescued; I am stepping into my identity as one called to reconcile people to God. I am anointed to bring transformation to every arena of this world—that the knowledge of Your glory would truly fill the earth.

September 23

The secret of the ministry of Jesus is in the relationship He has with His Father.

JESUS' PRIMARY MISSION was to reveal the Father by displaying His nature and His will. Jesus is the will of God. In doing so, He made startling statements like: *"The Son can do nothing of Himself, but what He sees the Father do...the Son also does in like manner"* (John 5:19) and *"I speak to the world those things which I heard from Him"* (John 8:26).

We are not discussing Jesus' identity as Messiah here. That is unparalleled, and there is nothing about His identity as Savior that humankind can model. He was the Messiah because God knew that we could never be able to do it. Regardless of how much of the law we tried to follow and how much good we strived to do, it all fell horribly flat, as our hearts were still rebellious in nature. We needed everything Jesus provided as Messiah and Savior of the world. There is none like the glorious, spotless Lamb of God.

That said, He is both Messiah *and* our model. Jesus Christ is our perfect sacrifice and He is our perfect revelation of the Father. His identity as the Christ refers to His anointing by the Holy Spirit. Want to know who God is and what He is like? Look at the Son. He is the standard, for both revealing the Father and for us to follow in living out the Christian life.

Daily Scripture Reading

John 5:19

Prayer

Open my eyes to behold You in a greater way, Father. Your Son did only what You showed Him. He is the exact representation of Your likeness! Keep my eyes fixed on Jesus. He is the safest place when it comes to discovering Who You are and learning Who I am called to represent in the earth.

September 24

Jesus put Heaven on a collision course with the orphaned planet called earth.

JESUS' DEPENDENCE UPON the Father brought forth the reality of His world into this one. This is how He could say, *"The Kingdom of Heaven is at hand!"*

This Kingdom is ruled by a King...Who is also a Father. It cannot be arbitrary that the language of Kingdom government and the identity of the Father is mentioned in the same prophetic passage:

> *For a child will be born to us, a son will be given to us; and the government will rest on His shoulders; and His name will be called Wonderful Counselor, Mighty God, Eternal Father, Prince of Peace. There will be no end to the increase of His government or of peace* (Isaiah 9:6-7 NASB).

As the Kingdom of God increases on the earth, the Father's house enlarges. The planet that was previously orphaned through the fall is restored to the original family design. Wherever the Kingdom expands, the result is family. Those who are translated into the Kingdom are brought into the love and goodness of a King Who is also the perfect Father.

Daily Scripture Reading

Isaiah 9:6-7

Prayer

Enlarge Your house, Father! May the earth be filled with Your glory as Your people bring Your Kingdom into every corner of the planet. Bring Your sons and daughters home, that they would know Your love and the significance that comes from being adopted into Your family.

All the acts of Jesus were expressions of His Father for all humanity to see.

PREVIOUS TO JESUS, all humankind saw the devastating nature of sin and the consequences for such actions. But Jesus came and furnished the one missing element—the Father. The writer of Hebrews called Jesus the exact representation of His Father's nature (see Heb. 1:3).

This reinforces the fact that everything Jesus said and did gave the world a pure picture of what the Father was like. In John 12:49, He shares, *"For I did not speak on My own initiative, but the Father Himself who sent Me has given Me a commandment as to what to say and what to speak"* (NASB). Jesus' words were far more intentional than we could ever imagine, for each one was first spoken by the Father. Likewise, everything that Jesus did was first displayed by the Father. He went as far to say, *"If I do not do the works of My Father, do not believe Me"* (John 10:37).

Scripture uses strong language to communicate the measure to which Jesus represented the Father. He was not the partial, but the *exact* representation of God's nature. We would do well to carefully study the example of Jesus throughout the Gospels. These stories, testimonies, and teachings are such a gift for us as they help us to clearly see the One Who shows us the Father.

Daily Scripture Reading

John 12:49

Prayer

Everything that Jesus did reveals Who You are. Help me to build my theology and understanding of Your ways, Father, by carefully looking at the life of Jesus. There is no greater or more clear expression of Who You are than the works of Jesus Christ.

September 26

The life of Jesus is the most complete and accurate revelation of the Father ever seen in this world.

JESUS SAID, "IF you've seen Me you've seen My Father" (see John 14:9). It is still true. It is the heart of this perfect Father to give life to humankind and destroy all the works of the destroyer (see John 10:10; 1 John 3:8). The Holy Spirit is the one who reveals the heart of the Father to and through us (see John 16:12-15).

In the same way that Jesus did what He saw the Father doing, we have been called to do the same works of Jesus (see John 14:12). By doing so, we are modeling the Father. The Holy Spirit is responsible for revealing Jesus to us and empowering us to represent Jesus in our lives by doing the same works that He did.

To this day, the works of Jesus unveil an accurate revelation of the Father to the world. What a privilege to participate in this most glorious revealing!

DAILY SCRIPTURE READING

JOHN 14:7-14

PRAYER

Every word and work of Jesus shows me Who You are, Father. He saves and reveals You are Savior. He heals and reveals You are healer. He delivers and reveals You are the deliverer. He touches lepers, raises the dead, and performs creative miracles over nature, revealing that You are compassionate, kind, and all powerful!

September 27

The Holy Spirit who always rested upon Jesus revealed in the moment what the Father wanted from Him.

THERE IS LITTLE doubt that Jesus heard directly from the Father about what He wanted Jesus to do in a particular situation. My personal belief is that much of that direction came in the nights Jesus spent in prayer that preceded the days of ministry.

But it is also true that the Holy Spirit who always rested upon Him revealed in the moment what the Father wanted from Him. Learning the many ways that God speaks helps us to be more in tune with this possibility.

Daily Scripture Reading

Luke 6:12

Prayer

As I spend time in Your Presence, Father, You reveal Your plans and Your divine strategy. Thank You for the ability to hear Your voice.

September 28

I can see what the Father is doing by observing the faith in others.

ONE OF THE more encouraging possibilities that Jesus displayed is the fact that He didn't always seem to know what to do ahead of time, but got His direction by seeing faith in another person. To me, this means that sometimes I can receive direction by seeing the heart's response of another to the Holy Spirit's work in them. Faith can exist in a person only through the work of God. We are able to see what the Father is doing as we watch faith at work in other people. But if I'm not familiar with the realm of faith in me, it will be harder to see it in another.

The centurion is a great example of this. Jesus was stunned by the faith he saw in that man and responded to his request by releasing the word to heal his servant. *"Now when Jesus heard this, He marveled and said to those who were following, 'Truly I say to you, I have not found such great faith with anyone in Israel'"* (Matt. 8:10 NASB). Jesus released the reality of the Kingdom to this man according to his faith. *"And Jesus said to the centurion, 'Go; it shall be done for you as you have believed.' And the servant was healed that very moment"* (Matt. 8:13 NASB).

Daily Scripture Reading

Matthew 8:5-13

Prayer

Holy Spirit, You reveal how You are moving through the faith of others. I ask for the ability to see You at work in these people, just as Jesus saw faith in the Roman centurion. Where I see You at work, help me to participate in what You are doing.

September 29

We make the distinction between the natural and the supernatural. Those are the two realms we live in. But God only has one realm—the natural. It's all natural for Him.

JOHN THE BAPTIST saw the dove come upon Jesus and remain. There is no record of anyone else seeing the dove. Yet everyone saw the result of the dove's presence—both in purity and power, displayed to reveal the heart of God for this orphaned planet.

As the Holy Spirit revealed the Father's will to Jesus, so He reveals the Father's heart to us. And His Presence and power reveal the Father through us. Revealing His will is revealing Him. Jesus became the ultimate revelation of the will of God on earth. But it's not just through what He accomplished. It is through His relentless and consistent hosting of the dove.

Giving place to the Presence of God as our greatest joy and treasure is not a trick we use to get miracles. But the Father cannot be adequately represented without miracles. They are essential in revealing His nature.

DAILY SCRIPTURE READING

2 CORINTHIANS 4:6

PRAYER

Father, help me to work with Your Spirit to give the world a clearer picture for how You move. You are good. I pray that Your Presence upon me would show Your goodness and break all false ideas about Who people think You are. May the works of Jesus in my life show Your glory to a world that desperately needs Your Presence.

September 30

WE WILL ALWAYS fall short in this miracle realm if we only respond to the things that become perfectly clear.

Some of the greatest breakthroughs I've ever seen came as we responded to a slight impression or an idea of what God might be doing. Our own faith will take us into the discovery of what the Father is doing. The key is saying "Yes" without a complete blueprint.

We often want God to download a complete plan and clear strategy before we give Him the unqualified "Yes" He deserves. The nature of faith is to say "Yes" first because we trust the nature of the One calling us out—even if we don't fully understand all that His invitation entails. It is amazing how a small step can lead to significant breakthrough. The problem is many allow their understanding to prevent them from taking the small steps and responding to the slight impressions.

DAILY SCRIPTURE READING

HEBREWS 11:8

PRAYER

Just like Abraham said "Yes" to You when he did not know where he was going, help me to always give You my complete "Yes" and total surrender—even when I am not clear on what You are doing.

OCTOBER

Releasing the Dove

October 1

Seeing what is possible through Jesus' example has freed me to hunger for what I know is within reach.

IT'S HARD TO put into words how moved I am by the story of the Holy Spirit resting upon Jesus like a dove...and remaining (see John 1:33). A holy jealousy gets stirred up in me—a jealousy to live in the reality that Jesus lived in.

It has been a growing experience for the last many years, one that continues to progress. Hunger prevails. Jesus was the first One upon Whom the dove *remained*. This reality cannot help but stir my heart to desire more than I am presently enjoying. I am reminded that the One Who remained upon Jesus is the very One the Father has sent to abide (or remain) with us *forever* (see John 14:16).

Daily Scripture Reading

John 14:16-31

Prayer

I want to know You more, Holy Spirit. Help me to grow in my relationship with You each and every day. You are always with me. You are God, right here—on the earth. You are the Promised One sent from Heaven to reveal Jesus and lead me into all truth. I ask You to take me deeper in the knowledge of Your ways and how You operate. I know there is so much more of You to know, experience, and release!

Jesus doesn't always tell us what to pursue. Some things only become a part of our lives because we see the ways of God and pursue accordingly.

JESUS DIDN'T TEACH people to touch His clothing to get well. They observed the nature of God working through Him and responded to what they saw was available through that example. We can now use the same principle to see what Jesus carried continuously that really set the precedent for how each of us is to live.

We do well to pursue according to His commands. But romance is no longer romance when it is commanded. Some things must be pursued only because they are there. Moses was able to distill the cry of his heart in this simple prayer: *"Let me know Your ways that I may know You"* (Exod. 33:13 NASB).

Daily Scripture Reading

Exodus 33:12-13

Prayer

Show me Your ways, Father. Grant me eyes that see Your ways in every miracle, sign, and wonder. Help me to see Your nature in every breakthrough and Your character in every blessing. I celebrate the works of Your hand. I offer thanksgiving for the great and glorious things that You do. But above all, Lord, may my heart always be hungry to know Your ways—Who You are and what You are like.

October 3

Revelations of God's nature are invitations to experience Him.

DISCOVERING GOD'S WAYS is the invitation to come to Him and know Him in the way revealed. As He reveals His nature to us through the moving of the Holy Spirit, He will often leave us without command. Instead, He longs to discover what is actually in our hearts, as it is in the nature of the heart in love to always respond to the open door for encounter.

There was never a formal command issued in Scripture for a person to receive healing by touching one's garments. Yet, with the woman with the issue of blood, this was her unique response to Jesus' Presence. She was not implementing a formula; she was responding to the Presence of the One Who released healing virtue. Her thought process is laid bare in the Gospels, as we read that "*she thought, "If I just touch His garments, I will get well*" (Mark 5:28 NASB). What provoked this thought process? There was no formulaic teaching circulating about how Jesus' clothes released healing power. It was testimony. At the beginning of her account in Mark, we see that she began her journey of faith "*after hearing about Jesus*" (Mark 5:27 NASB). She heard about the Person. It was not a command. It was not a seven-step process. It was not a principle. Simple testimony of Jesus is what birthed faith in her heart to respond to Him as she did. He did not despise or reject her unique response. It was obvious that the focus of her faith was not "anointed clothing." It was the Man Whose very Presence caused garments to be saturated with miracle-working power.

Daily Scripture Reading

Mark 5:25-34

Prayer

Lord, You have invited me to know You through experience. Help me to never box You in, assuming that I have figured out how You move and operate. You are God. You can do whatever You like. Your character never changes, but how You do things does.

October 4

Sometimes you don't get to know a person until you work with them.

THIS IS CERTAINLY the setting Jesus created for His disciples in Matthew 10:1 and then later for the 70 in Luke 10. They were to develop a relationship with the Holy Spirit in ministry that would later set them up for the most amazing promotion imaginable—they would become the dwelling place of God on earth.

However, the Holy Spirit couldn't live in the disciples until they were born again. This couldn't happen until Jesus had died and was raised from the dead. But even though the Spirit of God wasn't in the twelve, He was *with* the twelve.

> *The Spirit of truth, whom the world cannot receive, because it does not see Him or know Him, but you know Him because He abides with you and will be in you* (John 14:17 NASB).

He said to them: *You know Him*. This is amazing to me as they were not yet born again. They had a measure of relationship with the Holy Spirit before they were born again. This is where they *started* to get to know Him, as Jesus "*gave them authority over unclean spirits, to cast them out, and to heal every kind of disease and every kind of sickness*" (Matt. 10:1 NASB).

Daily Scripture Reading

John 14:16-17

Prayer

Help me to catch a fresh glimpse of how Your Spirit moves and how Your Presence works as I study the works of Jesus. Father, bring a season of fresh revelation of the Gospels. Open their pages to me like never before as I watch the Son of God live as a Kingdom citizen, anointed by the Holy Spirit. He is my model for living the Christian life. What a privilege to remember that I have been given the same Spirit that was upon Him—to do the same works in His Name!

October 5

Some of the things that have been hidden from us in the Scriptures are now being revealed because we have a place to put them.

JESUS WAS THE perfect teacher. His time with the twelve disciples was critical for many reasons. One reason is that during those times He gave practical instruction for the rest of their lives. Both by His instruction and His example He revealed the priority of this wonderful adventure with God the Holy Spirit. But in all honesty, some of Jesus' instruction seems extremely abstract to me and somewhat hard to understand.

Sometimes lessons seem impractical to us because we live in a different atmosphere than when the lesson was given. Having Jesus illustrate how to protect the Presence of the dove, for example, is much more practical when the evidence of that Presence is witnessed moment by moment by the disciples for over three years. When we grow up in an environment where little Presence is displayed, we don't always understand what Jesus taught. The atmosphere created by His manifest Presence and lifestyle contributes amazingly to a lesson being given. Having said that, we are in a season of increased Presence and power—all of this is changing for us.

Daily Scripture Reading

Luke 10:9

Prayer

Show me how to live and declare the message of Your Kingdom. The Kingdom does not just come with power; it comes through a Person. Holy Spirit, You carry and release the Kingdom, and You live in me.

October 6

The goal wasn't for the disciples to have powerful meetings at home, even though they did. The goal was for them to learn to work with the Holy Spirit, who was with them.

AFTER GIVING A commission to the 70 disciples, Jesus sent them out in pairs to their hometowns. He instructed:

> *Carry neither money bag, knapsack, nor sandals; and greet no one along the road. But whatever house you enter, first say, "Peace to this house." And if a son of peace is there, your peace will rest on it; if not, it will return to you* (Luke 10:4-6).

Notice that Jesus sent the disciples out without provisions. No money, no hotel reservations, no rented auditoriums, nothing—just a geographical direction and a shove. One of the things I tried to do for my children is to take care of every possible problem ahead of time so they would be successful. Jesus didn't. He intentionally sent them in over their heads. They stepped into situations where they would need each other (sent out in pairs) and they would need to discover the direction of the Spirit of God, as a team. Jesus was interested in connecting them to the process of hosting the Presence more than He was interested in the outcome of meetings. He was raising up a company of people upon whom the Holy Spirit could also rest and remain.

DAILY SCRIPTURE READING

LUKE 10:3

PRAYER

Just as Jesus sent out the 70 disciples to learn the ways and movement of the Spirit, show me Your ways, Holy Spirit, as I step out to do Your works. Break any intimidation that I may be feeling that keeps me from serving others with Your love, compassion, and power.

October 7

One of the reasons it's so important to learn ministry at home is because of the value of serving where there is no honor.

MANY OF THE lessons we need to learn can only be learned in serving others. The end result was they had powerful meetings at home, which is the most difficult place to be successful in ministry. As Jesus had already noted, *"Truly I say to you, no prophet is welcome in his hometown"* (Luke 4:24 NASB).

We do not serve *for* honor. Even though Jesus served in His hometown, He was not honored or properly recognized. The people were overly familiar with the son of Joseph and Mary. The same may be true for you. There are people in our lives every day who we are called to serve. We may never receive honor from them for our service. That is not the end goal. We serve because in serving we model the nature of Jesus. In serving, we cooperate with the Presence of the Holy Spirit and draw ability from His power. We serve others because God values people and we have said "Yes" to upholding Heaven's value system.

Daily Scripture Reading

Luke 4:24

Prayer

I do not serve to receive honor. Holy Spirit, help me to serve people because I honor them. I honor people because You love them.

October 8

We must not become addicted to the praises of men. If we don't live by their praises, we'll not die by their criticisms.

JESUS WAS SENDING His disciples into environments that would be very unwelcoming to them and their message (see Luke 10:3). He actually set them up to expect hostility, explaining that there would be those who would resist the demonstration of the Kingdom. Consider the beginning of his instruction—"*But whatever city you enter, and they do not receive you*" (Luke 10:10). He was training the disciples to give proper place to the Holy Spirit and, by default, not be moved by the criticism and rejection of men.

If the disciples' primary mission was to accommodate the Holy Spirit, working with Him to perform the supernatural exploits that Jesus described—healing, delivering, raising the dead, etc.—then the criticisms of people would not be a matter of significance. Many are moved by criticism when they should be moved by the Spirit. We course-correct and adjust directions because we experience resistance from people rather than remaining faithful to the commission the Lord has given to us, even when staying the course means welcoming a backlash of criticism. When accommodating His Presence is our paramount priority, everything else falls into its appropriate place.

DAILY SCRIPTURE READING

LUKE 10:1-12

PRAYER

I will not live by the praises of man. My goal is to follow Your lead and give Your Holy Spirit first place of priority. I am moved by Your Presence, not praises and not criticism. Prepare my heart for criticism when it comes. Also, prepare my heart to receive praise correctly.

October 9

The world thinks of peace as the absence of something—a time without war, a time without noise, or a time without conflict. For a believer, Peace is a Person—the Presence of Someone.

As Jesus was commissioning the 70 disciples, it is interesting to note what He told them to do once they found a place to stay. They were to let their peace come upon that household. Is that merely a command to greet people with the word *shalom*? I doubt it. That lesson could have been taught with much less fanfare. I personally don't believe they really understood this instruction until later in their story. Regardless, they were to release peace and then, interestingly, take it back if there was no one there who was worthy (see Matt. 10:13).

Our ability to respond to this command of Jesus to release peace over a household is central in His instruction for ministry. It is tied directly to our ability to recognize the Presence of the Holy Spirit. It's hard to release with any consistency what you're not aware of. Consciousness of Presence will always increase our impact when it comes to influencing the world around us.

Daily Scripture Reading

Matthew 10:11-14

Prayer

May I always see when, where, and how You are moving, Holy Spirit. When You call me to release peace—through prayer, over a person, or into a situation—may I respond instantly. Help me to live ready to take risks and bring Your peace wherever You lead me to release it.

October 10

Those who desire principles above Presence seek a kingdom without a king.

When we reduce the joy of knowing God to the principles that bring breakthrough, we cheapen the journey. So much of what we do is done out of ministry principles instead of out of the Presence.

One of the mysteries of life is that a primary role of a believer is the stewardship of a Person, the abiding Presence, who is the Holy Spirit—the dove that remains.

He is a person, not an "it."

Daily Scripture Reading

John 14:26

Prayer

Holy Spirit, You are a Person. You are God! This means that I am never alone. Thank You, Father, that because of Your Holy Spirit, Jesus' promise is coming to pass every day in my life. He promised that He would never leave me or forsake me. He promised to send me a Comforter Who would abide with me forever. Holy Spirit, come. You are so welcome, honored, and loved!

October 11

Jesus is called the Prince of Peace in Scripture. The Holy Spirit is the Spirit of Christ, the Person of peace. And that Peace Who is a Person is the actual atmosphere of Heaven.

THIS IS WHY peace is like a double-edged sword—it is calming and wonderful for the believer, but highly destructive and invasive for the powers of darkness. *"The God of peace will soon crush Satan under your feet"* (Rom. 16:20 NASB).

That's quite an assignment given to His followers—release the Person of peace when you enter a home, for in doing so you will release the Presence that is the actual atmosphere of Heaven to yielded hearts while at the same time undermining the powers of darkness that are at work in that home. This atmosphere is expressed through the Person of the Holy Spirit. For Jesus, this was Ministry 101.

Daily Scripture Reading

Romans 16:20

Prayer

Holy Spirit, You release the very atmosphere of Heaven through Your peace. Thank You for this gift, this wonderful fruit of the Spirit. Because You live inside me, I have peace. Your peace carries Your power.

October 12

Because the Spirit of the resurrected Christ lives within us, miracles are expected. But that is not where His desires are focused for us. He wants our hearts.

WHILE THERE ARE many expressions of a surrendered heart, God is looking for those who will trust Him. Remember, without faith it is impossible to please Him (see Heb. 11:6). Trust is the issue.

To honor Him fully, we have to live in such a way that unless God shows up, what we are attempting to do is bound to fail. This kind of abandonment was the nature of Jesus' life on earth and is now the nature of the believing believer. This is how we are "co-missioned" into this assignment. Jesus told the disciples, "Go into a city. Find a place to stay. Don't bring any money. Don't take enough clothing that you can take care of yourself for extended periods of time. Make yourself vulnerable in your abandonment to My purposes, so that unless I show up to provide and direct, it will not work."

DAILY SCRIPTURE READING

EXODUS 33:14-15

PRAYER

Unless Your Presence goes with me, I am lost. Holy Spirit, You are the greatest provision I could ever receive. You did not simply leave me with direction, truth, or power—You have given me Your very Person. God, You are with me and have resourced me for every situation that comes against me.

October 13

The front lines of battle are really the safest place to be.

DAVID MISSED OUT on this truth in his greatest failure. At the time when kings went to war, David was living in disagreement with his royal identity and stayed behind. This is what set him up for his fall with Bathsheba.

Jesus gave the disciples understanding in this concept of the safety of being in the battle, the safety of living as sheep that wolves would like to devour. You would think that becoming vulnerable to risk would be the most unsafe place to be. But this Kingdom works differently. Just as we are exalted by humbling ourselves and we live by dying, so in this Kingdom we are the safest when we are the most vulnerable to danger because we said *"Yes"* to His assignment.

DAILY SCRIPTURE READING

MATTHEW 10:16-20

PRAYER

There is always safety in the battle because Your Presence is with me every step of the way.

October 14

David lost the battle with his eyes, which opened the door for him to lose the battle over his heart, all because he was not in the battle he was born for.

Then it happened in the spring, at the time when kings go out to battle...David stayed at Jerusalem. Now when evening came David arose from his bed and walked around on the roof of the king's house, and from the roof he saw a woman bathing; and the woman was very beautiful in appearance. So David sent and inquired about the woman. And one said, "Is this not Bathsheba, the daughter of Eliam, the wife of Uriah the Hittite?" David sent messengers and took her, and when she came to him, he lay with her (2 Samuel 11:1-4 NASB).

IT WAS THE season for kings to go out to war. In this season, war would have been a safer place than on David's rooftop. Because he lost the battle with his eyes, David became positioned to lose the battle over his heart. This is a reminder that we must persevere in the battle that we were born for. One of the keys is guarding our eyes. If our eyes are not fixed on Him, it is easy for us to sidestep battle, reposition ourselves, and become distracted from our assignments. This is what happened to David and it proved to be a most costly decision.

Maintaining the right focus would have kept David stationed in the battle that he was meant to be in. Surely, he would have fought and enjoyed victory instead of staying behind only to experience one of his most crippling defeats.

DAILY SCRIPTURE READING

2 SAMUEL 11:1-4

PRAYER

You make me aware of the times and seasons. Holy Spirit, help me to remain in the right place at the right time to fight the right battle. Above all, help me to remain focused on You. Being in Your Presence is always the right place at the right time.

October 15

When the manifest Presence of God is with you in your assignment, dangerous places become safe.

IT WOULD BE foolish to think the danger of frontlines kind of ministry isn't real. But all of that changes when *He* is with you.

The measure we are aware of our need for Him is usually the measure we become aware of Him. It really is all about the Presence. It's about hosting Him. This is what the 70 disciples discovered. Neither their ignorance nor lack of experience disqualified them. They had been sent by One who was going with them.

Daily Scripture Reading

Matthew 28:20

Prayer

I have been commissioned by You, Jesus. You have sent me in Your authority and You have equipped me with Your Presence. You will never leave me or forsake me. You have not only sent me out—You are with me and You are inside of me, empowering me to fulfill the divine assignment You have given me to complete.

October 16

Too many opinions easily undermine the purposes of God.

I AM CONSTANTLY AMAZED at how differently Jesus thinks. He sent the disciples on a journey that was fully prepared, but not in the ways that often matter to me. It was fully prepared because God would go with them. Two people would be enough; they would benefit from the principle of unity, but not fall to the possible conflict that the twelve spies had who spied out the land in Moses' day.

Two spies brought back a good report. I'm not saying that traveling in pairs is the only model for ministry. I'm saying that Jesus sent them fully prepared in ways we don't always recognize—God would go with them in their assignment to release peace on a house, heal the sick, raise the dead, etc. Jesus made sure that they stayed Holy Spirit centered. They were prepared the best way possible. They saw Jesus do it, and He commissioned them to an assignment that required them to stay dependent on the Holy Spirit.

Daily Scripture Reading

Luke 10:1-4

Prayer

Help me to see life from Your perspective, Father. Renew my mind. Help me to think the way You do and respond to life from Your vantage point. Your realm knows no impossibility! So Holy Spirit, I ask You to come and transform my mind so that I would think more and more like Jesus.

The provision of the Lord is not just food on the table. The supernatural provision of the Lord is divine protection and full impact in our assignment.

I WOULD HAVE PROVIDED all the natural things the disciples needed for their commission. Jesus provided the direction and the Presence as seen in the power and authority given to them. What He gave them ensures the natural provisions will be there because the Holy Spirit is at work. This is the concept that Jesus taught the multitudes in Matthew 6:33, *"Seek first the kingdom of God...and all these things shall be added."* His Kingdom works entirely on the first things first principle.

That is the whole issue: Giving up the reins of being in control of my life to become truly Holy Spirit empowered and directed. Jesus' commission was to go learn how the Holy Spirit moves. Go learn His ways. This was His supreme value, and through this commission He was ushering the disciples into Heaven's value system.

DAILY SCRIPTURE READING

MATTHEW 6:33

PRAYER

Your Kingdom is my first priority and my main assignment. I trust You, Father, for all of the other provisions of daily life, as You have promised to meet all of my needs according to Your riches in glory. Your are faithful and I trust You.

October 18

***The Holy Spirit is still looking for places to rest*—AND THOSE PLACES ARE PEOPLE.**

I **REMIND YOU THAT** the dove represents the Holy Spirit in Scripture. This is especially clear in the story of Jesus' water baptism. And here in the story of Noah we find an interesting description of Noah's connection with the dove:

> *So it came to pass, at the end of forty days, that Noah opened the window of the ark which he had made. Then he sent out a raven, which kept going to and fro until the waters had dried up from the earth. He also sent out from himself a dove, to see if the waters had receded from the face of the ground. But the dove found no resting place for the sole of her foot, and she returned into the ark to him, for the waters were on the face of the whole earth. So he put out his hand and took her, and drew her into the ark to himself* (Genesis 8:6-9).

The dove was released because she would look for a resting place. When she didn't find a place to rest, she returned to Noah and the ark. I believe for most of us this lesson is abstract because we receive so little teaching and experience in learning to recognize the Presence of God. Most would never know in a ministry situation if the dove was released, let alone if He came back. It would be really tough to know if the Holy Spirit that was released from us is now resting upon someone. I state this not to shame anyone but to create hunger for what is legally our privilege and responsibility. We are to know the ways and Presence of the Holy Spirit so we can cooperate with Him in a way that changes the world around us. This is true ministry.

Daily Scripture Reading

Genesis 8:6-12

Prayer

Holy Spirit, make my life Your resting place.

October 19

Great sinners have lost their innocence in so many areas of their lives. But for most of them, there remains deep in their hearts an innocence as it pertains to the Holy Spirit Himself.

FOR MOST CAUGHT in deep sin, this part of the heart is still virgin territory. I've seen it so many times. The most corrupt, the most immoral and deceptive are changed in a moment when the Holy Spirit comes upon them. Under all the callousness caused by sin was a place of deep tenderness. It is a place that none of us can see without help from the Holy Spirit.

Amazingly, their hearts responded to God when He showed up. It's the ones Jesus referred to when He said, *"Her sins, which are many, have been forgiven, for she loved much; but he who is forgiven little, loves little"* (Luke 7:47 NASB). And it's this response that declares they are worthy of the dove.

Daily Scripture Reading

Luke 7:40-50

Prayer

Holy Spirit, help me to daily live in awe of how deeply I have been forgiven.

October 20

Jesus is not to be tried in small portions. He is to be surrendered to completely and wholeheartedly. Anything less will often have the opposite result than what He desired for us.

IT IS OFTEN those who have been overexposed to the things of God who actually build a resistance to Him. Overexposure often happens when a person hears much teaching from the Word but doesn't come to a place of total surrender. This was the issue with the Pharisees. The ones who were the most trained to recognize the Messiah when He came missed Him altogether.

Total surrender draws us into encounters with God that keep us tender. Without that element, we become hardened to the very word that was given to transform us. It would be similar to the way a vaccination is made. We are exposed to small portions of a particular disease, which in turn causes our body to build a resistance.

Daily Scripture Reading

1 Corinthians 6:19-20

Prayer

Jesus, I desire all of You. I don't want to just try You out. I don't want to test the waters. I offer my life, completely surrendered to You. Holy Spirit, here I am. I am Your vessel and Your temple—filled with Your Presence. Use me. Mold me. Shape me into the image of Your Son, from glory to glory. Father, may I glorify You with the life You have given me.

October 21

We will always release the reality of the world we are most aware of.

IN HEAVEN THERE are no thoughts void of God. He is the light, the life, and the heart of His world. Heaven is filled with perfect confidence and trust in God. On the other hand, this world is filled with mistrust and chaos.

Living aware of God is an essential part of the command to abide in Him. Brother Lawrence of the 1600s illustrated this theme remarkably well. It is presented in the book *The Practice of the Presence of God*. It was said of him that there was no difference between his times of prayer and his times working in the kitchen. His awareness of God and his communion with Him were the same in either role. May the same be said of us as we pursue this practical lifestyle of hosting His Presence.

DAILY SCRIPTURE READING

2 CORINTHIANS 4:18

PRAYER

Keep my eyes fixed on the unseen realm of Your Kingdom. Everything that I can see is temporary and subject to change; everything in Your Kingdom is unshakeable and eternal. I remain mindful of the unshakeable realities of Your Kingdom so that I can stand upon them when I am dealing with the different trials and circumstances in my life.

October 22

I get concerned when people have the holiness ambition without discovering the cornerstone of our theology: God is good.

LIVING WITH A continual awareness of Him has got to be a supreme goal for anyone who understands the privilege of hosting Him. He is the Holy Spirit, making holiness a huge part of the focus of our lives. Yet He is as good as He is holy.

I have learned that all my ambition, discipline, and deeply felt repentance had little effect on my life as it pertains to holiness. A holy lifestyle has become the natural result of delighting in the One who is holy—the One who accepts me as I am. All the sweaty efforts have not changed anything in my life worth mentioning, except to make me prideful and miserable. I wish I had discovered this aspect of the Christian life much earlier in my walk with the Lord. It certainly would have saved me years of frustration.

DAILY SCRIPTURE READING

ROMANS 12:1-2 NIV

PRAYER

In view of Who You are, Lord, and what You have done for me at the Cross, I offer up my life. There is no other acceptable response. When I see You for Who You really are, I am compelled by Your delight, by Your beauty, and by Your goodness to give You my all. Protect me from legalism. Keep me from trying to work for You; instead, keep me living in the place of Your delight.

October 23

Every believer is aware of God, but not always at a conscious level. Developing this awareness is one of the most important aspects of our life in Christ.

Every believer experiences God's Presence in some way, but we often remain untrained. This is especially so in a culture that has emphasized cognitive strengths over spiritual and sensual (physical sense) capabilities. For example, our bodies were created with the ability to recognize God's Presence. The psalmist said even his flesh cried out for the living God (see Ps. 84:2). The writer of Hebrews taught that a sign of maturity was the ability to discern good and evil through our senses: *"But solid food is for the mature, who because of practice have their senses trained to discern good and evil"* (Heb. 5:14 NASB).

Those who are trained to recognize counterfeit money never study counterfeit money, as the possibilities for making fake money are endless. They immerse themselves in being exposed to the authentic currency. Then the bad automatically stands out. It's the same with developing our senses to discern good and evil. Immersion in the discovery of God's Presence upon us (the Spirit given without measure) will cause anything contrary to stand out.

Daily Scripture Reading

Hebrews 5:12-14

Prayer

Increase my awareness of Your Presence, Holy Spirit. Keep my focus on Who You are and what You are doing. Let my heart be rooted in the truth of Your unchanging nature and character so that I am able to know when You are moving and know when You are not.

October 24

Giving the Holy Spirit our nights is the way to start our day. Many would do better in the daytime if they'd learn to give Him their nights.

IT HAS BEEN a practice of mine for many years now to go to sleep at night with this simple act: Release my affection for Him until I sense His Presence rest upon me. Now because I'm interested in sleep, I don't use this time to sing praises or even intercede about some great need. I simply love Him until my heart is warmed by His Presence. If I wake in the night, I resume and turn my heart toward Him again and go to sleep engaged with Him.

It's important to know how life works. When God created everything, *"there was evening and there was morning, one day."* This is repeated many times in Genesis chapter one. The day starts at night. For many, the torment that is experienced in the night watches would end by this simple action. Start your day at night by giving Him your affection until He warms your heart. Learn to maintain that sense of Presence throughout the night, and it will affect your day.

Daily Scripture Reading

Psalm 119:148 NIV

Prayer

Holy Spirit, I give my nights over to You. Because the day truly begins at night, I give You my affection in these night hours. I offer my worship and press into Your Presence. You come and warm my heart. You set the tone for my sleep. I ask You to fill my dreams with Your thoughts. Your purposes. Your imagery. Your meditations. And may the seeds I sow during the night hours welcome a harvest during the day.

October 25

Jesus often comes differently than we expect.

AFTER HIS RESURRECTION, Jesus met with His disciples in a room where they were hiding. But it was not a meeting they were planning on. They were hiding because they feared that the religious leaders would kill them next. Jesus either walked through the wall or just appeared in the room. That couldn't have helped their fear issues. Jesus responded to their panic with *"Peace be with you"* (John 20:19).

They didn't catch what Jesus made available. When peace is given, it must be received in order to be of benefit. After that, Jesus showed them His hands and His side that they might see the scars of His crucifixion. *"Then the disciples were glad when they saw the Lord"* (John 20:20). Only after seeing those scars did they realize who He was. He then spoke peace to them again.

DAILY SCRIPTURE READING

JOHN 20:19-20

PRAYER

Father, I ask You for open eyes. May I constantly be watching for the movement of Your Spirit, even if it doesn't make sense to me and seems different than I would expect.

October 26

While it is the resurrection that correctly illustrates and empowers the Christian life, it is the Cross that brings us there. There is no resurrection without the Cross.

BOTH TIMES, ON the Emmaus Road and in the Upper Room, Jesus' followers realized who He was only after He drew their attention to the Cross—the scars from the spear in His side and the nails in His hands, and the bread, which spoke of His broken body.

Moves of God must have the Cross as the central point to maintain their genuineness—keeping first things first. The throne is the center of His Kingdom, and on His throne sits the Lamb of God. The blood sacrifice will be honored and celebrated throughout eternity.

DAILY SCRIPTURE READING

JOHN 20:24-29

PRAYER

Thank You for the Worthy Lamb Who will be praised throughout eternity. Your Spirit empowers me to live the resurrected life, and for this I am so grateful. But may I always remember that there would be no resurrected life apart from the Cross.

October 27

We have authority over any storm we can sleep in. "Peace be with you."

IN JOHN 20, Jesus returned to the lesson that He gave the disciples in their first commission back in Matthew 10:8-12. He taught them to release peace when they entered a house. We also see that Jesus calmed a storm with peace. *"Then He arose and rebuked the wind, and said to the sea, 'Peace, be still!' And the wind ceased and there was a great calm"* (Mark 4:39). Keep in mind, this was the very storm that He slept in. The key for Jesus was living more aware of a world defined by peace than the one marred by its absence.

You have to have peace in order to give it away. Abiding in peace is what makes you a threat to any storm. Here, Jesus was commissioning the disciples to carry the very currency of Heaven, *peace*, into every house and every storm that required what His Presence released.

Daily Scripture Reading

Mark 4:35-41

Prayer

Your Presence gives me the peace to stay at rest in a storm. Thank You, Father, for this peace that passes all understanding. Truly, You offer peace that does not make any natural sense. This peace gives me protection through the storm and power over the storm.

October 28

I'd like to suggest that Jesus was modeling the nature of all ministry in this one act. To do what He did involves releasing the dove (Holy Spirit) until He finds places (people) to rest upon.

AFTER JESUS SHOWED His disciples the scars, they believed. He spoke peace to them again, as He is the God of the second chance. They apparently were open to it this time because He followed it with the greatest commission anyone has ever received. *"So Jesus said to them again, "Peace to you! As the Father has sent Me, I also send you"* (John 20:21). There it is: As the Father has sent Me, I also send you. Stunning. There is no greater call than to walk in the call of Jesus. But if that wasn't enough, we come to the part that makes it possible. *"And when He had said this, He breathed on them, and said to them, 'Receive the Holy Spirit'"* (John 20:22).

If Jesus were to say that as the Father sent Him, He also sends us, and then follow it by having a banquet for the poor, we'd emphasize feeding the poor as the primary ministry of Jesus we are to walk in. If He followed this great commission with a two-hour worship service, we'd say that was the primary function we are to walk in. Whatever action follows the command will be emphasized as primary; that is, unless it is abstract, which is the case in this situation. Because it is something so unusual, this action of Jesus gets lost in the long list of activities that only God can do—release the Spirit of God. In this one act, Jesus summarizes the life of those who follow Him in the greatest commission—as the Father sent Me, I also send you—*now release the Spirit of God.*

Daily Scripture Reading

John 20:19-22

Prayer

The goal of ministry is to release Your Spirit. Just as Jesus breathed upon the disciples and commissioned them with the Spirit, I have also received the same Holy Spirit. He is the Great Gift I have freely received in order to freely give away Your Presence.

October 29

Ministry should flow out of the relationship with the Person Who lives in us for our sakes, but rests upon us for the sake of others.

JESUS HAD ALREADY given His disciples power and authority while He was still on the earth. They cooperated with the Spirit while on the "mission trips" as well as during the earthly ministry of Jesus. Interestingly, what He gave them would not carry through after His death and resurrection. He brought them into His experience and enabled them to function under the umbrella of His authority and power, which they did well. Now they would have to have their own experience with God to have these two necessary ingredients.

Power and authority introduce us to the nature of the Holy Spirit with a primary focus on hosting His Presence. During His earthly ministry, Jesus faithfully showed the disciples what would become available to them after the Cross. Even though they experienced a temporary empowerment while Jesus was still with them, these task-oriented commissions were given to Jesus' followers as opportunities to learn how the Holy Spirit moves and operates.

Daily Scripture Reading

Acts 1:4-8

Prayer

I rely on a personal encounter with Your Presence to fulfill the destiny and calling You have prepared for me. I cannot depend on anyone else's experience with You, Holy Spirit, to help me fulfill my purpose. Thank You for those destiny-defining moments in Your Presence that launch me into new levels of anointing, calling, purpose, and bringing Your Kingdom to this world.

October 30

Authority comes with the commission, but power comes with the encounter.

WHEN THE DISCIPLES received the Holy Spirit in John 20, they were born again. They received a commission from God that was reaffirmed and expanded in Matthew 28, *"Go therefore and make disciples of all the nations, baptizing them in the name of the Father and of the Son and of the Holy Spirit, teaching them to observe all things that I have commanded you; and lo, I am with you always, even to the end of the age"* (Matt. 28:19-20).

Following this experience they were commanded not to leave Jerusalem until they were clothed with power from Heaven. *"And behold, I am sending forth the promise of My Father upon you; but you are to stay in the city until you are clothed with power from on high"* (Luke 24:49 NASB). They were commanded not to leave until they had their encounter with the Spirit of God.

In Matthew 28, they received authority, but in Acts 2, they received power. Even Jesus underwent the same experience. As the Son of God, He received authority from the Father to perform the works that He was purposed to do during His ministry on earth. However, it was at His water baptism where Jesus Himself had an encounter with the Holy Spirit Who empowered Him to do what He had been authorized to do.

Daily Scripture Reading

Luke 24:44-49

Prayer

I cannot fulfill Your call without Your empowerment. I recognize that apart from the power of Your Presence, I cannot fulfill Your commission. It takes Your ability to accomplish Your assignment. I am authorized. I am anointed. But it is in the place of encounter where I am empowered, filled, and re-filled.

October 31

I can't think of any greater privilege than to carry the Presence of the Holy Spirit into this world and then look for open doors to release Him.

I ONCE HAD A prophet friend tell me, "If you know of a church that you think I should go to, let me know, and I'll go there." He was basically saying to me, "You have favor in my eyes. And if there is a church that you want me to go to, I'll show them the same favor that I would show to you."

Somehow that is the nature of this supreme call. As we steward the Holy Spirit's Presence properly, in relationship, He will allow us the increasing privilege of releasing His Presence into various situations and people's lives in ministry. He will show them the same favor He has shown us.

DAILY SCRIPTURE READING

LUKE 4:18-19

PRAYER

Your Spirit is upon me to preach good news and find open doors where I can release His Presence. As You have freely given me the Presence of Your Holy Spirit, help me to freely give Him away to those who need what only He can bring. What a glorious stewardship to carry Your Presence—Your very Person!

NOVEMBER

Keys to Practically Hosting the Presence

November 1

Releasing God's Presence through Words

JESUS USED THIS method frequently. He only said what His Father was saying. That means every word He spoke had its origins in the heart of the Father. When He spoke His most confusing message, the crowds abandoned Him en masse. This all happened in John 6.

In this message, He spoke of how the people would have to eat His flesh and drink His blood to have any part in Him. Never before had Jesus taught on something so grotesque. To the listener He was speaking of cannibalism. We know that wasn't His intent. But we live after the fact. And the most amazing part to me is that Jesus didn't bother explaining what He meant. There's probably not a teacher or pastor alive that wouldn't have made sure the people understood what He was referring to, especially when we saw the crowd murmuring and ultimately leaving. Yet it served His purpose as they intended to make Him king by force.

When He asked His disciples if they were leaving too, Peter responded, *"Lord, to whom shall we go? You have the words of eternal life"* (John 6:68). To my point of view, Peter was saying, "We don't understand Your teaching more than those who left. But what we do know is that whenever You talk, we come alive inside. When You talk, we find out why we're alive!"

DAILY SCRIPTURE READING

JOHN 6:68

PRAYER

Father, You have the words of eternal life. As I align my words with Yours, I will watch Your will come to pass in my life and in those around me. These words carry Your Presence because they come out of You.

November 2

Words that Release Spirit and Life

JESUS EXPLAINED AN especially important part of the Christian life of ministry when He said, *"The words that I speak to you are spirit, and they are life"* (John 6:63). Jesus is the Word made flesh. But when He spoke, the word became Spirit. That is what happens whenever we say what the Father is saying.

We've all experienced this: We are in a troubling situation, and someone walks in the room and says something that changes the atmosphere of the entire room. It wasn't merely because they came in with a great idea. They spoke something that became material—a substance that changed the atmosphere. What happened? They spoke something timely and purposeful. They said what the Father was saying. Words become spirit.

Words are the tools with which God created the world. The spoken word is also central to creating faith in us (see Rom. 10:17). His spoken word is creative in nature. Saying what the Father is saying releases the creative nature and Presence of God into a situation to bring His influence and change.

DAILY SCRIPTURE READING

JOHN 6:63

PRAYER

Your very words release the Presence and life of the Holy Spirit. Help me to say what You are saying so that, my words would be infused with Your supernatural power.

November 3

Releasing God's Presence through Acts of Faith

GOD'S PRESENCE ACCOMPANIES His acts. Faith brings a substantial release of Presence, which is visible time after time in Jesus' ministry. An act of faith is any action on the outside that demonstrates the faith on the inside.

For example, I've told people to run on a severely injured ankle or leg. As soon as they do, they are healed. How? The Presence is released in the action. That is something I would never do out of the principle of faith. I am only willing to give that direction out of the Presence. Many leaders make a huge mistake at this point. I will never require someone to put themselves at risk out of a principle. If I am experiencing what appears to be a roadblock in my walk with Christ, I will at times require a bold act of myself out of principle—but never someone else.

Daily Scripture Reading

Mark 2:1-5

Prayer

I ask You, Father, to show me areas in my life where I need to perform an act of faith to experience an increase of Your Presence. Thank You for the breakthrough that is available on the other side of stepping out in faith.

November 4

Releasing God's Presence through Prophetic Acts

THE PROPHET ACT is a unique facet of the Christian life as it requires an action that by appearance has no connection to the desired outcome. Whereas stepping on an injured ankle is connected to the desired outcome—a healed ankle—a prophetic act has no connection.

A great example would be when Elisha was told about a borrowed axe head that fell into the river. It says, *"He cut off a stick, and threw it in there; and he made the iron float"* (2 Kings 6:6). You can throw sticks in the water all day long and never make an axe head swim. The act is seemingly unrelated. The strength of the prophetic act is that it comes from the heart of the Father. It is a prophetic act of obedience that has a logic outside human reasoning.

I've seen this happen many times when someone is wanting a miracle. I've had them move from where they were sitting and stand in the aisle of the church. It wasn't because there was more power of the Holy Spirit in the aisle. It's because it was a prophetic act that would release the Presence of the Holy Spirit upon them. Jesus operated in this many times. He once told a blind man to wash in the pool of Siloam (see John 9:7). There is no healing power in the pool. The miracle was released in the act of going and washing—logically unrelated to the desired outcome.

DAILY SCRIPTURE READING

JOHN 9:1-7

PRAYER

As I am directed, Lord, help me to obediently perform whatever prophetic act You are leading me to do. It may not make sense. It may appear strange. If You direct me to do it, I trust You and believe that the very act will release Your Presence and bring breakthrough.

November 5

Releasing God's Presence through Touch

THE LAYING ON of hands is one of the primary doctrines of the Church specifically referred to as a doctrine of Christ (see Heb. 6:1-2). It was a practice in the Old Testament, too. The priest laid his hands on a goat to symbolically release the sins of Israel on that goat that would then be released into the wilderness. The laying on of hands upon the goat was to release something that would help Israel come into their purpose. It was also used to impart authority, as in the case of Moses and his elders.

The apostle Paul laid his hands on Timothy to release apostolic commissioning. In Acts, hands were laid on people for the release of the Holy Spirit upon them (see Acts 8:18). The point is this: Laying hands on people is a tool that God uses to release the reality of His world, His Presence, upon another.

Daily Scripture Reading

Hebrews 6:1-2

Prayer

Your Word says that as we lay hands on the sick, they shall recover. Embolden me to step out and take risks in this area, laying hands on the sick and releasing Your Presence through touch.

November 6

Releasing God's Presence through Shadow and Clothing

PETER'S SHADOW IS one of the great stories about the overflow of Presence upon a person. There is no indication that this was directed or expected by Peter. But people learned to access what rested upon him. Our shadow will always release whatever overshadows us.

Being a resting place of the Spirit makes both the shadow and the anointed cloth/articles of clothing items of great power in our lives. I don't believe this principle has anything to do with our shadow. It has to do with the proximity to the anointing. Things become possible through us that have nothing to do with our faith. They have everything to do with Who is resting upon us—Who we're giving place to. In this context more good things happen by accident than ever used to happen on purpose.

The same is true with clothing. The manifest Presence of God upon a person makes unimaginable things possible. His Presence saturates cloth.

Daily Scripture Reading

Acts 5:12-16

Prayer

Holy Spirit, completely overshadow my life like You did with Peter. May Your Presence upon me increase in such a measure that every area of my life releases Your transforming power.

November 7

Releasing God's Presence through Compassion

COMPASSION IS ANOTHER non-intentional means of releasing God's Presence because it comes from within, almost like a volcano. The Bible often says that Jesus was moved by compassion and healed someone. Being willing to love people with the love of Christ brings the miraculous to the forefront.

Often people confuse compassion and sympathy. Sympathy gives attention to a person in need, but cannot deliver them. Compassion, on the other hand, comes to set them free.

DAILY SCRIPTURE READING

MATTHEW 9:35-38

PRAYER

Father, help me to live as Jesus did—motivated by compassion. This truly reveals Your heart. Protect me from operating out of sympathy, where I elevate problems more than the solutions You offer. Compassion releases Your Presence and brings freedom to those who are bound.

November 8

Releasing God's Presence through Worship

WORSHIP HAS AN unusual effect on our surroundings. We know that God inhabits our praise (see Ps. 22:3). It stands to reason that Presence is released. Atmosphere is changed. In fact, the atmosphere of Jerusalem came about in part because of worship. *"We hear them in our own tongues speaking of the mighty deeds of God"* (Acts 2:11 NASB). Such praise contributed to an atmospheric shift over an entire city where the spiritual blindness was lifted, followed by 3,000 souls being saved.

I've seen this myself when we've rented a particular facility for church services, only to have the people who use it afterward comment on the Presence that remains. A friend of mine used to take people onto the streets in San Francisco many years ago. They met with heavy resistance. But when he realized that when God arises, His enemies are scattered, he strategically used this approach for ministry (see Ps. 68). He split his team into two. One half went out to worship, and the other half would minister to people. The police told him that when he was on the streets, crime stopped. This is an amazing result from the dove being released over a part of the city. The atmosphere changes as the Presence is given His rightful place.

Daily Scripture Reading

Psalm 22:3

Prayer

Your Presence inhabits the praises of Your people and has a powerful impact on the atmosphere. You bring supernatural transformation, healing, freedom, and miracles simply by being hosted in our worship.

November 9

The physical presence of a Bible should never become the replacement of the Spirit of God upon His people.

I'M NOT SURE when it happened or even how it happened, but somewhere in church history the focus of our corporate gatherings became the sermon. I'm sure the change was subtle and was even justified—it's the high value we have for the Word of God. But to me, it's not a good enough reason. That is not to devalue the Scriptures. Unfortunately, something as precious as studying the Scriptures can become negative when it becomes divorced from relationship with a Person.

Being Presence-centered as a church, a family, and as an individual must be put on the front burner again. It is the heart of God for us, as it helps us mature in that all-important issue of trust.

Daily Scripture Reading

John 5:39

Prayer

God, Your Word reveals Who You are in me. Help me never to replace this relationship with Bible knowledge. Just because I have knowledge and information, this does not mean I am walking out everything that You have made available in the Spirit. As I spend time reading Your Word, I thank You that You are increasing my hunger to experience every promise and reality revealed in its pages.

November 10

Israel camped around the Presence of God, while the church often camps around a sermon.

ISRAEL CAMPED AROUND the tabernacle of Moses, which housed the Ark of the Covenant. This is where the Presence of God dwelt. This was the absolute center of life for the nation. It was practical for them. Somehow we must adjust whatever is necessary to rediscover the practical nature of the Presence of God being central to all we do and are.

It's been said of the early church that 95 percent of their activities would have stopped had the Holy Spirit been removed from them. But it is also stated that 95 percent of the modern church's activities would continue as normal because there is so little recognition of His Presence. Thankfully, these percentages are changing, as God has been retooling us for His last-days thrust of Presence and harvest. But we have a ways to go.

Daily Scripture Reading

Numbers 9:17

Prayer

I want to recognize Your Presence in everything I do. Like Israel, may I build my life around You. Your voice. Your movements. Your Presence. Your friendship.

November 11

One of the most arrogant thoughts to ever enter the mind is that the Presence of God isn't practical.

THIS LIE KEEPS us from discovering God's nearness. He is the author of the book, the designer of life, and the inspiration for the song. He is the ultimate in practicality.

Living conscious of His Presence with us is one of the most essential parts to this life. His Name is Emmanuel, which means God with us. The "God with us" lifestyle is one we inherited from Jesus. We must live it with the same priority of Presence to have the same impact and purpose as He did.

DAILY SCRIPTURE READING

PSALM 16:11

PRAYER

Continue to show me the path of life, Father. Because You are with me and live inside of me, there is clarity, direction, and practical wisdom to make everyday decisions. Thank You for this unending spring welling up within me!

November 12

Trust will take us beyond understanding into realms that only faith can discover.

Trust in the Lord with all your heart and do not lean on your own understanding. In all your ways acknowledge Him, and He will make your paths straight (Proverbs 3:5-6 NASB).

TRUST IS BUILT on interaction and the resulting discovery of His nature, which is good and perfect in every way. We don't believe because we understand. We understand because we believe. Discovering a fuller expression of God's nature and Presence is exponentially increased with this simple element called trust.

To acknowledge Him is the natural result when we trust Him. The One we trust above our own existence is to be recognized in every aspect and part of life. The word *acknowledge* actually means to know. It is an unusually big word in Scripture, with a broad range of meanings. But the thing that stands out to me the most is that this word often points to the realm of personal experience. It is bigger than head knowledge. It is beyond concepts alone. It is a knowing through encounter.

Daily Scripture Reading

Proverbs 3:5

Prayer

Help my trust for You to increase as we spend time together in the secret place.

November 13

Trust makes God's Presence more discoverable. He becomes much more tangible to the one who looks to Him with reliance and expectation.

AS I'VE MENTIONED, my strongest tool for discovering God's Presence is my affection for Him. Even so, He is the initiator. He is the great lover of humanity and chooses to draw near in these glorious moments. I cannot imagine life without the wonderful privilege of loving Him. He draws near. So very near.

My personal loose paraphrase of Proverbs 3:5-6 would go something like this: "In every part of your life recognize Him until it becomes a personal encounter with Him. He'll make life better." I never like the idea of presenting formulas that cheapen our walk with the Lord, and I certainly don't mean to imply that in this case. Yet acknowledging God's Presence and encountering Him will certainly make things work better in life. It's a given. The author, designer, and inspiration for life itself is essential to have on board—with full recognition from us.

Daily Scripture Reading

Proverbs 3:6

Prayer

I look for You in every single part of my life. You are always at work, Father. Your Spirit is always moving. Help me to simply recognize what You are doing until I am ushered into a personal encounter in Your Presence.

November 14

Use your faith to discover God's abiding Presence on your life.

MANY OF US have pursued a life of faith for many important reasons. The miracle realm is certainly one of them. Miracles are now a regular part of our lives in numbers I never thought were possible. It is wonderful. But of late I've wondered whether we might not surpass what we've seen in the miraculous if we used our faith to discover the Presence of God as much as we have used it to get breakthrough for miracles.

The same faith that has tapped into this realm of the miraculous is also our escort into discovering the greater depths of God's Presence. There is so much more of Him available for us to know and experience. If we continue to make our acquaintance with His Presence the main pursuit of our faith, everything else will come into perspective. His Presence is not the key to our breakthrough; He *is* the breakthrough. He never disappoints. The overwhelming outcome is learning to live from the Presence of God toward the issues of life. This Jesus did perfectly.

Daily Scripture Reading

Mark 7:24-30

Prayer

Father, show me how to model Jesus. He was always looking for what You were doing and how You were moving. Develop within me vision that quickly sees the activity of Your Spirit so I can participate in Your work.

November 15

The Presence of God upon us is due north.

WHEN THE COMPASS of my heart discovers the Presence of God, everything else falls into place much more easily. While I may not have the answer I am looking for in every specific area of need, I recognize the Presence that keeps me from the fear and anxiety that blocks my access to answers.

Divine order fills the life of the one who has the Presence of God as the priority. More than anything, may we be intentional about looking for Him in the midst of every situation or circumstance. Even though the environment around us may be filled with confusion, the Presence within keeps us anchored in the Truth that remains constant and unshakeable—*the King's advancing Kingdom.*

Just remember *how* the Kingdom of God is advanced: through the person and Presence of the Holy Spirit. In essence, as we keep His Presence our central priority, our hearts will be grounded in this lifelong quest to pursue and demonstrate His Kingdom.

DAILY SCRIPTURE READING

MATTHEW 6:31-33

PRAYER

Holy Spirit, I want Your Presence to be my primary pursuit in life. You are the solution. Y ou are the answer. I need Your Presence more than anything.

November 16

Trust is the natural expression of the one in deep repentance.

THE NATURE OF these two realities is portrayed well in Hebrews 6:1, *"repentance from dead works and of faith toward God."* In this one verse we see the nature of both repentance and faith—from and toward. The picture is of one making an about face, from something and toward something. Here it is from sin toward God Himself. His Presence is discovered in repentance.

Repentance means to change the way we think. Our perspective changes regarding sin and God. With deep sorrow we confess (fully own up to our sin without excuse) and turn to God (upon whom we place our entire trust).

DAILY SCRIPTURE READING

HEBREWS 6:1

PRAYER

My complete trust is in You, Lord. I have made the ultimate "about-face" in my life, turning away from old ways of thinking and toward You. I turn from sin. I turn from dead works that were unable to save me and are unable to keep me saved. Break off these old mindsets so that I can live fully dependent upon the work of Jesus—for every day of my life.

November 17

Repentance is the lifestyle of being face to face with God.

We witness the language of repentance in the Book of Acts, "*Therefore repent and return, so that your sins may be wiped away, in order that times of refreshing may come from the presence of the Lord*" (Acts 3:19 NASB).

Note the end result—that times of refreshing may come from the Presence of the Lord. In this passage, we see the pattern—the order that God created to lead us to Himself, to His manifest Presence. While we were sinners, God chose us to experience Him in such a way that we were fully restored to our original design—to live in and carry His Presence.

We are either walking in repentance or we need to repent.

Daily Scripture Reading

Acts 3:19

Prayer

I walk away from sin and toward Your way of life, Lord. I long to live face to face with You. My identity is no longer defined as sinner. That old nature was crucified and remains at the Cross. Help me to live a lifestyle of repentance, facing toward You and looking away from sin.

November 18

Christianity was never to be known for its disciplines; it was to be known by its passions.

THE PRESENCE OF God is discovered in prayer. And while that is an obvious truth, many people learn to pray without the Presence, thinking their discipline is what God is looking for. Discipline has an important part in walking with Christ, for sure. Yet, discipline was never meant to be the key cornerstone for the Christian life to be built upon. Our prayer lives are sustained not where there is discipline, but where there is passion. There are many who discipline themselves into keeping healthy Kingdom practices. The problem is that they are disciplining themselves to pray to One they have not encountered lately. Passion is the fruit of encounter.

Discipline is not a negative thing; it is a vital element when it comes to sustaining our passion. However, if there is no passion for us to sustain, we need to do a serious about-face.

DAILY SCRIPTURE READING

MATTHEW 22:34-40

PRAYER

May passion for You fuel everything that I do. From reading Scripture to praying to serving, may my love for You be the driving passion of my life. And Lord, help me to always live in response to Your love for me. I don't work for Your love; I work from love.

November 19

So many spend their lives praying to God, when they could be praying with God.

PRAYER IS THE ultimate expression of partnership with God. It is the adventure of discovering and praying His heart. This partnership, with its answers and breakthroughs, is supposed to be the source of our fullness of joy.

> *But you, beloved, building yourselves up on your most holy faith, praying in the Holy Spirit* (Jude 20).
>
> *With all prayer and petition pray at all times in the Spirit* (Ephesians 6:18 NASB).
>
> *He who speaks in a tongue edifies himself* (1 Corinthians 14:4).

When we pray anointed prayers, we are praying the heart of God. His heart is being expressed through words, emotion, and decree. Finding the heart of God is a sure way of locking into His Presence. This privilege of co-laboring is a part of the assignment given for those who would give themselves to carry His Presence well.

Daily Scripture Reading

Romans 8:26-27

Prayer

Father, I ask You to help me pray anointed prayers. Prayers that produce results. Prayers that partner with Your plans and purpose. These prayers are in alignment with Your heart and Your will. Holy Spirit, You are the One sent to lead and guide my prayers, even when I do not know what to pray in my own ability. I ask You to do this even now. May I be one who prays the words of the Father and sees His works manifest as a result.

November 20

Releasing God's Presence by Praying in Tongues

PRAYING IN TONGUES brings us edification and personal strength. In that kind of praying the Presence of God washes over us to bring great refreshing. I think it's a bit sad when people emphasize that tongues is the least of the gifts, which seems to give them the right to ignore it while they pursue the greater gifts.

If one of my children took the birthday or Christmas gift I gave them and refused to open it because they discerned it was one of lesser value than the others, they'd hear a sermon from me they'd not soon forget. Any gift from God is wonderful, glorious, and extremely necessary to live in His full intentions for us. This particular gift is brilliantly useful for living in the Presence continually.

Daily Scripture Reading

1 Corinthians 14:1-4

Prayer

Spend some time today praying in tongues.

If you have not yet received your prayer language, invite the Holy Spirit to come and release this wonderful blessing in your life. You don't need to work for it or try to earn it. It is received just like anything else in the Kingdom of God—by faith. Remember, He is a good Father Who only gives His children good gifts (see Luke 11:13).

If you are hungry to unlock every gift that available in the Holy Spirit, come before your Father and simply ask Him.

November 21

One of the great mysteries in life is to see the descendants of the Creator show so little creativity in how we do church and life in general.

I DON'T THINK THAT lack comes from people who like to be bored or who like to control things to death. It usually comes from a misunderstanding of who the Father is and what He is like.

People often fear being wrong so much that they fail to try something new, thinking they will displease God. If more people would relax in His goodness, we'd probably give a more accurate expression of the God who is never boring. He is still creative. And it's in our nature to be the same.

Daily Scripture Reading

Genesis 1:26-28

Prayer

I have been created in the image and likeness of You, the Creator. May I imitate Your nature by being creative myself. Thank You for inspired ideas. Thank You for supernatural solutions. Thank You for inventions and strategies that come straight from Heaven.

November 22

God measures prayer through time spent in interaction.

DURING MY PRAYER times I have to have paper and pen with me because of the ideas I get while I'm praying. I used to think it was the devil distracting me from praying. That's because I measured prayer by how much time I spent doing a one-way conversation.

Time in God's Presence will release creative ideas. When I spend time with God, I remember phone calls I need to make, projects I long forgot about, and things I had planned to do with my wife or my children. Ideas flow freely in this environment because that's the way He is. I get ideas in the Presence I wouldn't get anywhere else. Insights on how to fix problems or people that need to be affirmed all come in that exchange of fellowship between God and man. We must stop blaming the devil for all those interruptions. (Many of us have too big a devil and too small a God.) And while the enemy of our souls will work to distract us from the Presence, he's often blamed when he is nowhere near because we misunderstand our Father and what He values. When we realize that often it's God interacting with us, we are able to enjoy the process much more and give Him thanks for having concern for these parts of our lives that we might often think are too small for His input. If it matters to you, it matters to Him. These ideas are the fruit of our two-way conversation. But in order to keep from leaving the privilege of interaction with God to work on other things, I write these things down so I can return to my worship and fellowship with Him. The notes I write give me directions I can return to later.

DAILY SCRIPTURE READING

1 THESSALONIANS 5:17

PRAYER

Thank You for the blessing of prayer. May I never treat it as a one-way type of interaction where I am the only one speaking. Help me to listen. I come before You with ears that long to hear—whatever You want to say.

November 23

My personal life must be one of continuous worship to experience the transformations that I long for. We always become like the one we worship.

MY PRAYER TIMES are less and less about issues of need and more and more about discovering this wonderful Person Who has given Himself so freely and completely to me. I remember hearing Derek Prince speak on this subject about 40 years ago. It impacted me so profoundly. He said if you have ten minutes to pray, take about eight minutes for worship. It's amazing what you can pray for in two minutes.

Worship has become a primary part of life. It's wonderful when it's in the corporate gathering. But it's shallow when it's only corporate. I still believe in prayer and intercession. It is a joy. But my heart has this bent toward the Presence that is bigger than the answers I am seeking. There's a Person to be discovered daily. He must be enjoyed and discovered yet again. And it's all His idea. I can seek Him only because He found me.

Daily Scripture Reading

Romans 8:29

Prayer

May my life overflow in worship to You. This is the only fitting response to Who You are and what You have done through the Cross. As I live to worship You, I will experience Your Presence in greater dimensions. May each encounter conform me more and more into the image of Jesus.

November 24

There are only two basic emotions in life—love and fear. Turning my attention toward His love for me only increases my love for Him.

ONE OF THE more meaningful parts of my life is the five-minute vacations I take. They can happen any time or anywhere. The amount of time I take varies, but the activity does not. For example, if I'm in my office I'll ask my secretary to hold my calls for a few minutes. I will sit down and generally close my eyes and pray something like this, "God, I'm going to sit here quietly, just to be the object of Your love."

The flow of His love for us is huge, likened to the water that flows over Niagara Falls—except Niagara is too small. Becoming aware of that love and experiencing that love is wonderful beyond words. It has the side benefit of driving out all fear.

Daily Scripture Reading

Psalm 46

Prayer

I will be still and know that You are God. You are good. You are faithful. Help me to take a five-minute vacation right now and simply be the object of Your love. Here I am, Father—the one You have set Your love upon. I simply receive in a place of stillness and rest.

November 25

There would be more joy in the house if we became more aware of the One Who was in the house.

MANY OF US have been raised thinking there was a lot of work in prayer. Actually, I still value that model, but now only when it comes out of the lifestyle of Presence and romance. It is most effective when I'm in love. Discovering His Presence daily is the surest way to stay in love.

> *I have set the Lord always before me; because He is at my right hand I shall not be moved* (Psalm 16:8)

This psalm of David is a favorite for a number of reasons. It is a psalm of discovery of Presence. It concludes in verse 11 with, *"In Your presence is fullness of joy; in Your right hand are pleasures forever."* Fullness of joy. Where? In the Presence!

DAILY SCRIPTURE READING

PSALM 16

PRAYER

I have set You before me, Lord. Because my eyes are locked upon You, I will not be moved and I will not be shaken. You go before me and Your Presence is within me. You have completely equipped me for victory. I will trust and You will triumph.

November 26

Read until He speaks.

WHILE WORSHIP IS the number one way that God has used to teach me about His Presence, a very close second would be my encounters with Him through His Word. I love the Scriptures so much. Most of what I have learned about the voice of God has been learned in the reading of His Word. And while I believe in the intense study of Scripture, I mostly read for pleasure. In fact, I always read for pleasure.

God has spoken to me countless times through the years from the pages of His book. It is now a habit to immediately go to His Word when I need direction, comfort, insight, or wisdom. If I'm troubled by something, I go to the Psalms. Every emotion is well represented in that book. And I read until I hear my voice in a psalm. Once I hear my heart's cry, I know I have found the place for me to stop and feed. It's probably much like sheep that have found a pasture of bounty to feed from. They just stop and enjoy. That's my life. I stop and feed on the wonderful interaction, the voice, the actual Presence of God that is manifested in and through His Word.

Daily Scripture Reading

Psalm 29

Prayer

Holy Spirit, I come before the Word with expectation that You will speak. Help me to persevere until I hear Your voice and receive what You want to say to me.

November 27

There are times when God will only allow us to recognize His Presence in a crowd. It's not a rejection. He just longs for us to share His joy in the whole.

GOD LOVES THE Church. He loves the idea, the potential, and everything to do with the Church, His Son's body on earth. In fact, He stated that zeal for this house has consumed Him! He has devoted His strength, wisdom, and His intense emotions to this house on earth—His eternal dwelling place.

What I experience with God at home on my own is priceless. I wouldn't trade it for anything in the world. But neither would I trade the amazing moments I've experienced through the years in the gatherings of hundreds or thousands. They are also priceless moments that prepare us for eternity where people from every tribe and tongue will lift up praises to the Lord. This is indescribable joy.

Some things are reserved for the individual. And yet some things are actually too precious to be given to only one. They must be shared with a company of people, a body, the Church. And there are aspects of His Presence that will only be experienced in the corporate gathering. The exponential release and discovery of Presence is equal to the size of the group of people united in the purpose of exalting Jesus in praise.

Daily Scripture Reading

Psalm 109:30

Prayer

I will praise You in the midst of the assembly, Lord. Help me to understand the multiplied power that is released through corporate praise. Prepare my heart. When I come together with Your people, either in church, a small group, or among friends, and we praise You, help me to see what You are doing in the midst of this praise.

November 28

Gifts are free; maturity is expensive.

MANY HAVE COME to me through the years asking for a prayer of impartation, which is the release of a gift for ministry through the laying on of hands, often accompanied by prophecy. It has been one of the great privileges of life to see how God uses both their hunger and the anointing on my life to impact another willing vessel. And while impartation has become rightfully more important in recent years, for some it has become a shortcut to maturity, which really can only be developed through faithful service over time. Getting an instant answer is almost always preferred by those of us raised in this culture of immediate gratification.

I believe that giving and receiving impartation is such an amazing privilege. But like many, I also have seen it abused. That abuse is probably why many in my parents' generation rejected the concept of impartation altogether. But the testimonies of this great principle are bringing forth undeniable fruit to the glory of God. Learning how to access great anointing on another person's life is a great key to personal breakthrough.

Daily Scripture Reading

Romans 11:29

Prayer

Thank You for extending such amazing grace! Even though the gifts are free, help me grow in maturity in how to use them most effectively. Help me to collaborate with You, Lord, in being a good steward of the gifts You have graced me with. I want to see an increased flow of Your anointing in my life. I want to see a greater demonstration of Your Presence resting upon me, that others would be impacted by Your power.

November 29

I can lay hands on you and impart an anointing into your life as God wills. But I can't give you my history with God.

THE RELEASE OF a gift through the laying on of hands is entirely God's doing. Spiritual leaders are not spiritual vending machines where you put in your request, push a button, and out comes the desired gift. Often someone will tell me that they want twice what I have. Well, so do I! If it were that easy, I would lay hands on myself and pray, "Double it!"

There is something priceless in a person's life that must be developed and protected at any cost—it's our private history with God.

Daily Scripture Reading

2 Corinthians 3:18

Prayer

Thank You for the gift of impartation and laying on of hands. I ask for even greater release of Your Presence and power in my life through these wonderful experiences. But Lord, help me to never depend on what someone else carries to build my maturity.

November 30

If you make history with God, God will make history through you.

THIS HISTORY IS created when no one is watching—it's who we are when we are alone. It's seen in the cry of our hearts, how we think, what we pray, and how we value God Himself. Our lives are shaped when there is no one able to applaud our sacrifice or efforts.

These are the moments that we learn the most about hosting His Presence. It's when there's no one to pray for, no one to serve—that's where the relational boundaries are determined. Am I in this for how God can use me, or am I surrendered because He is God and there is no greater honor in life? Jesus had His encounter with the Holy Spirit at His water baptism. A crowd watched. Probably very few, if any, had an idea of what was happening. But it was on the nights on the mountain, when no one was watching, that His greatest breakthroughs came. History was made in Him before history was made through Him. He loved the Father before He could reveal the Father.

Daily Scripture Reading

Matthew 6:5-6

Prayer

History is made in the secret place with Your Presence. This is where no one is watching...except You. It is here that You shape me into the person You have created me to be. You speak to me. You reveal destiny. You share visions. You birth dreams. Help me to return to this place time after time to experience Your refreshing and to keep my perspective right.

DECEMBER

Your Baptism of Fire

December 1

John the Baptist needed and desired the baptism of fire—the baptism in the Holy Spirit.

JOHN THE BAPTIST was the greatest of all the Old Testament prophets. His responsibility, his anointing, and his place in history all put him at the top of the list. Jesus is the One Who pointed out this fact in His remarkable affirmation of John in Matthew 11. Over half the chapter was dedicated to his honor.

John had so much going for him—he walked in the spirit and power of Elijah, he ended Heaven's silence with his cries of the Kingdom of Heaven being at hand, and he was given the privilege to pave the way for the Messiah. Yet according to John, he was lacking one primary ingredient—*Jesus' baptism*. This desire came to light when Jesus came to John to be baptized in water. John had trouble figuring out how he could baptize Him as Jesus was not the one in need.

In the overwhelming contrast with Jesus' perfection, John realized his need. He confessed his desire with, *"I need to be baptized by You"* (Matt. 3:14). Interestingly, this all came about right after John had prophesied, *"He will baptize you with the Holy Spirit and fire"* (Matt. 3:11). It was fresh on his mind. This was the context for his confession. Jesus carried what John longed for—*the baptism of fire*.

DAILY SCRIPTURE READING

MATTHEW 3:11-12

PRAYER

Jesus is the One Who baptizes in the Holy Spirit and fire. The very encounter that John the Baptist longed for has been given to me freely because of Jesus' blood. Thank You, Lord, for this baptism. I am filled with Your Spirit.

Holy Spirit, You are living within me. I celebrate this, but I also desire a greater demonstration of You resting upon me. You are in me for my sake, but You desire to rest upon me to change the world around me.

December 2

It's the baptism of fire that makes it possible for every New Testament believer to be greater than the greatest of the Old Testament prophets.

THE BAPTISM OF fire is this one essential gift from God that makes it possible for the one who is *"least in the kingdom of heaven* [to be] *greater than he"* (Matt. 11:11). John had no access to that baptism. He was aware that One was coming Who would administer what he could not. Water represented a baptism of repentance, but fire would introduce a whole new level of supernatural living. The water is essential for the fire. A baptism of repentance necessarily precedes a baptism of fire, for one cannot be filled unless he or she has first been cleansed.

John was facilitating a powerful prophetic act. Water baptism was a prophetic picture of what the *True Baptizer* would ultimately accomplish—a cleansing that no natural water would perform. The stain of sin would be removed so that cleansed humanity could receive the fire of His Presence. Such is normal life in the Kingdom. By simply being born into the Kingdom, you have received full cleansing of your sin and have the very Presence of God living within you. This would explain why Jesus described the *least in the kingdom of heaven* as greater than the greatest of Old Testament prophets.

Even John the Baptist did not have access to what you have received because of Christ. He spoke of a coming reality but could not step into it while living on earth.

DAILY SCRIPTURE READING

MATTHEW 11:11-15

PRAYER

Lord, I thank You for the baptism of fire. Even today, I ask for You to fill me afresh. Come, Holy Spirit. Rise up within me. Saturate every area of my life with Your Presence and power. May the image of Jesus be all the more clearly revealed through my life because of Your fire upon me.

December 3

Jesus brought the disciples into the authority and power He lived in.

DURING JESUS' TIME on earth, the disciples had functioned under the umbrella of His experience and were deputized as a result. But before He left earth to live at the right hand of the Father, He made sure the disciples knew that the realm they had lived in for three and a half years with Him would never be enough for the days to come. They had to get their own power and authority.

Matthew 28 gives the most complete and well known of the Great Commission passages.

> *All authority has been given to Me in heaven and on earth. Go therefore and make disciples of all the nations, baptizing them in the name of the Father and of the Son and of the Holy Spirit, teaching them to observe all things that I have commanded you; and lo, I am with you always, even to the end of the age* (Matthew 28:18-20).

Here, Jesus declares that He has all authority, which obviously implies that the devil has none. In that moment, He gives a commission to His followers. The secret of this moment is that authority is given in the commission. He then instructs them to wait in Jerusalem until they are clothed with power from on high.

They had received authority but were instructed to wait for an encounter with power.

DAILY SCRIPTURE READING

MATTHEW 28:18-20

PRAYER

Jesus, You have all authority in Heaven and on earth. This means that the devil has none. He is a defeated foe and You reign as the Victorious One. I go forward today in this knowledge—that the One who has all authority lives within me. Thank You, Holy Spirit, for helping me represent Jesus well in every area of my life. May my life bring a clearer demonstration of Jesus' victory to the world as I continue to make hosting Your Presence my great quest in life.

December 4

There is nothing to replace a divine encounter. Everyone must have their own.

JUST AS AUTHORITY comes in the commission, so power comes in the encounter. We see it in Jesus' life, and so it is for the disciples. And it's no different for us. There is nothing that training, study, or association with the right people can do to make up for this one thing—the *need* to have a personal encounter with God. This is what builds our personal history.

Many fail to realize that what is needed in this pursuit of more is an abandonment to God that attracts something that cannot be explained, controlled, or understood. We must encounter One Who is bigger than we are in every possible way until He leaves a mark.

It is wonderful, glorious, and scary.

Daily Scripture Reading

John 1:29-34

Prayer

Thank You for the divine encounters that empower me to fulfill my assignment and Your commission. Keep my heart in a hungry posture, recognizing that even though I am commissioned and authorized to accomplish Your mission, I need Your power. I am dependent on Your anointing. I long for Your Presence. Apart from You, I can do nothing. But with You, all things are possible. Thank You for the Holy Spirit Who is with me and inside of me.

December 5

True learning comes in the experience, not the concept by itself.

TRAGICALLY, MANY STOP short of a divine encounter because they're satisfied with good theology. Once a concept is seen in Scripture, it can be shared with others even though there's no personal experience to back it up.

Often we can become guilty of only looking for something to happen to us that is on our list of what constitutes a "biblical" encounter with God. The lists of various experiences discovered in Scripture do not contain God; they reveal Him. In other words, He is bigger than His book, and is not limited to doing something for us the exact same way He did for someone else. He continues to be creative, each time revealing the wonder of who He is.

DAILY SCRIPTURE READING

2 CORINTHIANS 3:4-6

PRAYER

You change me from glory to glory in Your Presence. It does not come from my working, striving, or religious efforts. It is not the result of how much of the Bible I read, memorize, know, or study. Help me to approach Your Word as the blueprint for what is available in Your Presence. Your Word is alive. It is living. It causes my heart to burn. Time after time, Your Word shows me what is available in my relationship with You and causes me to pursue You with renewed passion.

December 6

God has used my experiences in traveling to other places to set me up for life-changing encounters at home.

ONCE, IN THE middle of the night, God came in answer to my prayer for more of Him, yet not in a way I had expected. I went from a dead sleep to being wide awake. Unexplainable power began to pulsate through my body, seemingly just shy of electrocution. It was as though I had been plugged into a wall socket with a thousand volts of electricity flowing through my body. My arms and legs shot out in silent explosions as if something was released through my hands and feet. The more I tried to stop it, the worse it got. I soon discovered that this was not a wrestling match I was going to win. I heard no voice, nor did I have any visions. This was simply the most overwhelming experience of my life. It was raw power...it was God. He came in response to a prayer I had been praying for months—*God, I must have more of You at any cost!*

Expect Him to answer your cries for more. This is one prayer that He truly loves to answer. Don't be discouraged if you find yourself praying and feel like you are not experiencing instant response. God visited me in response to a prayer I had been consistently praying over a period of time. Also, be open to receive His visitation in whatever way He chooses to reveal Himself.

Daily Scripture Reading

Psalm 84:1-3

Prayer

My very flesh cries out for Your Presence. My body was formed to experience You, just as my soul and spirit were. Every touch and taste of Your Presence stirs me to hunger even more. Every time You draw near, I am both satisfied and left desiring more. Thank You for the gift of Your Presence. It not only fills the deep places of my spirit and soul, but actually satisfies the cry of my flesh.

December 7

All I knew was I was hungry for God. It had been my constant cry day and night.

I WANT TO CONTINUE sharing my story for the purpose of stirring up your expectation. Remember, your God delights in satisfying the hungry with good things (see Ps. 107:9). If you find yourself longing for more of God, this testimony is your license to press in with expectation. He comes and encounters us differently, but make no mistake—His touch changes everything.

The evening before my encounter was glorious. We were having meetings with a good friend and prophet, Dick Joyce. The year was 1995. At the end of the meeting, I prayed for a friend who was having difficulty experiencing God's Presence. I told him that I felt God was going to surprise him with an encounter that could come in the middle of the day or even at 3 a.m. When the power fell on me that night, I looked at the clock. It was 3 a.m. exactly. I knew I had been set up.

For months I had been asking God to give me more of Him. I wasn't sure of the correct way to pray, nor did I understand the doctrine behind my request. All I knew was that I was hungry for more. God does not answer our cries because we asked perfectly or offered up the appropriate spiritual jargon. It is the longing that motivates the prayer that He is looking at and responding to.

Daily Scripture Reading

Psalm 107:9

Prayer

Father, You delight in satisfying the thirsty soul. Your Word promises that You will fill the hungry with what is good. I am hungry for more, Lord. I am hungry to experience every part of the glorious inheritance I received the day I was filled with Your Spirit. I refuse to put limits or boundaries on what is available in the here and now. You said, "On earth as it is in Heaven." I make it my aim to experience as much Heaven on earth as is possible through Your Spirit.

December 8

The favor of God sometimes looks different from the perspective of earth than from Heaven.

THIS DIVINE ENCOUNTER was glorious, but not pleasant. At first I was embarrassed, even though I was the only one who knew I was in that condition. As I lay there, I had a mental picture of me standing before my congregation, preaching the Word as I loved to do. But I saw myself with my arms and legs flailing about as though I had serious physical problems. The scene changed—I was walking down the main street of our town, in front of my favorite restaurant, again arms and legs moving about without control.

I didn't know of anyone who would believe that this was from God. I recalled Jacob and his encounter with the angel of the Lord. He limped for the rest of His life. And then there was Mary, the mother of Jesus. She had an experience with God that not even her fiancé believed, although a visit from an angel helped to change his mind. As a result she bore the Christ child...and then bore a stigma for the remainder of her days as the mother of the illegitimate child.

My request for more of God carried a price. Even though an encounter like this often makes little sense to our natural reasoning, it is one I am willing to embrace regardless of the cost attached. Remember, experiencing more of Him makes *any* price required of no consequence. Why? Consider the reward we get in return: *Him.*

Daily Scripture Reading

Genesis 32:24-32

Prayer

God, help me to see Your favor from Heaven's perspective, not earth's. Even though I receive favor from You, this does not mean everyone in my life will understand it or even celebrate it. Help me to be like Mary—saying "Yes" to whatever You ask, no matter the cost or stigma.

December 9

If I lose respectability and get Him in the exchange, I'll gladly make that trade.

TEARS BEGAN TO soak my pillowcase as I remembered the prayers of the previous months. At the forefront was the realization that God wanted to make an exchange—His increased Presence for my dignity. It's difficult to explain how you know the purpose of such an encounter. All I can say is you just know. You know His purpose so clearly that every other reality fades into the shadows as God puts His finger on the one thing that matters to Him.

The power surges didn't stop. They continued throughout the night, with me weeping and praying, *More, Lord, more, please give me more of You*. It all stopped at 6:38 a.m., at which time I got out of bed completely refreshed. This experience continued the following two nights, beginning moments after getting into bed.

In the midst of the tears came a point of no return. I gladly yielded, crying, *More, God. More! I must have more of You at any cost!*

Daily Scripture Reading

1 Corinthians 3:18-23

Prayer

Lord, I will gladly give anything, knowing that I get more of You in return. Whatever this means—respectability, reputation. If people call me foolish for going after You, I gladly embrace it knowing that foolishness is wisdom to You. Any price that I pay is more than worth it. Your Presence is my treasure.

December 10

There are many interesting encounters that God has had with His people throughout the years. It's a mistake to use one as the standard for all.

THE TWO MOST life-changing encounters I've had with God couldn't be more different from one another. Over the past few entries, I related the story of being electrocuted in His Presence.

The other one was so subtle that it would have been as easy to miss as it was to catch. It was because I "turned aside." The Bible says that when Moses turned aside, God spoke (see Exod. 3:1-4). My burning bush was a Scripture that the Holy Spirit highlighted to me. I stopped and considered it, pursuing what God might be saying. That was May of 1979, and I've never been the same since. It started small, much like a seed. But it has been increasing continuously, having tremendous impact for how I think and live. (It was Isaiah 60:1-19, where God showed me the purpose and nature of the Church.)

Keep your heart postured in a mode to receive. The specifics of the different encounters vary, but their fundamental purpose is singular—drive us into a deeper pursuit and experience of His Presence.

Daily Scripture Reading

Exodus 3:1-4

Prayer

God, I ask You to give me eyes and ears to recognize those divine moments of encounter. They may be extremely noticeable. But also, they may be so subtle that if I don't turn aside, I could miss them. Help me not pursue a certain type of encounter—the encounter is not my pursuit anyway. You are! I am after You, Father. Your Presence is my desire.

December 11

It's not how extreme an encounter is with God. It's how much of us He apprehends in the experience—and how much of His Presence He can entrust to us.

Your encounter with God may stir up a holy jealousy in me; it isn't healthy to judge what God has done in me by comparing it to what He's done for you. In the electrocution experience that I have been sharing about, I didn't know if I'd ever get out of bed again. It seemed that my circuits were fried and that I had lost the ability to function in life as a normal human being. That, of course, wasn't the case. But I only learned that after the fact—after I said "Yes" to "more at any price."

Keep in mind that Jesus manifested a lifestyle, as a Man, that is intensely practical and can no longer be avoided or considered unattainable. It is possible to carry the Presence of the Holy Spirit so well that the Father is revealed to this orphaned planet. That satisfies the quest for divine purpose quite well. Doing exactly as He did is what Jesus had in mind when He commissioned us in John 20:21.

Daily Scripture Reading

John 20:19-22

Prayer

Father, as You sent Jesus, You are sending me. In the same way You equipped Him for the task, You have equipped me with Your very Spirit. Thank You, Lord, that Jesus gave me the picture of a lifestyle that would become available. Thank You for the work of Calvary that cleansed me from all sin. Thank You for the Holy Spirit Who has filled me with Your Presence. Your work alone has qualified me to be an empowered sent one, just as Jesus was.

December 12

God wants to be found by us, but we must seek Him where He may be found.

PSALM 37 IS one of my favorite psalms. I turn to it frequently to feed on over and over again. In it, I discovered that waiting on the Lord was quite different from what I had originally thought. Waiting is not sitting still. It is more clearly seen in setting up an ambush for the one who promised, *"I will be found by you"* (Jer. 29:14). Where is He found?

This is a place of rest that comes out of the conviction of who He is in us and who we are in Him. For that reason, waiting makes sense. Psalm 37:7 tells us to *"rest in the Lord, and wait patiently for Him."* Resting is a beautiful picture of people who no longer feel the pressure to strive to prove themselves. They are comfortable in their own skin.

Daily Scripture Reading

Psalm 37

Prayer

Lord, I wait upon You with expectation. Your Word says that You are found by those who seek You. Help me to seek You from a place of rest, waiting patiently for You to reveal Yourself to me.

December 13

Intense focus restricts what you are willing and able to see. And while this approach will keep you from seeing many things, it will also open your eyes to see more of what you hunger for.

THE HEBREW WORD translated as *patiently* in Psalm 37:7 has two meanings: "pain in childbirth" or "whirling in the air in dance." Both of these activities require incredible focus and strength. We are to wait on God with an unflinching resolve and focus, much like what Jacob had when he wrestled the angel.

Patience also demands a singularity in focus.

There are seasons in life when being involved in many diverse activities is not only acceptable, it's good. But there are also seasons when it is deadly.

I was once driving from Northern California to Southern California on Interstate 5. South of Bakersfield I found myself in a dust storm that almost completely blinded me. It covered the entire freeway. There were cars immediately behind me, so I knew stopping could be disastrous. As I got into this cloud of dust I could faintly see cars and trucks scattered all over both sides of the freeway with people waving frantically. Talking with friends, listening to music, and the like are acceptable activities while driving, but they could have been deadly in this moment. Absolute silence filled the car as I worked to maintain my speed and focus on the lane ahead of me. After a minute or two, we made it through that terrifying cloud of death by God's grace alone. This demanded self-control on my end, recognizing that a singleness of vision was demanded to navigate the danger.

Self-control is not the ability to say *"No"* to a thousand other voices. It's the ability to say *"Yes"* to the one thing.

Daily Scripture Reading

Philippians 3:7-11

Prayer

I press toward the upward call in Christ Jesus. My vision and focus is single. More than anything, Holy Spirit, let my life serve as Your place of habitation on the earth.

December 14

Each of us has become the target of God for a specific encounter that redefines our purpose on planet earth.

IT'S THE BAPTISM of fire. We were born to burn. And while the danger of turning our attention from the Person to the experience, it's worth the risk. No amount of miracles, no amount of insight, no amount of personal success will ever satisfy the cry of the heart for this baptism. And while many would like to just get it over with, oftentimes there is a deep process involved.

For the one hundred and twenty, it was ten days of continuous prayer. For me it was an eight-month season where my prayers actually woke me up. I didn't wake up to pray. I woke up praying.

Such a singleness of focus is rewarded. I personally don't think that these encounters are supposed to be a one-time event. We must have frequent encounters with God that continuously recalibrate our hearts that we might be entrusted with more and more of God. What a person values they will protect. God will give us the measure of His Presence that we are willing to jealously guard.

DAILY SCRIPTURE READING

PSALM 108:1-5

PRAYER

Father, help my heart to remain steadfast. May my focus be single and directed completely on pursuing You. You reward this focus with encounter. You satisfy the longing heart. You reveal Yourself to those who are intent on finding You.

December 15

When Jesus appeared to two men on the road to Emmaus, He opened the Scriptures to explain why the Christ had to die.

AS YET THEY didn't know who He was, but they persuaded Him to stay for a meal. When He broke the bread, their eyes were opened, and then He vanished. Their response is one of my favorite ones in all of the Bible. *"Were not our hearts burning within us while He was speaking...?"* (Luke 24:32 NASB).

That is exactly what happens to me when I read of what this same Jesus has done in the lives of those who have given themselves for more.

My heart burns.

Daily Scripture Reading

Luke 24:13-35

Prayer

You are the One Who causes my heart to burn with passion and desire. As I continue in Your Word, Lord, may my hunger for more of You increase. I deeply long to encounter the One revealed in the pages of Scripture. Every reality that Your Word has made available to me, I want to press in to experience and release it in my life.

FOR THE REST of our time together, I want to stir up your hunger for this baptism of fire. I am going to share some historic encounters with God that have radically transformed the lives of some notable individuals—including D.L. Moody, Evan Roberts, John G. Lake, and others.

Over the following entries, there will be a Prayer, but no Daily Scripture Reading. The goal is to see Scripture come alive in the testimonies you read and become hungry to experience this same baptism of fire in your life.

December 16

D.L. Moody: Experiencing the Baptism of Fire

IT WAS SOME months later, while walking the streets of New York, that Dwight L. Moody finally experienced the breakthrough for which he and Sarah Cooke had been praying together. It was shortly before his second and most important trip to England.

R.A. Torrey had this to say about this significant advance in Moody's life:

> Not long after, one day on his way to England, he was walking up Wall Street in New York; (Mr. Moody very seldom told this and I almost hesitate to tell it) and in the midst of the bustle and hurry of that city his prayer was answered; the power of God fell upon him as he walked up the street and he had to hurry off to the house of a friend and ask that he might have a room by himself, and in that room he stayed alone for hours; and the Holy Ghost came upon him, filling his soul with such joy that at last he had to ask God to withhold His hand, lest he die on the spot from very joy. He went out from that place with the power of the Holy Ghost upon him, and when he got to London the power of God wrought through him mightily in North London, and hundreds were added to the churches; and that was what led to his being invited over to the wonderful campaign that followed in later years.

PRAYER

Your Presence is overwhelming, Holy Spirit. Thank You, Lord, for creating me in such a way that I am built to carry and contain Your Presence. Even though there are moments when I don't feel like I can withstand an increase, You have designed me to be Your temple. I am filled with Your glory so I can freely release it through my life.

December 17

D.L. Moody Describes His Hunger for the Baptism of Fire

MOODY DESCRIBES HIS experience in this way:

> I was crying all the time that God would fill me with His Spirit. Well, one day, in the city of New York—oh, what a day!—I cannot describe it, I seldom refer to it; it is almost too sacred an experience for to name. Paul had an experience of which he never spoke for fourteen years. I can only say that God revealed Himself to me, and I had such an experience of His love that I had to ask Him to stay His hand. I went to preaching again. The sermons were not different; I did not present any new truths, and yet hundreds were converted. I would not now be placed back where I was before that blessed experience if you should give me all the world—it would be as the small dust of the balance.

Prayer

Father, You always respond to the cries of Your people. As I cry out for more, I thank You that You will satisfy.

December 18

Evan Roberts: Contending for More

FOR A PERIOD of time Evan Roberts had been seeking and finding a more intimate relationship with the Lord. William Davies, a deacon at the Moriah Chapel, had counseled young Evan never to miss the prayer meetings in case the Holy Spirit would come and he would be missing. So Evan faithfully attended the Monday evening meeting at Moriah, Tuesday at Pisgah, Wednesday at Moriah, and Thursday and Friday at other prayer meetings and Bible classes. For thirteen years he did this and faithfully prayed for a mighty visitation for the Holy Spirit.

One day before school, in the spring of 1904, Evan found himself in what he later referred to as a Mount of Transfiguration experience. The Lord revealed Himself in such an amazing and overwhelming manner that Evan was filled with divine awe. After this he would go through periods of uncontrollable trembling that brought concern to his family. For weeks God visited Evan each night. When his family pressed him to tell about the experiences he would only say it was something indescribable. When the time drew near for him to enter Grammar School at New Castle Emlyn, he was afraid to go because he was afraid that he would miss these encounters with the Lord.

Prayer

You faithfully reveal Yourself to those who seek You out. Help me to be a lifelong seeker. I never want to be satisfied. May my joy and satisfaction come from not being satisfied. There is always more. I celebrate what I have experienced and praise You for what I have tasted so far. At the same time, I praise You, Father, because You have made it impossible for me to become stagnant. Glory to glory is the only direction I can move in.

Evan Roberts: Receiving the Fire

AT THIS TIME a convention was being held at Blaenenerch a few miles from Evan Roberts' school. An evangelist named Seth Joshua was leading the meetings. On Thursday morning, September 29, 1904, Roberts and nineteen other young people, including his friend Sydney Evans, attended the meeting. On the way to the meeting the Lord moved on the small company and they began to sing: "It is coming, it is coming—the power of the Holy Ghost. I receive it, I receive it—the power of the Holy Ghost."

During the seven o'clock meeting, Evan was deeply moved and he broke down completely at the close of the service. When Seth Joshua used the words "*Bend us, oh Lord,*" Evan entered such travail that he heard nothing more. He later testified that the Spirit of God whispered to him: "This is what you need."

"Bend me, oh Lord," he cried. But the fire did not fall. At the 9 o'clock meeting the spirit of intercession was moving on the congregation in great power. Evan was bursting to pray. Then the Spirit of God told him to do so publicly. With tears streaming down his face Evan just began to cry: "*Bend me! Bend me! Bend me! Bend us.*" Then the Holy Spirit came upon him with a mighty baptism that filled Evan with Calvary's love and a love for Calvary.

That night the message of the Cross was so branded upon Evan's heart that there would be no other theme of the great revival he would soon help lead. From that night on, Evan Roberts could focus on one thought—the salvation of souls. Historians would refer to that night as "Blaenanerch's great meeting."

PRAYER

Bend me, O Lord. May my life be dedicated to hosting Your Presence. You are my one desire—my great pursuit. Spirit of God, fill me with Calvary's love and a love for Calvary, just as You did for Evan Roberts.

December 20

Evan Roberts: Empowered to Carry Revival

One midnight shortly after this, Evan's roommate and closest friend, Sydney Evans, came into the room to find Evan's face shining with a holy light. Astonished, he asked what had happened. Evan replied that he had just seen in a vision the whole of Wales being lifted up to Heaven. He then prophesied: "We are going to see the mightiest revival that Wales has ever known—and the Holy Spirit is coming just now. We must get ready. We must have a little band and go all over the country preaching." Suddenly he stopped and with piercing eyes he cried: *"Do you believe that God can give us 100,000 souls, now?"*

The Presence of the Lord so gripped Sydney that he could not help but believe. Later, while sitting in a chapel, Evan saw in a vision some of his old companions and many other young people as a voice spoke to him saying: "*Go to these people.*" He said, "Lord, if it is Thy will, I will go." Then the whole chapel became filled with light so dazzling that he could only faintly see the minister in the pulpit.

Prayer

Holy Spirit, Your anointing empowers me to win the lost. Stir up the desire within me to see my city and region come to Christ, just as you did for Evan Roberts. I am in (name your city) for such a time as this. While I live here, I possess a voice of authority in prayer. I am yet another vessel carrying Your Presence in this region. Lord, give me a vision to see this city transformed by Your power and goodness—and help me, through the enabling of Your Spirit, to participate in Heaven's assignment for my region.

George Whitefield: Encountering the Sovereign Spirit

WHITEFIELD WAS A major player in the Great Awakening started by Jonathan Edwards. Many were saved in his missions, and it is estimated that he preached to six million without the use of radio or television. Whitefield's meetings were criticized for their emotional expressions of worship.

John Wesley describes a prayer meeting with Whitefield in which the Spirit of God moved on them in 1739. "About three in the morning, as we were continuing instant in prayer, the power of God came mightily upon us, insomuch that many cried out for exceeding joy, and many fell to the ground. As soon as we were recovered a little from the awe and amazement at the Presence of His majesty, we broke out with one voice, 'We praise Thee, O God, we acknowledge Thee to be the Lord.'"

Understand that we are not referring to hype or a striving, emotional attempt to garnish experience from God. This is about the sudden, undeniable surprises of His sovereignty.

PRAYER

Your Spirit moves sovereignly. He also moves in response to faith. Help me not to try and work something up through hype or striving. Show me how to live in a place of rest, trusting the encounters and defining moments to You.

William Seymour: The Spirit Poured Out on Azusa Street

THE SPIRIT BEGAN to fall in Los Angeles as people were radically filled and walked out into the streets speaking in tongues. Crowds began to grow at these home meetings, where Seymour was living with a host family. Before long, they were preaching from the front porch as people filled the streets to listen. Eventually, they moved into an old horse stable at 312 Azusa Street. It was in this stable in 1906 that the Pentecostal movement was officially born.

People would fall over and weep. They would speak in tongues. They would laugh, jerk, dance, and shout. They would wait on the Lord for hours, sometimes saying nothing. Seymour would often preach from his knees.

"No one could possibly record all the miracles that occurred there," writes charismatic historian Roberts Liardon. John G. Lake said of William Seymour that, "He had more of God in his life than any man I had ever met up to that time."

PRAYER

Father, may I serve as an accurate representative of Your nature and character to a world who desperately needs to see You. I ask that Your light would shine brightly upon me, that those looking at my life would see Your life radiating through me. Help them to get hungry for what I have. Thank You for enlisting me in this glorious ministry of reconciliation.

December 23

William Seymour: Recognizing the Priority of the Presence

PRAYER LASTED ALL day and all night. Firemen were even dispatched to Azusa Street, because people saw a "fire" which was actually just the visible glory of God resting on the exterior of the building.

Missionaries began coming to Azusa Street from around the world to catch the fire. People would fall over, get saved, and begin speaking in tongues blocks away from the building, even though no one prayed for them and they had no idea what was going on in the Azusa mission. Parishioners would also hit the streets, knocking on doors with little bottles of oil and asking to pray for the sick.

Seymour sought first and foremost to cultivate the Presence of God in his meetings. If someone felt led, they would stand up and begin to pray or preach. If the anointing did not seem to be on a particular speaker, that person would sometimes get a gentle tap on the shoulder to hush up.

Truly, the Spirit of God was the leader of those meetings.

PRAYER

Your Presence is my supreme desire. Thank You for all of the signs and the wonders. Thank You for the breakthroughs and miracles. Thank You for the blessings. But above all, thank You, Holy Spirit, for Your Presence. Help me to be one like William Seymour who celebrates and accommodates Your Presence above everything else.

December 24

John G. Lake: Experiencing Currents of Power

As recounted by John G. Lake:

> One afternoon a brother minister called and invited me to accompany him to visit a lady who was sick. Arriving at the home we found the lady in a wheelchair. All her joints were set with inflammatory rheumatism. She had been in the condition for ten years. While my friend was conversing with her, preparing her to be prayed with, that she might be healed, I sat in a deep chair on the opposite side of a large room. My soul was crying out to God in a yearning too deep for words, when suddenly it seemed to me that I had passed under a shower of warm tropical rain, which was not falling upon me but through me. My spirit and soul and body, under this influence, was soothed into such a deep still calm as I had never known. My brain, which had always been so active, became perfectly still. An awe of the presence of God settled over me. I knew it was God.
>
> Some moments passed; I do not know how many. The Spirit said, "I have heard your prayers, I have seen your tears. You are now baptized in the Holy Spirit." Then currents of power began to rush through my being from the crown of my head to the soles of my feet. The shocks of power increased in rapidity and voltage. As these currents of power would pass through me, they seemed to come upon my head, rush through my body and through my feet into the floor. The power was so great that my body began to vibrate intensely so that I believe if I had not been sitting in such a deep low chair I might have fallen upon the floor.

Prayer

Your power gives me the ability to serve others better. Show me those in my sphere of influence who need a touch of Your Presence to bring healing, wholeness, and freedom!

December 25

John G. Lake: Releasing the Fire

As recounted by John G. Lake:

> My friend was motioning me to come and join him in prayer for this woman who was sick. In his absorption he had not noticed that anything had taken place in me. I arose to go to him, but I found my body trembling so violently that I had difficulty in walking across the room, and especially in controlling the trembling of my hands and arms. I knew that it would not be wise to thus lay my hands upon the sick woman as I was likely to jar her. It occurred to me that all that was necessary was to touch the tips of my fingers on the top of the patient's head and then the vibrations would not jar her. This I did. At once the currents of holy power passed through my being, and I knew that it likewise passed through the one that was sick. She did not speak, but apparently was amazed at the effect in her body.
>
> My friend who had been talking to her in his great earnestness had been kneeling as he talked to her. He arose saying, "Let us pray that the Lord will now heal you." As he did so he took her by the hand. At the instant their hands touched, a flash of dynamic power went through my person and through the sick woman, and as my friend held her hand the shock of power went through her hand into him. The rush of power into his person was so great that it caused him to fall on the floor.

Prayer

Holy Spirit, You are the One Who empowers me to lay hands on the sick and see them recover. You are the One Who breaks every stronghold and bondage. I draw from Your grace and strength at work within me. I cannot bring healing or deliverance to anyone; You can, You want to, and You live inside of me.

December 26

John G. Lake: Sustaining the Baptism

AS RECOUNTED BY John G. Lake:

> My friend looked up at me with joy and surprise, and springing to his feet said, "Praise the Lord, John, Jesus has baptized you in the Holy Ghost!" Then he took the crippled hand that had been set for so many years. The clenched hands opened and the joints began to work, first the fingers, then the hand and the wrist, then the elbow and shoulder.
>
> These were the outward manifestations. But oh! Who could describe the thrills of joy inexpressible that were passing through my spirit? Who could comprehend the peace and presence of God that thrilled my soul? Even at this late date, ten years afterward the awe of that hour rests upon my soul. My experience has truly been as Jesus said: "He shall be within you a well of water, springing up into everlasting life." That never-ceasing fountain has flowed through my spirit, soul and body day and night, bringing salvation and healing and the Baptism of the Spirit in the power of God to multitudes.

PRAYER

Father, thank You for the living water that flows in my life a river. Show me how to sustain my encounters with Your Presence—that they would be key benchmarks in my Christian life that shape my future. Also, help me not to make them memorials that I simply remember, but defining moments that keep me pressing in for more.

December 27

Charles Finney: Carrying the Presence

FINNEY WRITES OF the following unusual experience in his own autobiography:

> He entered a factory one morning after breakfast. In a room filled with young ladies working on their weaving machines, looms, and spinning devices, two in particular stood out to him. They looked a bit agitated, but seemed to cover it with laughter. He said nothing, but walked closer, noticing that one was trembling so badly that she couldn't mend her thread. When he got to within about eight to ten feet they burst out in tears and slumped down. In moments nearly the whole roomful of workers was in tears. The owner, who was yet unconverted himself, recognized that this was a divine moment and ordered that his factory be shut down to give his workers a chance to come to Christ. A mini-revival broke out, which lasted several days. Nearly the entire mill was converted during this time. It all started with a man upon whom the Spirit of God loved to rest. And so without words a room full of workers came under the conviction of the Holy Spirit and a revival was born.

While this exact experience did not happen every day, I can't help but wonder if maybe the Lord is trying to draw us into a greater hunger for more, now that we know what else is possible. This testimony is in God's resume. It reveals how He is willing to affect the surroundings of those who host Him well.

PRAYER

Holy Spirit, help me to be one who You love to rest upon. I am not content simply reading about the anointing or studying it; I desire to walk this out in my everyday life. May I be one, like Charles Finney, who is so saturated and drenched in Your Presence that I release a noticeable shift wherever I go.

Smith Wigglesworth: An Atmosphere Saturated in God's Presence

HERE IS THE final story that is one of my favorite stories in all of church history. Smith was truly a man of the Presence.

> There were eleven leading Christians in prayer with our Brother at a special afternoon meeting. Each had taken a part. The Evangelist then began to pray for the Dominion, and as he continued, each, according to their measure of spirituality, got out. The power of God filled the room and they could not remain in an atmosphere supercharged by the power of God.
>
> The author on hearing of this from one who was present registered a vow that if the opportunity came, he at any rate would remain whoever else went out. During the stay in the Sounds a special meeting was called to pray for the other towns in New Zealand yet to be visited. A like position to the other meeting now arose. Here was the opportunity, the challenge, the contest was on. A number prayed. Then the old saint began to lift up his voice, and strange as it may seem, the exodus began. A Divine influence began to fill the place. The room became holy. The power of God began to feel like a heavy weight. With set chin, and a definite decision not to budge, the only other one now left in the room hung on and hung on, until the pressure became too great, and he could stay no longer. With the flood gates of his soul pouring out a stream of tears, and with uncontrollable sobbing he had to get out or die; and a man who knew God as few do was left alone immersed in an atmosphere that few men could breathe in.

PRAYER

Father, I hunger to experience more of Your tangible, manifest Presence in my life. Show me what it looks like to carry this measure of Your glory wherever I go so that I can bring transformation to whatever atmosphere I am placed in.

December 29

Normal people became heroes of the faith, not because of their giftedness, their intelligence, or their pedigree. They are heroes because they learned the value of their greatest gift—the Holy Spirit.

I HOPE YOU NOTICED that the stories of deep personal encounters resulted in outpourings, movements, societal transformation, and ultimately an increased awareness of His Presence, sometimes over a city, region, or nation.

Those experiences affected everything about their lives and eventually impacted their surroundings. The historic transformations of culture didn't happen merely because people got into political office and made changes according to their convictions.

While that can be good, there's something much better. *Presence.*

Prayer

You take normal people and transform them into history makers. I am so grateful that You don't look at my giftedness or ability. These do not determine whether or not I will be used by You. I pray that my greatest value, even above being used by You, would be honoring the Holy Spirit—the greatest gift You have given to humanity.

December 30

How can I experience more of God's Presence when I have already received the Holy Spirit?

SIMPLE. YOU HAVE received the fullness of God in the Holy Spirit. The question is, how much of the fullness are you experiencing and releasing in your life today? The Holy Spirit is willing to give you the measure you will jealously guard. There is no lesser or downgraded Holy Spirit. When you receive the Spirit, you receive God. Period.

The pursuit of *more* involves you becoming further awakened to the reality that the Presence of God lives inside of you. The Presence that dwelt in the tabernacle—that was always meant to be carried and transported by God's priests—is the Presence that you have received. I pray that you have become more aware of the Presence of the Holy Spirit resting upon your life and that a relentless pursuit has been birthed within you to go after Him.

PRAYER

Holy Spirit, I ask for more. I know I have received Your fullness—but I know there is more of You to be released through me. Thank You for making me Your eternal dwelling place. Empower me to surrender more of my life to You so that I can see every area of my life under the influence of Your Presence.

December 31

The courts of Heaven have concluded once and for all that the kind of life represented in the lives of these heroes of the faith is available for all.

TESTIMONIES OF DIVINE encounters make me feel like I've just entered that dust cloud on Interstate 5 again. But this time it's not the danger of an accident that has my eyes fixed on the road ahead. It's the chance I could miss the purpose for which I was apprehended by God by being preoccupied with other things. Lesser things. Stories of God encounters are testimonies that prophesy of what God has made available for us in our lifetime. As such, they set a legal precedent.

We are the ones upon whom the promises of the ages have come to rest. And they are contingent upon our being a people who have discovered our eternal purpose. We have been chosen to be His eternal dwelling place. We have been chosen to host His Presence.

Prayer

Father, thank You that the testimony of Jesus is the spirit of prophecy. Every single encounter that I read about in Scripture and throughout history is a prophecy, revealing what is available for me. Stir my hunger to keep pressing in for everything that Your Spirit has made available to me.

ABOUT BILL JOHNSON

BILL JOHNSON IS a fifth-generation pastor with a rich heritage in the Holy Spirit. Together Bill and his wife serve a growing number of churches that have partnered for revival. This leadership network has crossed denominational lines, building relationships that enable church leaders to walk successfully in both purity and power.

Bill and Brenda (Beni) Johnson are the senior pastors of Bethel Church, Redding, California. All three of their children and spouses are involved in full-time ministry. They also have nine wonderful grandchildren.